The Torch
in My Ear

Elias Canetti

The Torch in My Ear

Translated from the German

by Joachim Neugroschel

ANDRE DEUTSCH

Originally published in German as *Die Fackel im Ohr*
Copyright © 1980 by Carl Hanser Verlag, München
English translation copyright © 1982 by Farrar, Straus
and Giroux, Inc.

This edition first published 1989 by
André Deutsch Limited
105-106 Great Russell Street
London WC1B 3LJ

British Library Cataloguing in Publication Data

Canetti, Elias, *1905*-
The torch in my ear
1. German literature. Austrian writers.
Canetti, Elias, 1905
I. Title II. Die Fackel im Ohr. English
838'.91209'0924

ISBN 0 233 98434 8

Printed in Great Britain by
Billing and Sons Limited, Worcester

Part One

Inflation and Impotence

Frankfurt 1921-1924

The Pension Charlotte

I absorbed the changing locations of my earlier life without resistance. Never have I regretted that as a child I was exposed to such powerful and contrasting impressions. Every new place, no matter how exotic it seemed at first, won me over with its particular effect on me and its unforeseeable ramifications.

There was only one thing I felt bitter about: I never got over leaving Zurich. I was sixteen and I felt so deeply attached to the people and places, the school, the land, the literature, even Swiss German (which I had acquired despite my mother's tenacious resistance), that I never wanted to leave. After just five years in Zurich, I felt, at my tender age, that I should never go anywhere else, that I should spend the rest of my life here, in greater and greater intellectual well-being.

The break was violent, and any arguments I had put forward to my mother about remaining had been derided. After our devastating conversation, which decided my fate, I stood there, ridiculous and pusillanimous, a coward who refused to look life in the face because of mere books, an arrogant fool stuffed with false and useless knowledge, a narrow-minded, self-complaisant parasite, a pensioner, an old man who hadn't proved himself in any way, shape, or form.

The new environment had been chosen under circum-

stances that I was left in the dark about, and I had two reactions to the brutality of the change. One reaction was home-
sickness; this was a natural ailment of the people in whose
land I had lived, and by experiencing it so vehemently, I felt
as if I belonged to them. My other reaction was a critical
attitude toward my new milieu. Gone was the time of unhindered influx of all the unknown things. I tried to close myself
off to the new environment, because it had been forced on
me. However, I wasn't capable of total and indiscriminate rejection: my character had become too receptive. And thus
began a period of testing and of sharper and sharper satire. Anything that was different from what I knew seemed
exaggerated and comical. Also, very many things were presented to me at the same time.

We had moved to Frankfurt; and since conditions were
precarious and we didn't know how long we'd be staying, we
lived in a boardinghouse. Here, we were rather crowded in
two rooms, much closer to other people than ever before. We
felt like a family, but we ate downstairs with other roomers
at a long boardinghouse table. In the Pension Charlotte, we
got to know all sorts of people, whom I saw every day during
the main meal, and who were replaced only gradually. Some
remained throughout the two years that I ultimately spent in
the boardinghouse; some merely for one year, or even just
six months. They were very different from one another; all
of them are etched in my memory. But I had to pay close
attention to understand what they were talking about. My
brothers, eleven and thirteen years old, were the youngest,
and I, at seventeen, was the third youngest.

The boarders didn't always gather downstairs. Fräulein
Rahm, a young, slender fashion model, very blond, the stylish
beauty of the Pension, had only a few meals. She ate very
little because she had to watch her figure; but people talked
about her all the more. There was no man who didn't ogle
her, no man who didn't lust after her. Everyone knew that,
besides her steady beau, a haberdasher who didn't live in the

boardinghouse, she had other gentleman callers; and thus many of the men thought of her and viewed her with the kind of delight one feels at something that one is entitled to and that one might someday acquire. The women ran her down behind her back. The men, among themselves or risking it in front of their wives, put in a good word for her, especially for her elegant figure. She was so tall and slender that your eyes could climb up and down her without gaining a foothold anywhere.

At the head of the dining table sat Frau Kupfer, a brown-haired woman, haggard with worry, a war widow, who operated the boardinghouse in order to make ends meet for herself and her son. She was very orderly, precise, and always aware of the difficulties of this period, which could be expressed in numbers; her most frequent phrase was: "I can't afford it." Her son Oskar, a thickset boy with bushy eyebrows and a low forehead, sat at her right. At her left sat Herr Rebhuhn, an elderly gentleman, asthmatic, a bank official. Although exceedingly friendly, he would scowl and get nasty whenever the conversation turned to the outcome of the war. He was Jewish, but very much a German nationalist; and if anyone disagreed with him at such times, he would quickly start carrying on about the "knife in the back," contrary to his usual easygoing ways. He grew so agitated that he'd get an asthma attack and have to be taken out by his sister, Fräulein Rebhuhn, who lived with him in the boardinghouse. Since the others knew about this peculiarity of his and also about how terribly he suffered from asthma, they generally avoided this touchy political subject, so that he seldom had a fit.

Only Herr Schutt—whose war injury was in no way less critical than Herr Rebhuhn's asthma and who walked on crutches, suffered awful pains, and looked very pale (he had to take morphine for his pains)—never minced his words. He hated the war and regretted that it hadn't ended before he got his serious wound; he stressed that he had foreseen it and had always regarded the Kaiser as a menace to society, he professed to being a follower of the Independent Party, and, he said, had he been a member of Parliament, he would have unhesitatingly voted against the military loans. It was really quite awkward that the two of them, Herr Rebhuhn and Herr Schutt, sat so near one another, separated only by Herr Rebhuhn's oldish sister. Whenever danger threatened, she would turn left to her neighbor, purse her sweetish old-maid lips, put her forefinger on them, and send Herr Schutt a long, pleading look, while cautiously pointing the forefinger of her right hand at an angle toward her brother. Herr Schutt, otherwise so bitter, understood and nearly always broke off, usually in midsentence; besides, he spoke so low that you had to listen very hard to catch anything. Thus, the situation was saved by Fräulein Rebhuhn, who always heeded Herr Schutt's words very alertly. Herr Rebhuhn hadn't yet noticed anything; he himself never began. He was the gentlest and most peaceful of men: it was only if someone brought up the outcome of the war and approved of the ensuing rebellions that the "knife" came over him like lightning and he blindly threw himself into battle.

However, it would be all wrong to think that this was what meals were generally like here. This military conflict was the only one I can recall; and I might have forgotten it if it hadn't grown so bad that, a year later, both opponents had to be led from the table, Herr Rebhuhn as always on his sister's arm, Herr Schutt far more arduously on his crutches, with the help of Fräulein Kündig, a teacher, who had been living in the Pension for a long time. She had become his lady friend, and actually married him later on, so as to provide a home for him and take better care of him.

Fräulein Kündig was one of two teachers in the boardinghouse. The other, Fräulein Bunzel, had a pock-marked face and a somewhat whining voice, as though lamenting her ugliness with every sentence. They were no spring chickens, perhaps fortyish; the two of them represented Education in the Pension. As sedulous readers of the *Frankfurter Zeitung*, they knew what was what and what people were talking about; and one sensed that they were on the lookout for people to converse with, people who promised not to be too unworthy. Still, they were by no means tactless if they couldn't find a gentleman with something to say about Unruh, Binding, Spengler, or Meier-Graefe's *Vincent*. They knew what they owed the landlady and they would then keep still. Fräulein Bunzel's whining voice never showed even a trace of sarcasm; and Fräulein Kündig, who seemed a lot bouncier and tackled men as well as cultural themes with great vivacity, would always wait for both possibilities to overlap; a man she couldn't *talk* to would have been interested only in Fräulein Rahm, the model, anyway. A human being whom Fräulein Kündig couldn't enlighten about this, that, or the other was out of the question for her. And, as she confessed to my mother tête-à-tête, this was also the reason why she, an attractive woman in contrast to her colleague, was as yet unmarried. A man who never read a book was, so far as she was concerned, not a man. It was better to remain free and not have to run a household. Nor did she yearn for children; she saw too many of them anyhow, she said. She went to plays and concerts and talked about them, usually adhering to the reviews in the *Frankfurter Zeitung*. How strange, she said, that the critics always shared her opinion.

My mother had been familiar with the German cultural tone since Arosa; and, in contrast to Vienna's aesthetic decadence, it appealed to her. She liked Fräulein Kündig and believed her; nor did she find fault with her when she noticed Fräulein Kündig's interest in Herr Schutt. He may have been much too bitter to get into conversations about art or literature. He had nothing to offer but a half-stifled grunt for Binding, whom Fräulein Kündig esteemed no less than Unruh (both authors were frequently mentioned in the *Frankfurter Zeitung*). And when Spengler's name came up, unavoidable in those days, Herr Schutt declared: "He wasn't at the front. Nothing is known about it." Whereupon Herr Rebhuhn mildly tossed in: "I should think that's unimportant for a philosopher."

"Maybe not for a philosopher of history," Fräulein Kündig protested; and one could see that, with all due respect for Spengler, she was taking Herr Schutt's part. However, the two men didn't get into an argument; the very fact that Herr Schutt *expected* active military duty from someone, while Herr Rebhuhn was willing to overlook it, had something conciliatory about it; it was as if the two of them had traded opinions. Still, the actual question of whether Spengler had been at the front wasn't settled in this way; and I still don't know the answer even now. Fräulein Kündig, it was obvious, felt sorry for Herr Schutt. For a long time, she managed to hide her pity behind free and easy remarks like "our war boy" or "he got through it." You could never tell how responsive he felt. He acted as neutral to her as if she'd never said a word to him; nonetheless, he greeted her with a nod when he entered the dining room, while he never even deigned to glance at Fräulein Rebhuhn to his right. Once, when my brothers and I were late from school and still not at the table, he asked my mother: "Where's your cannon fodder?" Which she later reported not without indignation. She said she had angrily replied: "Never! Never!" And he had mocked her: "No more war!"

However, Herr Schutt did acknowledge that my mother stubbornly opposed war, even though she had never experienced it personally; and his baiting remarks were actually meant to confirm her stance. Among the boarders, there was a very different sort, whom he ignored altogether. For instance, the Bembergs, a young married couple, who sat to his left. Herr Bemberg was a stockbroker with an unflagging sense of material profits; he even praised Fräulein Rahm for being so "able," referring to her knack for maneuvering countless suitors. "The chicest young lady in Frankfurt," he said, and yet he was one of the very few men who wasn't after her. What impressed him about her was "her nose for money" and her skeptical reaction to compliments. "She won't let anyone turn her head. She first wants to know what's on your mind."

His wife, composed of fashionable attributes, with the bobbed hair looking the most natural, was easygoing, but in a different way from Fräulein Rahm. She came from a solid middle-class background, but there was nothing incisive about her. You could tell she bought anything she felt like buying, but few things looked right on her; she went to art exhibits, was interested in women's clothing in paintings, admitted to having a weakness for Lucas Cranach, and explained that she liked his "terrific" modernity, whereby the word *explain* must sound too deep for her meager interjections. Herr and Frau Bemberg had met at a dance. One hour earlier, they'd been perfect strangers, but both knew—as he confessed not without pride—that there was more to each of them, much more to her than to him, but he was already considered a promising young broker. He found her "chic," asked her to dance, and promptly nicknamed her Pattie. "You remind me of Pattie," he said. "She's American." She wanted to know whether Pattie had been his first love. "It all depends on what you mean," he said. She understood and found it terrific that his first woman had been American, and she kept the name Pattie. That was what he called her in front of all the boarders, and whenever she didn't come down to a meal, he said: "Pattie isn't hungry today. She's watching her figure."

I would have forgotten all about this inoffensive couple if Herr Schutt hadn't managed to treat them as if they didn't exist. When he came hobbling along on his crutches, he acted as if they weren't there. He ignored their greeting, he overlooked their faces; and Frau Kupfer, who put up with his residing in the house only in memory of her husband, who had died in action, never once dared to say "Herr Bemberg" or "Frau Bemberg" in his presence. The young couple put up uncomplainingly with this boycott, which was started by Herr Schutt but spread no further. They sort of felt sorry for the cripple, who seemed poor in every respect; and although their pity wasn't much, it nevertheless countered his scorn.

At the farthest end of the table, the contrasts were less sharp. There was Herr Schimmel, a department-store official, radiant with health, sporting a stiff mustache and red cheeks, an ex-officer, neither embittered nor dissatisfied. His smile, never vanishing from his face, was virtually a spiritual state; it was reassuring to see that there are spirits that always stay exactly the same. His smile didn't change even in the worst weather, and the only thing at all surprising was that so much contentment remained alone and needed no human companionship to survive. Such companionship could easily have been found: not far from Herr Schimmel sat Fräulein Parandowski, a salesgirl; proud, beautiful, with the head of a Greek statue, she was never discomfited by Fräulein Kündig's reliance on the *Frankfurter Zeitung,* and Herr Bemberg's praises of Fräulein Rahm rolled off Fräulein Parandowski like water off a duck's back. "I just couldn't," she said, shaking her head. That was all she said, and it was clear what she couldn't. Fräulein Parandowski listened, but barely spoke; imperturbability suited her. Herr Schimmel's mustache (he sat diagonally across from her) looked as though it had been brushed into shape just for her. These two people were virtually made for one another. Yet he never spoke a word to her, they never came or left together; it was as though their nontogetherness was always precisely planned. Fräulein Parandowski neither waited for him to get up from the table nor hesitated to come to a meal way before him. They did have something in common, their silence. But he always smiled without giving it a second thought, while she, her head raised high, remained earnest, as if always thinking of something.

It was clear to everyone that there was more here than met the eye. Fräulein Kündig, who sat nearby, tried to get to the bottom of it, but foundered on the monumental resistance of these two people. Once, Fräulein Bunzel forgot herself and said "caryatid" just within earshot of Fräulein Parandowski, while Fräulein Kündig cheerily greeted Herr Schimmel with: "Here comes the cavalry."

But Frau Kupfer instantly rebuked her: she couldn't afford personal remarks at her boardinghouse table, and Fräulein Kündig used the reproach to ask Herr Schimmel point-blank whether he objected to being referred to as "cavalry." "It is an honor," he smiled. "I was a cavalryman."

"And he'll remain one till his dying day." That was how scornfully Herr Schutt reacted to any escapade of Fräulein Kündig's before it was settled that they liked one another.

It was only after about six months that a superior mind appeared in the Pension: Herr Caroli. He knew how to keep everyone at bay: he had read a great deal. His ironic comments, which emerged as carefully candied reading-fruits, delighted Fräulein Kündig. She couldn't always hit on where a line of his came from, and she would humble herself to ask for enlightenment. "Oh, please, please, now just where is that from? Please tell me, otherwise I won't get a wink of sleep again."

"Where do you think it's from?" Herr Schutt then replied in place of Herr Caroli. "From Büchmann's *Dictionary of Quotations,* like everything he says."

But this was way off target and a disgrace for Herr Schutt; for nothing that Herr Caroli uttered derived from Büchmann. "I'd rather take poison than Büchmann," said Herr Caroli. "I never quote anything that I haven't actually read." This was also the boardinghouse consensus. I was the only one to doubt it, because Herr Caroli took no notice of us. He even disliked Mother (who certainly had as good a background as he): her three boys took away seats from adults at the table, and one had to suppress the wittiest remarks because of them.

At that time—I was reading the Greek tragedies—he quoted *Oedipus* after attending a performance in Darmstadt. I continued his quotation, he pretended not to hear; and when I stubbornly repeated it, he whirled toward me and asked sharply: "Did you have that in school today?" I seldom had said anything; his rebuke, to muzzle me once and for all, was unfair and felt to be unfair by the others at the table. But since he was dreaded for his irony, no one protested, and I held my tongue, humiliated.

Herr Caroli not only knew a lot by heart, he cleverly varied entire quotations and then waited to see if anyone understood what he had pulled off. Fräulein Kündig, an eager playgoer, was hottest on his trail. A witty man, he was particularly skillful at distorting superserious things. But Fräulein Rebhuhn, the most sensitive boarder, told him that nothing was sacred to him; and he was impudent enough to reply: "Certainly not Feuerbach." Everyone knew that Fräulein Rebhuhn lived only for her asthmatic brother—and Feuerbach, and she said about Iphigenia (Feuerbach's, of course): "I would gladly have been she." Herr Caroli, who looked Southern and was about thirty-five, and had to put up with being told by the ladies that he had a forehead like Trotsky's, never spared anyone, not even himself. He'd rather be Rathenau, he said, three days before Rathenau's assassination; and this was the only time I ever saw him shaken. For, with tears in his eyes, he looked at me, a schoolboy, and said: "It will soon be over!"

Herr Rebhuhn, that warmhearted and Kaiser-possessed man, was the only one not rattled by the assassination. He esteemed old Rathenau a lot more than the son and never forgave the younger one for serving the Republic. However, he did concede that Walther had been something of a credit to Germany earlier, in the war, when Germany still had its honor, when it was still an empire. Herr Schutt said fiercely: "They're going to kill everyone, *everyone!*" For the first time in his life, Herr Bemberg mentioned the working class: "The workers won't put up with it!" Herr Caroli said: "We ought to leave Germany!" Fräulein Rahm, who couldn't stand assassinations because something often went awry, said: "Would you take me along?" And Herr Caroli never forgot this; his claim to intellect abandoned him on that day. He quite openly courted her, and to the annoyance of the ladies, he was seen going into her room and then not coming out again until ten o'clock.

An Important Visitor

At the noon meal in the Pension Charlotte, Mother played a respectable but not dominating part. She was marked by Vienna, even if part of her resisted Vienna. All she knew of Spengler was the title of his opus, *The Decline of the West*. Painting had never meant much to her; when Meier-Graefe's *Vincent* came out and Van Gogh became the chief topic of conversation at the boardinghouse table, Mother couldn't join in. And if ever she did let go and say something, she didn't cut a very good figure. Sunflowers, she said, had no fragrance, and the best thing about them was the seeds: you could at least munch them. There was an embarrassed hush, led by Fräulein Kündig, the supreme authority on current culture and truly moved by many of the things brought up in the *Frankfurter Zeitung*. Around this time, the Van Gogh religion began; and Fräulein Kündig once said it was only now, after learning about Van Gogh, that she understood what Jesus was all about—a statement which Herr Bemberg emphatically protested against. Herr Schutt found it extravagant, Herr Schimmel smiled. Fräulein Rebhuhn pleaded: "But he's so unmusical," meaning Van Gogh; and when she realized that no one understood what she was talking about, she undauntedly added: "Can you imagine him painting Feuerbach's *Concert*?"

I didn't know anything about Van Gogh and I asked Mother about him upstairs in our rooms. She had so little to say that I was embarrassed for her. She even said something she would never have said before: "A madman who painted straw chairs and sunflowers, everything always yellow. He didn't like any other colors, until he got sunstroke and put a bullet through his brain." I was very unsatisfied by this information. I sensed that the madness she ascribed to him referred to me. For some time now, she had been against any kind of eccentricity; every second artist was "crazy," as far as she was concerned, but this referred only to modern artists (especially those still alive); the earlier ones, with whom she'd been brought up, escaped unmolested. She allowed no one to touch a hair on her Shakespeare's head; and she had great moments at the boardinghouse table only when Herr Bemberg or some other incautious soul complained how awfully bored he'd been at some performance of Shakespeare—it was really time to put an end to him and replace him with something more modern.

Mother would then at last become her old admired self again. With a few sparkling sentences, she demolished poor Herr Bemberg, who woefully cast about for help; but no one came to his rescue. When Shakespeare was at stake, Mother didn't give a damn about anything. She threw caution to the winds, she didn't care what the others thought of her, and when she concluded by saying that for the shallow people of this inflation period, who had only money on their minds, Shakespeare was certainly not the right thing, she conquered all hearts; from Fräulein Kündig, who admired her élan and her spirit, to Herr Schutt, who embodied the tragic, even if he had never called it by its name, and even Fräulein Parandowski, who supported any pride and visualized Shakespeare as proud. Why, even Herr Schimmel's smile took on a mysterious quality when, to the amazement of the entire table, he said "Ophelia," repeating the name slowly lest he had mispronounced it. "Our cavalrist at *Hamlet*," said Fräulein Kündig. "Who would have thought." Whereupon Herr Schutt promptly broke in: "Just because a man says 'Ophelia' doesn't necessarily mean that he's seen *Hamlet*." It turned out that Herr Schimmel didn't know who Hamlet was, which provoked great mirth. Never again did he sally out so far. None-theless, Herr Bemberg's attack on Shakespeare was beaten off; his own wife solemnly declared that she liked the women disguised as men in Shakespeare, they were so chic.

In those days, the name Stinnes often cropped up in the papers. It was the period of inflation. I refused to under-stand anything of economic matters; behind anything that smelled of economy, I sensed a trap laid by my Manchester uncle, who wanted to drag me into his business. His major attack at Sprüngli's restaurant in Zurich, just two years ear-lier, was still in my bones [see *The Tongue Set Free*]. Its effect had been intensified by my terrible argument with Mother. Anything I felt threatened by I blamed on him. It was natu-ral that he should overlap with Stinnes for me. The way peo-ple talked about Stinnes, the envy I sensed in Herr Bemberg's voice when he mentioned his name, the cutting scorn with which Herr Schutt condemned him ("Everyone keeps getting poorer, he keeps getting richer"), the unanimous sympathy of all the women in the boardinghouse (Frau Kupfer: *"He* can still afford things"; Fräulein Rahm, who found her long-est sentence for him: "What do we know about his sort?"; Fräulein Rebhuhn: "He's never got time for music"; Fräulein Bunzel: "I feel sorry for him. No one understands him"; Fräulein Kündig: "I'd like to read the begging letters he re-ceives"; Fräulein Parandowski would have liked to work for him: "You know where you are with a man like him"; Frau Bemberg enjoyed thinking about his wife: "A woman has to dress chicly for a man like him")—they always talked about him for a long time. My mother was the only one who didn't say a word. This one time, Herr Rebhuhn concurred with Herr Schutt and even used the harsh word *parasite;* more precisely: "A parasite in the nation." And Herr Schimmel, mildest of all smilers, gave an unexpected twist to Fräulein Parandowski's comment: "Maybe we've already been bought up. You can't tell." When I asked Mother why she held her tongue, she said it would be inappropriate for her as a foreigner to meddle with internal German matters. But it was obvious that she was thinking of something else, something she didn't want to get off her chest.

Then, one day, she was holding a letter in her hand and saying: "Children, the day after tomorrow, we're having company. Herr Hungerbach is coming to tea." It turned out that she knew Herr Hungerbach from the forest sanatorium in Arosa. She said she felt a bit embarrassed that he was visiting her in the boardinghouse; he was used to a completely different life style, but she couldn't very well say no. It was too late anyway; he was traveling and she didn't even know where to reach him. As usual, when I heard the word *travel*, I imagined an explorer and I wanted to know through what continent he was traveling. "He's on a business trip, of course," she said. "He's an industrialist." Now I knew why she had been silent at the table. "It would be better if we didn't speak about him in the boardinghouse. Nobody will recognize him when he comes."

Naturally, I was biased against him. I wouldn't have needed the mealtime talk to dislike him. He was a man who belonged to my ogre-uncle's sphere; what did he want here? I sensed an uneasiness in my mother and I felt I ought to protect her against him. But I didn't realize how serious the matter was until she said: "When he is here, my son, do not leave the room. I would like you to hear him out from start to finish. This is a man who's in the thick of life. In Arosa, he promised to take you boys in hand when we came to Germany. He's got an endless number of things to do. But I can now see that he's a man of his word."

I was curious about Herr Hungerbach; and expecting a serious collision with him, I looked forward to an opponent who would make things hard for me. I wanted to be impressed by him in order to stand my ground against him all the better. My mother, who had a keen scent for my "youthful prejudices" (as she called them), said I shouldn't believe that Herr Hungerbach was a spoiled brat from a rich background. On the contrary, he had had a difficult time as the son of a miner, and he had worked his way up step by step. In Arosa, he had once told her his life story, and she had finally learned what it means to start way on the bottom. She had finally said to Herr Hungerbach: "I'm afraid my boy has always had it too easy." He then asked about me and eventually declared that it's never too late. He knew just what to do in such a case: "Throw him in the water and let him struggle. All at once, he'll know how to swim."

Herr Hungerbach had an abrupt manner. He knocked and was already in the room. He shook Mother's hand, but instead of looking at her, he focused his gaze on me and barked. His sentences were short and abrupt; it was impossible to misunderstand them; but he didn't speak, he barked. From the instant he arrived to the instant he left (he stayed a full hour), he kept barking nonstop. He asked no questions and expected no answers. Mother had been his fellow patient in Arosa, but he never once inquired about her health. He didn't ask me what my name was. Instead, I got a rehash of all the horrifying things my mother had thrown at me in our argument one year earlier. The best thing, he said, is a tough apprenticeship as early as possible. Don't bother going to university. Throw away the books, forget the whole business. Everything in books is wrong, all that counts is life, experience, and hard work. Work till your bones ache. Nothing else deserves to be called work. Anyone who can't take it, anyone who's too weak, should perish. And good riddance. There are too many people in the world anyway. The useless ones should vanish. Besides, it's not out of the question for someone to turn out useful after all. Despite a totally wrong start. The main thing is to forget all this foolishness, which has nothing to do with real life. Life is struggle, ruthless struggle, and that's a good thing. Otherwise, mankind can't progress. A race of weaklings would have died out long ago without leaving a trace. Nothing will get you nothing. Men have to be raised by men. Women are too sentimental, they only want to dress up their little princes and keep them away from any dirt. But work is dirty more than anything else. The definition of work: something that makes you tired and dirty; but you still don't give up.

I find it terribly distorting to translate Herr Hungerbach's barking into intelligible utterances; but even if I didn't understand certain phrases and words, the meaning of every individual directive was more than clear. He absolutely seemed to expect you to jump up on the spot and get down to hard work (no other kind counted).

Nevertheless, tea was poured. We sat around a low, circular table; the guest brought the teacup to his lips, but before he could manage to take a sip, a new directive occurred to him, and it was too urgent for him to wait one sip. The cup was brusquely set down, the mouth opened to new terse phrases, from which at least one thing could be gleaned: their indubitableness. Even older people could hardly have contradicted him, much less women or children. Herr Hungerbach enjoyed his impact. He was dressed all in blue, the color of his eyes. He was immaculate, not the tiniest spot on him, not a speck of dust. I thought of various things I'd have liked to say, but what crossed my mind most often was the word *miner*, and I wondered if this cleanest, hardest, most self-assured of men had really worked in a mine when he was young, as Mother claimed.

Since I never opened my mouth even *once* (when would he have granted me a split second?), since he had hurled out everything, he added (and this time it sounded like a directive to himself) one last thing: He said he had no time to lose and left. He did shake Mother's hand, but he no longer paid me any heed; he had, so he thought, shattered me much too thoroughly to consider me worth saying goodbye to. He prohibited Mother from seeing him downstairs; he said he knew the way and absolutely refused to hear a word of thanks. She should first wait and see the effect of his surgery before expressing her gratitude. "The operation was a success, but the patient died," he added. This was a joke to mellow the previous seriousness. Then it was over.

"He's changed a lot. He was different in Arosa," said Mother. She was embarrassed and ashamed. She realized she could hardly have picked a worse ally for her new methods of upbringing. But, while Herr Hungerbach had been talking, I had had a terrible suspicion, which tormented me and left me speechless. It was quite a while before I felt capable of blurting it out. Meanwhile, Mother recounted all sorts of things about Herr Hungerbach, the way he'd been *earlier,* just a year ago. To my amazement, she emphasized—for the first time—his faith. He had spoken to her several times about how important his faith was to him. He had said he owed his faith to his mother; he had never faltered, not even in the most difficult times. He had always known that everything would turn out all right, and it always did: He had gotten so far, he said, because he had never faltered.

What did all this have to do with his faith, I asked.

"He told me how bad things look in Germany," she said, "and that it will have to keep getting worse before it gets better. You have to pull yourselves up by your own bootstraps; there's just no other way. And in such a crisis, there's no room for weaklings and Mamma's boys."

"Did he talk the same way back then?" I asked.

"What do you mean?"

"I mean did he always bark and without looking you in the eye?"

"No, it surprised me, too. He was really different back then. He always inquired about my health and asked me whether I'd heard from you. He was impressed that I spoke about you so much. He even listened. Once—I remember clearly— he sighed . . . Just imagine this man sighing. And he said it had been different in his youth. His mother hadn't had time for such niceties, with fifteen or sixteen children, I've forgotten how many. I wanted him to read your play. He took the manuscript, read the title, and said: '*Junius Brutus*—not a bad title. You can learn something from the Romans.' "

"Did he even know who that was?"

"Yes. Just imagine. He said: 'Why, that was the man who sentenced his own sons to death.' "

"That's all he knows about the story. He liked that part, it suits him. But did he read it?"

"No, of course not. He had no time for literature. He always studied the business section of the newspaper, and he kept telling me to move to Germany. 'You can live there very cheap, dear Frau Canetti, cheaper all the time!' "

"And that's why we left Zurich and moved to Germany?" I said it with such bitterness that even I was startled. It was worse than I had feared. The thought of leaving the place I loved more than anything in the world, leaving it just to live *more cheaply* somewhere else, was utterly humiliating. She instantly noticed that she had gone too far, and retreated: "No, that's not why. Not at all. It may have been a factor sometimes when I was considering the matter, but it wasn't decisive."

"What *was* decisive?"

She felt cornered, on the defensive, and since we were still under the impact of the disgusting visit, it did her good to account to me and clear up a few things for herself.

She seemed uncertain, as though groping through her mind, groping for answers that would stand up and not melt on the spot. "He always wanted to talk to me," she said. "I think he liked me. He was respectful and, instead of joking around like the other patients there, he was always earnest and spoke about his mother. I liked that. You know, usually women don't like it if a man compares them with his mother, because it makes them feel older. But I liked it because I felt he was taking me seriously."

"But you impress everyone because you're beautiful and intelligent." I really thought so, otherwise I wouldn't have said it at this point. I was in no mood for friendly words. On the contrary, I felt a terrible hatred. I was finally on the trail of what had been my gravest loss since my father's death: our departure from Zurich.

"He kept saying it's irresponsible of me, as a lone woman, to bring you up. He said you ought to feel a man's strong hand. 'But this is the way things *are* now,' I used to answer him. 'Where in the world do you expect me to get him a father?' I've never remarried, so that I could devote myself fully to you boys, and now I was being told that this was bad for you: my sacrifice for you would ultimately harm you. I was terrified. *Now,* I believe he *wanted* to terrify me in order to make an impression on me. He wasn't very interesting intellectually, you know. He always kept repeating the same things. But he did frighten me, as far as you were concerned, and he promptly offered to help me. 'Come to Germany, my dear Frau Canetti,' he said. 'I'm a terribly busy man, I have no time whatsoever, not a minute, but I'll see about your son. Why don't you come to Frankfurt? I'll visit you and have a serious talk with him. He doesn't know what the world is like. His eyes will open in Germany. I'll take care of him, and thoroughly. Then you can throw him into life! He's studied enough. No more books! He'll never be a man! Do you want to have a woman for a son?' "

The Challenge

Rainer Friedrich was a tall, moony boy, who, when he walked, never thought about how or where he was going. It wouldn't have surprised you if his right leg had gone in one direction and his left leg in another. He wasn't weak, mind you, just totally uninterested in physical things, and that's why he was the worst athlete in class. He was always lost in thought—in fact, two kinds of thought. His real gift was mathematics. He had a knack for it such as I have never seen.

No sooner was a problem stated than he had solved it; the rest of us still hadn't quite understood what it was all about, and he had already come up with the answer. But he didn't show off; his answer came softly and naturally, as if he were translating fluently from one language to another. It was no strain whatsoever; mathematics seemed like his native tongue. I was surprised by both aspects: his facility and his lack of conceit. It wasn't just knowledge, it was ability, which he was always prepared to demonstrate in any frame of mind. I asked him whether he could solve formulas in his sleep. He earnestly deliberated and then said simply: "I think so." I greatly respected his ability, but I didn't envy him. It was impossible to feel envy about something so unique; the very fact that it was so astonishing, so miraculous, raised it far above the region of any lower envy. However, I did envy his modesty. "It's so easy," he would say when someone expressed amazement at his instinctive solution. "You can do it, too." He acted as if he really believed that you could do anything he could, but that you just didn't *want* to—a kind of unwillingness that he never tried to explain except perhaps on religious grounds.

For the second thing that occupied his thoughts was *toto caelo* remote from mathematics. It was his faith. He went to a Bible group; he was a pious Christian. Since he lived near me, we walked home from school together, and he made an effort to convert me to his faith. This had never happened to me at school. He didn't try arguments, it was never a discussion; there was no trace of the rigorous logic of his mathematical mind. It was a friendly invitation, which was always preceded by my name, whereby he placed an almost adjuring stress on the first syllable. "Élias," that was how he began, almost with a drawl, "try it. *You* can believe, too. All you have to do is want to. It's very simple. Christ died for you, too." He regarded me as stubborn, for I didn't answer. He assumed it was the word *Christ* that went against my grain. How could he have known that "Jesus Christ" had been very close to me during my early childhood, in those wonderful English hymns that we sang with our governess [see *The Tongue Set Free*]. What repelled me, what struck me dumb, what horrified me wasn't the name, which I, perhaps unwittingly, still carried inside me; rather, it was the "died for you, too." I had never come to terms with the word *die*. If someone had died for me, I would have been burdened with the worst guilt feelings, as though I were profiting from a murder. If there was anything that kept me away from Christ, it was this notion of a sacrifice, the sacrifice of a life, which had been offered up for all mankind, of course, but also for me.

A few months before the secret singing of Christian hymns had begun in Manchester, Mr. Duke, the Jewish instructor, had taught me about Abraham's sacrifice of his son. I've never gotten over it, not even today—ridiculous as it might sound. It aroused a skepticism toward *orders* within me, a doubt that has never subsided. It alone sufficed to keep me from becoming an observant Jew. Christ's crucifixion, although voluntary, had no less a bewildering effect on me, for it meant that death had been *employed*, whatever the purpose. Friedrich, who believed he was saying the best for his cause and always stated with warmth in his voice that Christ had died for me, too, never had an inkling of how completely he was thwarting his efforts with that sentence. Perhaps he misinterpreted my silence, mistook it for indecision. For otherwise, it would be hard to tell why he kept repeating the same sentence every day on the way home from school. His obstinacy was astonishing, but never annoying, for I always sensed that it derived from a decent conviction: he wanted to let me feel that I wasn't excluded from the best thing he had, and that I could be as much a part of it as he. Also, his gentleness was disarming: he never seemed annoyed at my silence in this respect. We talked about lots of things and I was anything but silent. So he merely frowned, as though surprised that this one problem was so hard to solve, and then said when we parted: "Think it over, Elias"—this too more pleading than emphatic—and stumbled into his house.

I knew that our walk home would always end with this conversion attempt and I grew accustomed to it. But only gradually did I learn about a completely different mood that prevailed in his home, next to the Christian one and diametrically opposed to it. He had a younger brother, who also attended the Wöhler School, two years below us. I've forgotten his name, perhaps because he encountered me so nastily and treated me with undisguised hostility. He wasn't as tall as his brother, but a good athlete, who knew quite well what he did with his legs. He was as sure and resolute as Rainer was vague and dreamy. They had the same eyes; but while the elder brother always had a waiting, inquisitive, benevolent look, the younger one's gaze had something bold, quarrelsome, provoking in it. I knew him only by sight. I had never conversed with him, but from Rainer I found out indirectly what he had said about me.

It was always something unpleasant or insulting. "My brother says your real name is Kahn and not Canetti. He wants to know why you people changed your name." These suspicious queries always came from his brother; they were expressed in his name. Rainer wanted my answers in order to refute his brother. He was very fond of him, I believe; he liked me, too, and so he may have felt that by reporting every malicious remark, he was actually mediating and trying to make peace. I was supposed to refute the comments. My answers were reported to his brother. But Rainer was quite mistaken about any possibility of reconciliation. On our way home, the very first thing I got to hear from Rainer was a new suspicion and accusation from his brother. These comments were so silly that I never took them seriously, even though I answered them conscientiously. Their main thrust was always the same, namely, that I, like all other Jews, was trying to hide my Jewish background. This was obviously not the case, and it was even more obvious a few minutes later, when I responded with silence to Rainer's inevitable conversion attempt.

Perhaps it was his brother's inability to listen to reason that forced me to come up with patient and detailed replies. Rainer repeated all his brother's comments in parentheses, so to speak. He transmitted them tonelessly, without taking a position. He didn't say, "I believe it, too" or "I don't believe it"; he delivered his message as though he were merely the go-between. Had I heard these inexhaustible suspicions in his brother's aggressive tone, I would have lost my temper and never replied. But they were always perfectly calm, preceded by "my brother says" or "my brother wants to know." And then came something so awful that I was forced to speak—even though it hadn't really gotten my dander up—for it was so silly that you felt sorry for the person asking it. "Elias, my brother wants to know: Why did you people use Christian blood for the Passover Feast?" I answered: "Never. Never. Why, we celebrated Passover when I was a child. I would have noticed something. We had lots of Christian maids in the house, they were my playmates." But then his brother's next message came the next day: "Maybe not nowadays. Now, it's too well known. But in earlier times, why did the Jews back then slaughter Christian children for their Passover Feast?" All the old accusations were dug up: "Why did the Jews poison the wells?" When I said, "They never did that," he went on, "They *did*, at the time of the plague." "But they died of the plague just like everyone else." "Because they poisoned the wells. Their hatred of Christians was so great that they perished, too, because of their hatred." "Why do Jews curse all other human beings?" "Why are Jews cowardly?" "Why were there no Jews in active combat during the war?"

Thus it went. My patience was inexhaustible; I answered as well as I could, always earnest, never offended, as though I had checked my encyclopedia to find out the scholarly facts. These accusations seemed totally absurd, and my answers, I decided, were going to do away with them once and for all. And in order to emulate Rainer's equanimity, I once said to him: "Tell your brother I'm grateful to him. This way, I can get rid of these stupid ideas for good."

Now, even my gullible, innocent, and sincere friend Rainer was surprised. "That'll be tough," he said, "he's always got new questions." But the real innocent was I, because for several months, I failed to see what his brother was after. One day, Rainer said: "My brother wants to know why you always keep answering his questions. After all, you can go up to him in the schoolyard during recess and challenge him to a fight. You can fight with him if you're not scared of him!"

I would never have dreamt of being scared of him. I could only pity him because of his unspeakably stupid questions. But he wanted to pick a fight with me and had chosen the peculiar detour of his brother, who had never stopped his conversion attempts on a single day during this period. My pity changed to scorn. I didn't do him the honor of challenging him: he was two years my junior; it wouldn't have been fair to fight with a boy in a lower class. So I cut off my "dealings" with him. The next time Rainer began, "My brother says—" I interrupted him in midsentence: "Your brother can go to hell. I don't fight with little kids." However, we remained friends; nor did anything change in his conversion attempts.

The Portrait

Hans Baum, my first friend here, was the son of an engineer at the Siemens-Schuckert Works. He was a very formal person, raised in discipline by his father, intent on not compromising himself, always earnest and conscientious, a good worker, not very gifted, but painstaking. He read good books and attended the Saalbau concerts; there was always something we could talk about. One inexhaustible topic was Romain Rolland, especially his *Beethoven* and his *Jean-Christophe*. Baum, feeling a sense of responsibility for mankind, wanted to be a doctor, which I liked very much about him. He did have thoughts about politics, but they were moderate thoughts. He instinctively rejected any extremes; he was so self-controlled that he always seemed to be in uniform. Young as he was, he thought out every issue from all sides, "for justice's sake," as he put it, but perhaps more because he abhorred thoughtlessness.

When I visited his home, I was amazed at how spirited his father was, a vehement philistine with a thousand prejudices, which he never stopped voicing, good-natured, thoughtless, a prankster. His deepest affection was for Frankfurt. I visited them a few more times. Each time he read us poems by his favorite poet, Friedrich Stoltze (a local Frankfurt poet). "This is the greatest poet," he said. "Anyone who doesn't like him deserves to be shot." Hans Baum's mother had died years ago; the household was run by his sister, a cheery girl, corpulent despite her youth.

Young Baum's rectitude was something I mulled over. He would rather have bitten off his tongue than tell a lie. Cowardice was a sin in his world, perhaps the greatest. If a teacher called him to account—which didn't happen often; he was one of the best students—he would give completely open answers, heedless of the consequences for himself. If it wasn't about him, he was chivalrous and covered up for his friends, but without lying. If the teacher called on him, he would stand up straight as an arrow. He had the most rigid posture in class, and he buttoned his jacket, resolute, but formal. It would have been impossible for him to keep his jacket unbuttoned in a public situation; perhaps that was why he often made you think he was wearing a uniform. There was nothing you could really say against Baum. He already had integrity when young and was by no means stupid. But he was always the same; every reaction of his was predictable. You were never surprised by him. At best you were surprised by the fact that there was nothing surprising about him. In matters of honor, he was more than sensitive. A long time later, when I told him about the game that Friedrich's brother had indulged in with me, he was beside himself (Baum was Jewish) and he asked me in all seriousness whether he should challenge the brother. He understood neither the long, patient period of my replies nor my subsequent total scorn. The matter unnerved Baum. He felt there must be something wrong with me, because I'd put up with the game for so long. Since I wouldn't allow him to do anything direct in my name, he investigated and found out that Friedrich's deceased father had gotten into business difficulties, in which competitors of his, Jews, had had a hand. I didn't understand the details; our information wasn't precise enough for us to understand. But the father had died a short while later, and I now began to understand how the family had developed this blind hatred.

Felix Wertheim was a merry, spirited boy, who was quite indifferent to whether and how much he learned, for during classes, he was busy studying the teachers. No idiosyncrasy of any teacher eluded him; he mastered them all like roles, and he had very productive favorites. His particular victim was Krämer, the choleric Latin teacher, whom he played so perfectly that you thought he *was* Krämer. Once, during such a performance, Krämer arrived in class unexpectedly early and was suddenly confronted with himself. Wertheim had gotten into such a rage that he couldn't stop, and so he lashed out at Krämer, as though the teacher were the wrong one and were insolently arrogating his role. The scene went on for a minute or so. The two stood face to face, stared at each other incredulously, and lashed out at each other in the filthiest way, as was Krämer's wont. The class expected the worst, but nothing happened—Krämer, choleric Krämer, had to laugh. He had a hard time stifling his mirth. Wertheim sank back on his seat in the first row. He had lost his own desire to laugh because of Krämer's unmistakable desire to laugh. The incident was never mentioned; there was no punishment.

Krämer felt flattered by the perfect fidelity of the portrait and was incapable of doing anything against his likeness.

Wertheim's father owned a big clothing store. He was rich and uninterested in hiding his wealth. We were invited to their home on New Year's Eve, and we found ourselves in a house full of Liebermanns. Five or six Liebermanns hung in every room; I don't believe there were any other paintings. The highlight of the collection was a portrait of the host. We were charmingly regaled; it was nice and swanky. The host had no qualms about showing his portrait. He spoke—audible to everyone—about his friendship with Liebermann. I said, no less loudly, to Baum: "He sat for a portrait, that doesn't make him his friend by any stretch of the imagination."

This man's claim to friendship with Liebermann irritated me; indeed, I was irked by the very thought that a great painter had occupied himself with this ordinary face. The portrait bothered me more than the sitter. I felt that the collection would have been so much better without this painting. There was no way of skirting it. Everything was arranged to make you see it. Not even my impolite remark had whisked it away; aside from Baum, no one had paid me any heed.

In the ensuing weeks, Baum and I had a heated discussion about the portrait. I asked him: Did a painter have to paint everyone who approached him with a commission? Couldn't the painter say no if he didn't feel like making the person the subject of his art? Baum felt that the painter had to accept, but he had the possibility of revealing his opinion in the way he painted the picture. He had every right to do an ugly or repulsive portrait. This was within the precincts of his art, but a refusal would be a sign of weakness. It would mean that he was unsure of his abilities. This sounded moderate and just; my immoderateness, I felt, contrasted unpleasantly with his fairness.

"How can he paint," I said, "if he's shaken by disgust at a face? If he gets even and distorts the sitter's face, then it's not a portrait anymore. The man needn't have sat for him; the painter could have done it just as well without him. But if he accepts payment for this mockery of the victim, then he's done something very base for money. You could forgive a poor starving devil, because he's still unknown. But in a famous and sought-after painter, it's inexcusable."

Baum didn't dislike rigorous standards, but he was less interested in other people's morality than in his own. He said that you can't expect everyone to be like Michelangelo. There were people who were dependent and not so proud. I felt that all painters should be proud. Anyone who didn't have the grit could take up an ordinary trade. But Baum gave me something important to think about.

How did I imagine a portraitist to be? Should he depict people as they are, or should he paint ideal pictures of them? Yet for ideal pictures, you don't need portrait painters! Every human being was as he was, and that was what the painter should capture. This way, later generations would know how many different sorts of people there had been.

This made sense to me, and I admitted defeat. But I was left with a queasy feeling about the relationship between painters and their patrons. I couldn't shake the suspicion that most portraits were meant to flatter and therefore shouldn't be taken seriously. Perhaps that was one of the reasons why I then sided so resolutely with the satirists. George Grosz became as important to me as Daumier. The distortion that served satirical aims won me over completely. I was irresistibly addicted to it as though *it* were Truth.

A Fool's Confession

Six months after I entered the class, a new boy came in, Jean Dreyfus. He was taller and older than I, well built, athletic, handsome. He spoke French at home, and a little of it rubbed off on his German. He came from Geneva, but had already lived in Paris, and his cosmopolitan background made him stand out from the other schoolboys. There was something sophisticated and superior about him, but he didn't show off. Contrary to Baum, he did not value school knowledge; he didn't take the teachers seriously and treated them with exquisite irony; he made me feel he knew more about certain things than they did. He was extremely polite and yet appeared spontaneous. I could never tell in advance what he would say about something. He was never gross or childish; he was always controlled and made you feel his superiority without oppressing you with it. He was a strong boy; physical and mental things seemed well balanced in him. He struck me as perfect, but I was confused because I couldn't ferret out what he took seriously. Hence this mystery was added to all his other charms. I brooded a great deal about what it could be. I suspected it had something to do with his background, but I was so dazzled by this background that I could never untangle the mystery.

I believe that Dreyfus never realized what drew me to him. Had he known, he would have made fun of it. After our very first conversations, I made up my mind to be his friend; and since he was always cordial and civilized, the process of becoming friends took a certain amount of time. On the paternal side, his family owned one of the largest private banks in Germany; we imagined that his father must be very rich. Since I felt encircled and threatened by my own relatives, his situation would have inevitably aroused my distrust and dislike. But such a response was prevented by the fact—overwhelming for me—that his father had resisted the banking tradition and become a poet, quite simply a poet. Not a writer aiming for cheap success as a novelist, but a modern poet, intelligible to very few, writing, I presumed, in French. I had never read anything of his, but he had books out; I made no attempt to lay hold of them; on the contrary, it strikes me today that I felt qualms about getting them, because what I cared about was the aura of something obscure, unfathomable, so difficult that it would have been absurd for me to seek access to the poems at my age. Albert Dreyfus was also interested in modern art. He wrote art reviews and collected paintings, was friendly with many of the most original new painters, and was married to a painter, my classmate's mother.

At first, I didn't quite catch this fact. Jean mentioned it casually; it didn't sound like anything particularly honorable, more (so far as one could divine anything behind his well-formed sentences) like a problem. But when he invited me over and I came into a home full of paintings—powerful impressionist portraits, including childhood pictures of my friend—I found out that these were his mother's works. They were so lively and full of bravura that, despite my meager knowledge in this area, I instantly blurted out: "Why, she's a *real* painter! You never told me!" To which he replied, somewhat astonished: "Did you doubt it? I did tell you!" It all depended on what one meant by *tell;* he hadn't announced it, just tossed it in casually; and, given the great solemnity that I associated with any kind of artistic activity, his way of informing me had seemed to aim at *distracting* my attention, at apologizing cordially for his mother's painting. I had expected something like Fräulein Mina's flower pictures at the Yalta school [see *The Tongue Set Free*] and I was thunderstruck.

It wouldn't have occurred to me to ask whether Jean's mother was a *famous* painter; all that mattered was that I saw the paintings, that they existed, that they were vibrant and vital, and also that the whole rather large apartment was *brimming* with them. During a later visit, I met the painter. She looked nervous and a bit scattered; she appeared unhappy, even though she frequently laughed. I sensed something of her deep affection for her son. Jean seemed less balanced in her presence; he was worried, as anyone else would have been, and he inquired after his mother's health.

Her answer didn't satisfy him. He asked again. He wanted to know the whole truth, no trace of irony, sympathy (the very last thing I'd have expected of him) instead of superiority; if I had seen him and his mother together more often, I would have had a very different conception of him.

But I never saw her again; I saw him every day, and so I got from him what I needed most at that time: an intact, unquestioned notion of art and the lives of those who devote themselves to it. A father who had turned his back on the family business and become a poet, whose passion was paintings, and who had therefore married a real painter. A son who spoke marvelous French even though he went to a German school, and now and then (what could be more natural with such a father!) wrote a French poem himself, even though he was more interested in mathematics. Then there was the uncle, his father's brother, a physician, a neurologist, a professor at the University of Frankfurt, with an absolutely beautiful daughter, Maria, whom I met only once and would have liked to see again.

Nothing was missing: the science for which I had the greatest respect, medicine—I kept catching myself thinking that I would study medicine—and finally, the beauty of an apparently capricious cousin. Jean, who acted as if he knew a little about women, admitted she was attractive, but tended to apply more rigorous standards to a cousin.

It was nice to talk to Jean about girls: actually, he did the talking, and I listened. It took me a while to gain enough experience from his conversations to come up with my own stories. They were all made up. I was still as inexperienced as I'd been in Zurich; but I learned from Jean and took on his aura. He never noticed that I regaled him with tall tales, whereby I preferred to stick to very few—normally one continuous story, which dragged on through many vicissitudes. My story was so suspenseful that he always asked me for more, and he was keenly interested in one girl in particular, whom I had named Maria in honor of his cousin. Not only was she beautiful, but she also had the most contradictory qualities: on one day, you were sure she liked you—only to learn on the next day that she was totally indifferent to you. But this didn't end the matter. Two days later you were rewarded for your persistence with a first kiss, and then came a long list of insults, rejections, and the tenderest declarations. We puzzled a great deal about the nature of women. He confessed that he had never run into such an enigmatic girl as my Maria, yet he had had all sorts of experiences. He expressed a desire to meet her, and I didn't say no point-blank. For, thanks to her whims, I was able to put him off without arousing his suspicions.

These conversations went on practically uninterrupted, they had their own weight and continued for months on end; and they first aroused my interest in things that I basically still felt indifferent to. I knew nothing; I had no inkling of what went on between lovers aside from kissing. At the boarding-house, Fräulein Rahm lived in the next room, receiving her Friend evening after evening. Although Mother had taken the precautionary measure of placing the piano against the connecting door, one could hear enough without eavesdropping. It must have been because of the nature of this relationship that the sounds from next door surprised me, but didn't occupy me. First came Herr Ödenburg's pleas, which Fräulein Rahm answered with a harsh "No!" The pleading became a beseeching, then a whimpering and begging that wouldn't stop and was interrupted only by colder and colder "No!"s. Finally, it sounded as if Fräulein Rahm were seriously angry. "Get out! Get out!" she ordered, while Herr Ödenburg wept heartbreakingly. Sometimes she actually threw him out, in the middle of his tears, and I wondered whether he was still crying on the stairway when he ran into any of the boarders; but I didn't have the heart to go and see for myself. Sometimes he was allowed to stay; the weeping became a whimpering. He had to leave Fräulein Rahm at ten on the dot anyway, because women couldn't have male callers after 10 P.M.

When the weeping grew so loud that we couldn't read, Mother shook her head, but we never talked about it. I knew how unpleasant it was for her to have such a neighbor; but, so far as our childishly innocent ears were concerned, she wasn't really dissatisfied with this sort of relationship. Whatever I heard, I kept to myself; I never associated it with Jean's conquests; but perhaps, without my realizing it, it had a remote influence on the behavior of my Maria.

Things were never improper in Jean's accounts or my fictions. We recounted them as people used to do. Everything had a chivalrous tinge; what counted was admiration, not capture. If the admiration was clever and skillful enough to penetrate and not be forgotten, then you had won; conquering consisted in making an impression and being taken seriously. If the flow of beautiful things that you thought up and then *articulated* was not interrupted, if the chance to apply them depended not only on your own skill, but also on the expectation and receptivity of the girl in question, then this was proof that you were taken seriously, and you were a man. You had to prove yourself in this way; this attracted you more than the adventure itself. Jean told about an uninterrupted chain of incidents in which he'd proven himself. Although my own stories were invented from beginning to end, I believed every word he told me, just as he believed me. It never crossed my mind to doubt what he told me simply because I was making up *my* stories. Our reports existed in themselves; perhaps he embellished details; the things I created out of whole cloth may have stimulated him to juice up a few particulars. Our accounts were attuned to each other, they dovetailed, and they influenced his inner life at this time no less than mine.

My attitude was altogether different in my conversations with Hans Baum. Jean and Hans weren't friends, Jean considered Baum boring. He despised good students; and duty, which Hans fairly emanated, struck Jean as ludicrous, because it was rigid and lifeless and always remained the same. Their aloofness toward one another stood me in good stead; had they compared what I told them about love, I would have soon lost all prestige with them.

I *meant* what I said to Baum, while I was only playing in my conversations with Dreyfus. Perhaps I was intent on learning from Dreyfus, although I competed with him only in conversations and made sure not to emulate him otherwise. Once, I had a very serious talk with Baum when, to his astonishment, I told him my latest opinion on the topic: "There's no such thing as love," I declared. "Love is an invention of poets. Sooner or later, you read about it in a book and you believe it because you're young. You think it's been kept from you by adults, so you pounce on it and believe it before you experience it personally. No one would hit upon it on his own. There is really no such thing as love." He hesitated to reply. I could tell that he totally disagreed with me. But since he took everything so seriously and was extremely reserved to boot, he made no effort to refute me. He would have had to expose intimate experiences of his own, something he was incapable of doing.

My extreme negation was in response to a book that had been in Mother's possession since Zurich and that I had now read against her will: Strindberg's *A Fool's Confession*. She liked this book very much; I could tell because it always lay out by itself, while she heaped up all the other Strindberg volumes in one pile. Once, when in an antiquated and arrogant manner, I called Herr Ödenburg a "necktie salesman" and wondered how Fräulein Rahm could stand his company evening after evening (while my hand, by chance or design, played with *A Fool's Confession*, opened it, leafed through it, closed it, went back to it and opened it again), she said, assuming I meant to read this book after all because of the nightly scenes next door: "Don't read that! You'll destroy something for yourself that you'll never be able to restore. Wait until you've had your own experiences. Then it can't harm you."

For so many years, I had blindly believed her. She had never had to argue to prevent me from reading a book. But now, since Herr Hungerbach's visit, her authority was shattered. I had met him, and he was totally different from the man she had described and whose visit she had announced. Now, I wanted to see for myself what Strindberg was all about. I didn't promise her anything, but she felt confident, because I hadn't talked back either. The next chance I got, I took *A Fool's Confession* and raced through it behind her back, as quickly as I had once read Dickens, but with no desire to reread it.

I felt no sympathy with this confession; it struck me as one long lie. I believe there was a certain sobriety about it that repelled me, the attempt to say nothing that went beyond the moment, a reduction and restriction to the given situation. I missed an impetus, the impetus of invention, by which I meant invention in general, not in specifics. I didn't discern the true impetus: hate. I didn't see that the core was my most personal experience, my earliest one: jealousy. I was bothered by the lack of freedom at the beginning, because it was another man's wife. The story seemed "barricaded." I didn't like circuitous routes to people. With the pride of my seventeen years, I looked straight ahead and felt scorn for concealment. Confrontation was everything; only the other person counted. I could take side glances no more seriously than side cuts. This book, far too readable, would have slid off me as though I had never read it. But then came the passage that struck me like a club, the only passage I can still remember down to the tiniest detail, even though I have never picked the book up again, perhaps because of this scene.

The hero of the book, the confessor, Strindberg himself, is visited for the first time by the wife of his friend, an officer in the Guards. He undresses her and places her on the floor. He sees the tips of her breasts shimmering through the gauze.

This description of intimacy was something completely new for me. It took place in a room that could be any room, even ours. Perhaps that was one of the reasons why I rejected the passage so vehemently: it was impossible. The author wanted to talk me into something that he called "Love." But I wouldn't let him bulldoze me, and I called him a liar. Not only didn't I want to know anything about this business, which I found thoroughly reprehensible, for it took place behind the back of the woman's husband, a friend, who trusted both of them—but I viewed it as an absurd, a wretched, an implausible, an insolent invention. Why should a woman let a man put her on the floor? Why did he undress her? Why did she let him undress her? There she was on the floor, and he was looking at her. The situation was both incomprehensible and new to me. It made me furious at the writer, who dared to present something like this as if it had really taken place.

A sort of campaign against it began in me; even if all others weakened and let themselves be convinced that this was true, *I* didn't believe it, I would never believe it. Herr Ödenburg's whimpering next door had nothing to do with it. Fräulein Rahm walked through her room upright and straight as an arrow. Once, when I was on the balcony of my room, peering at the stars through opera glasses, I had seen Fräulein Rahm naked. Accidentally, as I thought, the opera glass had focused on the brightly lit window of her room. There she stood, naked, her head high, her body slender and shimmering in the reddish light. I was so surprised that I kept looking. She walked a few steps, straight as an arrow, just as she walked dressed. From the balcony, I couldn't hear the whimpering. But when I stepped back into the room, embarrassed, I instantly heard it again, as loud as ever. This meant that it had gone on all the time that I was on the balcony. While Fräulein Rahm had walked up and down in her room, Herr Ödenburg had continued whimpering. He had made no impact on her; she acted as if she didn't see him, as if she were alone. I didn't see him either; it was as if he hadn't been there.

The Fainting

Every night, I went out on the balcony and looked at the stars. I sought constellations that I knew and I was glad when I found them. Not all of them were equally clear; not all of them had a conspicuously blue star of their own, like Vega in Lyra overhead in the zenith, or a huge red star, like Betelgeuse in Orion rising. I felt the vastness that I sought. In the daytime, I couldn't feel the vastness of space; this feeling was aroused at night by the stars. Sometimes, I helped by uttering one of the enormous numbers of light-years separating me from this star or that.

Many things tormented me. I felt guilty about the poverty that we saw around us and didn't share. I would have felt less guilty if I had succeeded just once in convincing Mother of how unjust our "prosperity," as I called it, was. But she remained cold and aloof whenever I launched into such things. She deliberately closed herself off; and yet, just a moment earlier, she had been carrying on about some book or piece of music. It was quite easy to get her to talk again; all I had to do was drop the subject which she didn't want to hear about, and she would wax loquacious again. But I made it a point of honor to *force* her to say something. I told her about the distressing things I'd seen that day. I asked her point-blank if she knew about this or that: she lapsed into silence, a vaguely scornful or disapproving look on her face. It was only when I brought up something really terrible that she said: "I didn't cause the inflation," or "That's the result of the war."

I had the impression that it made no difference to her what happened to people she didn't know, especially when they were poor. Yet during the war, when people were being maimed and killed, she had been full of sympathy. Perhaps her commiseration had been exhausted by the war; at times, I felt as if something had been consumed in her, something that she had been all too lavish with. But that was still the more bearable conjecture; for what tormented me more and more was the suspicion that in Arosa she had come under the influence of people who impressed her because they "were in the thick of life," "stood their ground." She had never employed such locutions before. When I heard them too frequently now, I defended myself against them and attacked her ("In what way were they in the thick of life? They were patients in a sanatorium. They were sick and idle when they told you these things"). She became angry and accused me of being heartless toward sick people. It was as though she had withdrawn all commiseration from the world and limited it to the narrower mankind in her sanatorium.

However, there were far more men than women in this smaller world, because men pursued her as a young woman. And when they vied for her attention, they stressed their masculine features—perhaps precisely because they were ill—and made such a to-do about them that she *believed* them and accepted traits and characteristics that she had scorned, even loathed, just a short while ago, during the war. Her position among these men rested on her willingness to listen to them. She wanted to find out as much as possible from them. She was always ready for their confessions, but never exploited, or intrigued with, the intimate knowledge she thereby gained. Instead of the child with whom she was used to conversing for years, she now had many people to talk to and she took them seriously.

It was impossible for her to have a frivolous or shallow relationship with others. So, at the sanatorium, her best quality, her seriousness, removed her from mankind at large, who, next to her sons, had been everything to her. She had come to prefer a narrower group, whom she could not regard as privileged, for they were ill. Perhaps she had relapsed into what she had been at home: the spoiled favorite daughter of rich people. The great period in her life, when she had felt both unhappy and guilty, when she had atoned for her guilt—which seemed vague and almost ungraspable—by means of a superhuman effort for the intellectual development of her sons, an effort that reached its high point in the war when her energy concentrated on a wild hatred of war—that great period may have been over long before I realized it. And the letters passing back and forth between Arosa and Zurich may have been a game of hide-and-seek, in which we seemed to be clinging to a past that no longer existed.

Now in the Pension Charlotte, I wasn't really able to formulate all this with cool clarity, even though, after Herr Hungerbach's visit, I began to understand certain things and interpret them correctly. It all took place as a struggle, a dogged attack, in which I tried to bring her back to the "real" things of the world, the things I considered real. The conversations at the boardinghouse table were often a welcome occasion for such attacks. I learned to conceal my true goal and begin quite hypocritically: with questions about something I hadn't understood downstairs, with discussions about the conduct of boarders who weren't her cup of tea. We were in total harmony about the Bembergs, the young parvenu couple at the boardinghouse table. Mother's scorn for the nouveaux riches remained unshaken throughout her life. Had I realized that this scorn derived from her Sephardic notion of "good families," I would have felt less comfortable in these moments of excellent rapport.

However, my best approach was to try and ask Mother about something. An anything but childlike cunning prompted me to inquire about things that—as experience taught me—she was up on. This provided me with a better entrée, and I could gradually get to what I was after. But often, I was impatient and badgered her thoughtlessly about something I was really interested in. This led, for instance, to the Van Gogh fiasco, when she failed utterly and tried to conceal her ignorance with the most hidebound attacks on "that crazy painter." At such times, I lost my head and charged into her, provoking collisions embarrassing to us both. To her, because she was patently wrong; to me, because I mercilessly accused her of talking about something she knew nothing about—a conduct that she had always vehemently criticized in our discussions of writers. After these collisions, I felt such despair that I left the house and went biking—one great comfort in those Frankfurt years. My other comfort, far more necessary whenever she kept silence, when there was no collision, when nothing happened, was: the stars.

Something that she stubbornly denied, namely the responsibility for things happening around her, something that she warded off with a kind of deliberate, selective, and always available blindness, became so urgent at this point, so plain, that I had to discuss it with her; it grew into a permanent reproach. She feared my coming home from school, for it was quite certain that I would burst out with something new that I had seen or else heard from others. During my first sentence, I could already feel her closing off, and so my words came out all the more violently, assuming the reproachful tone that she could hardly endure. At first, I never rebuked her for causing things that were so unjust or inhuman as to infuriate me. But since she didn't want to listen, developing her own way of only half taking my words in, my report degenerated into a reproach after all. By giving my words a personal form, I compelled her to listen and to make some sort of reply. She tried to say, "I know. I know," or "I can imagine." But I wouldn't let her get away with that, I intensified what I had seen or heard, I reprimanded her for it. It was as if some power had assigned me to transmit a complaint to her. "Listen!" I then said, first impatiently and soon angrily. "Listen! You've got to explain this to me! How can it possibly happen with nobody noticing?"

A woman had passed out on the street and collapsed. The people helping her up said, "She's starving." She looked dreadfully pale and haggard, but other people walked by, paying no attention. "Did *you* remain?" my mother asked mordantly; she had to say *something*. And it was true: I had come home and sat down with her and my brothers at the round table at which we would have our afternoon tea. The full teacup stood in front of me, bread and butter lay at my place. I hadn't taken a bite yet, but I had sat down at the table as usual, and I had begun my account only when I was seated.

The incident I had witnessed that day was no everyday event; this was the first time in my life that I had seen a person faint on the street and collapse because of hunger and weakness. It had shocked me so deeply that I entered the room wordlessly and sat down at the table wordlessly. The sight of the bread and butter, and then especially the jar of honey in the middle of the table, had loosened my tongue, and I began to say something. She speedily recognized the ridiculous aspect of the situation; but, as was her wont, she reacted too vehemently. Had she waited a bit—until I'd picked up the bread and butter and bitten in or even spread it with honey—her scorn, nourished by the ludicrousness of my situation, would have shattered me. But she didn't take the situation seriously; perhaps she thought that since I was sitting, we would go through the usual process of afternoon tea. She had too much faith in established ritual, employing it like a weapon to strike me down as fast as possible; for she was annoyed that teatime should be disturbed by the picture of hunger and fainting—that was all, just annoyed. And so, in her lack of sympathy, she underestimated the earnestness of my frame of mind. I banged the table so hard that the tea splashed out of the cups onto the tablecloth, and I said: "I refuse to stay here!" And out I dashed.

I leaped down the stairs, jumped on my bicycle, and desperately pedaled in and out, through the streets of our neighborhood, as rapidly and senselessly as possible, without knowing what I wanted (for what could I have wanted?), but filled with abysmal hatred for our afternoon tea, haunted by the honey jar, which I bitterly cursed. "If only I'd hurled it out the window! Into the street! Not into the yard!" It would have had a meaning only if it had smashed on the street, in front of everyone; then everyone would have known that there were people here who had honey while others were starving. But I had done nothing of the sort. I had left the honey jar upstairs on the table, I hadn't even knocked over the teacup; a bit of tea had splashed on the tablecloth, that was all. The event had upset me deeply, but I hadn't really accomplished anything, there was so little violence in me—a peaceful lamb, no one hears its woeful bleating. And all that had happened was that Mother was annoyed because our afternoon tea was disturbed.

Nothing else had really happened. I finally went back. She punished me by sympathetically asking whether the event had really been all that bad; after all, a person recovers from fainting. It wasn't the end. I had probably been so scared because I had happened to see the woman just when she was collapsing. It's altogether different when you see people *die*. I was afraid she would start in again about the forest sanatorium and the people who had died there. She always used to say that those people had died *right before her eyes*. But this time, she didn't say it. All she said was that I ought to get used to such things; after all, I often said that I'd like to be a doctor. What kind of a doctor would *collapse* at the death of a patient? Maybe it was good, she added, that I had seen this woman fainting, so that I could start getting used to these things.

And so, a woman's collapse, which had infuriated me, became a general professional matter: a problem for physicians. She had responded to my brusque actions not with a reprimand, but with a reminder of my later life, when I would be bound to fail if I didn't become tougher and more self-controlled.

Since that event, I was marked: I wasn't fit to be a doctor. My soft heart would prevent me from ever getting used to such a profession. I was highly impressed—although I never admitted it—by this twist that she gave to my future plans. I thought about the matter and grew indecisive. I was no longer certain whether I could become a doctor.

Gilgamesh and Aristophanes

The Frankfurt period was not limited to my experiences with the sort of people I found in the Pension Charlotte. But since these experiences went on daily, as a steady process, they were not to be underestimated. You sat at the table, always at the same place, watching people who had become dramatis personae for you. Most of them remained the same; nothing unexpected ever came from their lips. But some maintained their fuller nature and could surprise you with leaps. It was a spectacle, one way or the other; and I never *once* entered the dining room without feeling curious and excited.

With one single exception, I couldn't really warm up to the teachers at school. The choleric Latin teacher blew up at the least provocation and then yelled at us, calling us "stinking asses." This wasn't his only insult. His pedagogical methods, based on "model sentences" that we had to rattle off, were laughable. It was astonishing that my dislike of him didn't make me forget the Latin I had learned in Zurich. Never in any school have I witnessed anything so embarrassing and vociferous as his outbursts. He had been deeply affected by the war. He must have been critically wounded; you said this to yourself in order to endure him. A number of teachers were stamped by the war, albeit not so dramatically. One of them was a hearty, stormy man, brimming over with feelings for the students. Then there was an excellent mathematics teacher with an air of distress, but his distress affected only him, never his students. He exhausted himself totally in teaching; there was something almost frighteningly conscientious about it.

One could feel tempted to depict the diverse effects of war on people by considering these teachers; but this would require some knowledge of their experiences, which they never talked to us about. All I had before me was their faces and bodies, and all I knew about them was the way they acted in class; everything else was mere hearsay.

However, I would like to speak about a fine, quiet man, to whom I am indebted. Gerber was our German teacher. In contrast to the others, he seemed almost timid. Because of the essays he assigned, a kind of friendship developed between us. At first, these essays bored me, whether the topic was Schiller's *Mary Stuart* or whatever. But they cost me no effort, and he was satisfied with what I did. Then the topics became more interesting, and I came out with my real opinions, which, as reactions against school, were already quite rebellious and certainly didn't fit in with his views. But he let me speak my mind. He wrote long remarks in red ink at the bottom, giving me food for thought; yet he was tolerant in these comments, never sparing his recognition for the way in which I said what I did. Whatever his objections, they never struck me as hostile; and even though I didn't accept them, I was happy that he expressed them. He was no inspiring teacher, but he was very understanding. He had small hands and feet and made small motions; although he didn't seem particularly slow, everything he did was slightly reduced. Nor did his voice have the pushy, virile tones that other teachers had when throwing their weight around.

As administrator of the faculty library, Gerber opened it up to me, letting me read anything I wanted. I was wild about ancient Greek literature, and I read one volume after another in German translation: the historians, the dramatists, the poets, the orators. I omitted only the philosophers—Plato and Aristotle. But I really read everything else, not only the great authors, but also those who were interesting solely because of their material, for instance Diodorus or Strabo. Gerber was surprised that I never stopped; I kept borrowing these books for two years. When I reached Strabo, Gerber inquired, with a slight shake of his head, whether I wouldn't like something medieval for a change, but he didn't have much luck.

Once, when we happened to be in the faculty library, Gerber asked me cautiously, almost tenderly, what I wanted to be. I sensed the answer he expected, but I replied, a bit unsure of myself, that I wanted to be a doctor. He was disappointed; after reflecting a bit, he hit on a compromise: "Then you'll be a second Carl Ludwig Schleich." Gerber liked Schleich's memoirs, but he would have preferred to hear me say, plain and simple, that I wanted to be a writer. After that, he often brought up writer-physicians, discreetly and in some sort of context.

In his classes, we read plays aloud, each student doing a part; and I can't say that these readings were pleasurable. But he was trying to have students without literary interests get excited about literature by taking over such roles. He seldom chose plays that were penetratingly dull. We read Schiller's *The Brigands*, Goethe's *Egmont*, and *King Lear*, and we got the chance to see performances of some of these plays at the Schauspielhaus.

The boarders at the Pension Charlotte talked a lot about theatrical productions. They discussed them in detail, and the connoisseurs always started with the reviews in the *Frankfurter Zeitung*, debating them even when they disagreed with the critics, but paying homage to the highbrow main opinion (printed). Hence, these conversations were on a high level and perhaps more serious than those on other topics. One sensed concern about the theater; they were also proud of it.

If anything went wrong, they felt personally affected and weren't content with just snide attacks. The theater was a recognized institution, and even people who otherwise were in enemy camps would have hesitated to cause any trouble. Herr Schutt hardly ever went to the theater because of his serious wounds; but you noticed, even in his few words, that he had Fräulein Kündig inform him about every performance. Anything he said sounded as sure as if he had been there himself. Whoever really had nothing to say held his tongue; the most embarrassing thing in the world was to compromise oneself in this area.

Since all other conversations appeared so uncertain—everything seesawing and opinions crossing not only because of the superficial chitchat—one had the impression, especially being so young, that at least one thing was regarded as inviolable: the theater.

I went to the Schauspielhaus fairly often, and I was so carried away by one production that I did all I could to go back several times. It starred an actress who was on my mind for a long time, and I can still see her before me today: Gerda Müller as Kleist's Penthesilea. *This* passion entered into me. I never doubted it; my initiation into love was *Penthesilea*. The play overwhelmed me like one of the Greek tragedies I was reading, *The Bacchae*. The wildness of the battling Amazons was like that of the Maenads; instead of the furies who tear the king to shreds, it was Penthesilea who sicced her pack of hounds on Achilles, burying her own teeth in his flesh. Since then, I've never dared to see another staging of this play; and whenever I've read it, I've heard *her* voice, which has never weakened for me. I've remained faithful to the actress who convinced me of the truth of love.

I saw no connection between her and the lamentable events next door in the boardinghouse, and I still regarded *A Fool's Confession* as a pack of lies.

One of the actors who performed frequently was Carl Ebert; at first, he appeared regularly, and then subsequently as a guest. Years later, he became famous for very different things. In my youth, I saw him as Schiller's Karl Moor, as Egmont. I got used to him in diverse parts. I would have gone to a production for his sake alone, and I can't even be ashamed of this weakness; for I owe it my most important experience in the Frankfurt period. One Sunday matinee, Ebert was scheduled to read from a work that I had never heard of. It was older than the Bible, a Babylonian epic. I knew that the Babylonians had had a Flood; supposedly, the legend drifted from them to the Bible. This was all I could expect, and this one reason would never have moved me to go. But Carl Ebert was reading, and so, as a fan of a lovable actor, I discovered *Gilgamesh,* which had a crucial impact on my life and its innermost meaning, on my faith, strength, and expectation such as nothing else in the world.

Gilgamesh's lament on the death of his friend Enkidu struck me to the core:

> I wept for him day and night,
> I let nobody bury him—
> I wanted to see whether my shrieks
> Would make my friend rise again.
> Seven days and seven nights
> Until the worms attacked his face.
> When he was gone, I did not find life again,
> I roamed the steppe like a brigand.

And then comes his enterprise against death, his wandering through the darkness of the celestial mountain and his crossing of the waters of death, his meeting with his forebear Utnapishtim, who escaped the Great Flood and was granted immortality by the Gods. Gilgamesh asks him how to attain everlasting life. It is true that Gilgamesh fails in his quest and even dies. But this makes the necessity of his enterprise seem all the more valid.

In this way, I experienced the effect of a myth: something I have thought about in various ways during the ensuing half century, something I have so often turned over in my mind, but never *once* earnestly doubted. I absorbed as a unity something that has remained in me as a unity. I can't find fault with it. The question whether I *believe* such a tale doesn't affect me; how can I, given my intrinsic substance, decide whether I believe in it. The aim is not to parrot the banality that so far all human beings have died: the point is to decide whether to *accept* death willingly or stand up against it. With my indignation against death, I have acquired a right to glory, wealth, misery, and despair of all experience. I have lived in this endless rebellion. And if my grief for the near and dear that I have lost in the course of time was no smaller than that of Gilgamesh for his friend Enkidu, I at least have one thing, one single thing, over the lion man: I care about the life of *every* human being and not just that of my neighbor.

The focus of this epic on just a few people contrasts with the turbulent period in which I encountered it. My memories of those Frankfurt years are structured by events of a public nature, which followed one another in quick succession. They were preceded by rumors—the boardinghouse table was a hive of rumors, not all of which proved to be false. I remember the boarders discussing the Rathenau assassination before we read about it in the newspapers (there was no radio). The French figured most often in these rumors. They had occupied Frankfurt, then withdrawn, and were now suddenly rumored to be coming back. *Reprisals* and *reparations* became everyday words. The discovery of a secret arsenal in our school basement caused a great sensation. When the matter was investigated, it turned out that these weapons had been stored there by a young teacher, whom I knew only by sight; he was very popular, the most popular teacher at school.

The first demonstrations I saw made a deep impact on me; they weren't infrequent and they were always against the war. There was a sharp separation between those who sided with the revolution that had ended the war and the others, who resented not the war, but the Versailles Treaty one year later.

This was the most important distinction; its effects were already tangible. A demonstration against the Rathenau assassination provided me with my first experience of a crowd. Since I articulated the consequences of my experience in discussions some years later, I would like to wait before talking about what happened (see pp. 79–82).

Our last year in Frankfurt was again a year of dissolution for our small family. Mother felt ill; perhaps the tension of our daily confrontations had become unendurable for her. She went south, as she had often done in the past. We three brothers left the Pension Charlotte and moved in with a family, whose caring female member, Frau Suse, welcomed us with warmth and kindness such as one doesn't even expect from one's own mother. This family consisted of a father, a mother, two children about our age, a grandmother, and a maid. I got to know every single one of them, plus the two or three foreign boarders they took in—I got to know them so well that it would take an entire book to explain what I came to understand about people during this period.

This was the time when the inflation reached its high point; its daily jump, ultimately reaching one trillion, had extreme consequences, if not always the same, for all people. It was dreadful to watch. Everything that happened—and a great deal happened—depended on one thing, the breakneck devaluation of money. It was more than disorder that smashed over people, it was something like daily *explosions;* if anything survived one explosion, it got into another one the next day. I saw the effects, not only on a large scale; I saw them, undisguisedly close, in every member of that family; the smallest, the most private, the most personal event always had one and the same cause: the raging plunge of money.

In order to stand my ground against the money-minded people in my own family, I had made it a rather cheap virtue to scorn money. I regarded money as something boring, monotonous, that yielded nothing intellectual, and that made the people devoted to it drier and drier, more and more sterile. But now, I suddenly saw it from a different, an eerie side—a demon with a gigantic whip, lashing at everything and reaching people down to their most private nooks and crannies.

Perhaps it was this extreme logical consequence of a thing that she would at first have coolly put up with, but which I reminded her of incessantly, that prompted my mother to flee Frankfurt. She felt like going back to Vienna. As soon as she was halfway recovered from her illness, she picked up my two younger brothers and found schools for them in Vienna. I remained in Frankfurt another six months, because I was about to graduate high school and was then to start university in Vienna.

During these last six months in Frankfurt, I stayed with the same family, feeling perfectly free. I often attended meetings, listening to the discussions that followed them on the streets at night; and I watched every opinion, every conviction, every faith clashing with others. The discussions were so passionate that they crackled and flared; I never took part, I only listened, with an intensity that strikes me as dreadful today, because I was defenseless. One's own opinions were not up to this immoderation, this excess pressure. Many things repelled me, but I couldn't refute them. Some things attracted me, but I couldn't tell why. I still had no sense of the separateness of *languages* colliding here. Among all the people I heard, there is none I could evoke or even mimic in his true guise. What I grasped was the separateness of *opinions*, the hard cores of convictions; it was a witches' cauldron, steaming and bubbling, but all the ingredients floating in it had their specific smell and could be recognized.

I have never experienced more disquiet in people than in those six months. It didn't much matter how they differed from one another as individuals; at this time, I barely noticed things that would have been the first I'd look for in later years. I was attentive to every conviction, even if it went against my grain. Some public speakers, who were certain of their tried-and-tested effect, seemed like charlatans. But then, in the discussions on the street, when everything had splintered, and people who were no orators tried to convince one another, their disquiet seized hold of me, and I took each of them seriously.

If I describe this period as my Aristophanic apprenticeship, I am not trying to sound arrogant or flippant. I was reading Aristophanes and was struck by the powerful and consistent way that each of his comedies is dominated by a surprising fundamental idea from which it derives. In *Lysistrata*, the first Aristophanic play I read, the women refuse to have sexual relations with their husbands, and their strike brings about the end of the war between Athens and Sparta. Such basic ideas are frequent in Aristophanes; since most of his comedies are lost, many of these brainstorms are not extant. I would have had to be blind not to notice the similarity with the things I perceived all around me. Here, too, everything derived from a single fundamental condition, the raging plunge of money. It was no brainstorm, it was reality; that's why it wasn't funny, it was horrible. But as a total structure, if one tried to see it as such, it resembled one of those comedies. One might say that the cruelty of Aristophanes' vision offered the sole possibility of holding together a world that was shivering into a thousand particles.

Since then, I have had an unshakable dislike for stage depictions of merely private matters. In the conflict between the Old and the New Comedy in Athens, I sided with the Old Comedy, though not quite realizing it. The theater, I feel, should depict only something that affects the public as a whole. Comedy of character, targeting some individual or other, usually embarrasses me a bit, no matter how good it is: I always feel as if I've retreated into some hiding place that I leave only when necessary, for eating or some similar purpose. Comedy lives for me, as when it began with Aristophanes, from its *universal* interest, its view of the world in larger contexts. However, it should deal boldly with these contexts, indulge in brainstorms that verge on madness, connect, separate, vary, confront, find new structures for new brainstorms, never repeat itself and never get shoddy, demand the utmost from the spectator, shake him, take him, and drain him.

It is certainly a very late reflection which leads me to conclude that the choice of drama, which would be so important to me, should have been decided back then. I do not believe I am mistaken; for how else could I explain that my memory of my final year in Frankfurt is bursting with the turbulence of public events and yet contains, as though they were the very same world, the Aristophanic comedies, overwhelming me when I first read them. I see nothing between these two aspects, they overlap; and their being so close together in my memory signifies that they were major things for me in that period, each having a determining influence on the other.

But something else was operating at the same time, connected with Gilgamesh, and serving as a counterpoise. It concerned the fate of the individual human being, separated from all other human beings, in his own way of being alone: the fact that he must die, and whether he should put up with the fact that a death is imminent for him.

Part Two

Storm and Compulsion

Vienna 1924-1925

Living with My Brother

In early April 1924, Georg and I moved into a room in Frau Sussin's apartment at 22 Praterstrasse, Vienna. It was the dark back room, with a window to the courtyard. Here we spent four months together, not a very long period. But this was the first time that I lived alone with my brother, and a great many things happened.

We became close. I took the place of a mentor with whom he conferred about everything, especially all moral problems. What one could do and what one should do, what one must despise under any circumstances, and also what one should find out, what one should get to know—almost every evening of those four months together, we discussed those things, in between our work at the large square table by the window, where we sat, each with his books and notebooks. We were at a ninety degree angle to one another, we only had to raise our heads to see one another right in the face. Back then, although six years my junior, he was already slightly taller than I. When we sat, we were nearly the same size. I had decided to begin studying chemistry in Vienna (without being certain that I would stay with it); the semester was to start in another month. Since I had had no chemistry at school in Frankfurt, it was high time that I acquired some knowledge in this field. In the remaining four weeks, I wanted to make up for what I had missed. I had the *Textbook of Inorganic*

Chemistry in front of me; and since it was theoretical, involving no practical tasks, it interested me, and I made rapid headway.

But no matter how absorbed I was, no matter what the topic, Georg was allowed to interrupt me at any time and ask me questions. He attended the Realgymnasium [secondary school emphasizing modern languages] in Stubenbastei and, being thirteen, was in a lower year. He learned willingly and easily, and had trouble only with drawing, which was taken very seriously in his school. But he was as eager for knowledge as I had been at his age, and sensible questions crossed his mind about every subject. They were seldom about something he didn't understand; he easily understood everything he read. What he asked about was details that he wanted to find out in addition to the more general contents of the textbooks. I could answer many of his questions on the spot without first thinking about them or looking them up. It made me happy to transmit information to him; previously, I had kept everything to myself; there was no one for me to talk to about such things. He noticed how glad I was about every interruption and that there need be no limits to his questions. A lot of things came up in just a few hours, and his questions enlivened chemistry for me, which seemed a bit alien and threatening because I would quite possibly be studying it for four years or longer. Thus he asked me about Roman authors, about history (whereby I always turned the conversation to the Greeks, if I could), about mathematical problems, about botany and zoology, and best of all, in connection with geography, about countries and their people. He already knew that this was what he could hear most about from me, and sometimes I had to bring myself up short— that's how willingly and thoroughly I repeated to him the things I had learned from my explorers. Nor did I refrain from judging the behavior of people. When I got to the struggle against diseases in exotic lands, I was beside myself with enthusiasm. I still hadn't gotten over giving up medicine, and I passed my old wish on to him, naïvely and without restraint.

I loved his insatiableness. When I sat down to my books, I looked forward to his questions. I would have suffered more from his silence than he from mine. Had he been domineering or calculating, he could easily have put me in his power. An evening at our table without his questions would have crushed me and made me unhappy. But that was it: there was no ulterior motive to his questions, any more than there was to my answers. He wanted to know; I wanted to give him what I knew; everything he found out led automatically to new questions. It was amazing that he never embarrassed me. His insatiableness stayed within my limits. Whether our minds ran in the same channels or whether the energy of my mediation kept him away from other things, he only asked me questions that I could answer and he never humiliated me—which would have been easy, had he stumbled upon my ignorance. We were both completely open, holding nothing back from each other. During this period, we were mutually dependent; there was no one else close to us; we had only one demand to fulfill: not to disappoint one another. On no account would I have missed our joint "learning evenings" at the large, square table, which had been pushed over to the window.

Summer came, the evenings grew long, we opened the windows facing the courtyard. Two stories below, right underneath us, was Fink the tailor's shop; his windows were open, too, and the fine hum of his sewing machine wafted up to us. He worked until late at night; he worked all the time. We heard him when we ate supper at our square table, we heard him when we cleared up, we heard him when we settled down to read, and we forgot him only when our conversation got so exciting that we would have forgotten *anything* else. But then, when we lay in bed, tired because the day had begun early, we again heard the humming of his sewing machine until we fell asleep.

Our supper consisted of bread and yogurt, for a while just bread; for our living arrangement had commenced with a minor catastrophe, which was all my fault. Our allowance was scanty, but everything that we needed to live on had been calculated, and it would have sufficed for a somewhat more generous supper. I received the monthly allowance in advance, part of it from Grandfather, the rest from Mother. I carried the entire amount on my person, planning to administer it well. I was experienced in this respect; I had spent six months in Frankfurt with my little brothers and without Mother, and during the final, raging phase of the inflation, it hadn't been at all easy to do everything right and make ends meet. Compared with that period, Vienna seemed like child's play.

And it would have been child's play. But I hadn't reckoned with the Prater Amusement Park. It was very close by, not fifteen minutes away; and because of its overwhelming significance during my childhood in Vienna [see *The Tongue Set Free*], the park seemed even closer. Instead of keeping my little brother away from its temptations, I took him along. One Saturday afternoon, I showed him the splendors, some of which had vanished. But even those I found again were rather disappointing. Georg had been five when we'd left Vienna the first time, and he had no memory of the amusement park; hence he was dependent on my stories, which I embellished as temptingly as possible. For it was somewhat shameful that I, the seemingly omniscient big brother, who had told him about the Prometheus of Aeschylus, the French Revolution, the law of gravitation, and the theory of evolution, was now regaling him with, of all things, the Messina Earthquake in the Tunnel of Fun and the Mouth of Hell in front of it.

I must have painted it in dreadful colors, for when we finally found the Tunnel of Fun and stood in front of the Mouth of Hell, into which the devils were leisurely feeding sinners skewered on pitchforks, Georg looked at me in surprise and said: "And you were really scared of that?"

"I wasn't. I was eight already, but you two were scared; you were both still very little."

I noticed he was about to lose his respect for me. But he didn't feel right about it. He was very fond of our evening conversations, even though they had only just begun, and so he showed no desire to view the Earthquake of Messina, which had lured us here in the first place. I was relieved to get out of it. I didn't want to see the earthquake either now, and I pulled him away quickly. In this way, I could preserve my memory in all its old magnificence.

But I didn't get off the hook so easily; I had to offer him something to make up for the disappointment. So I threw myself into the games of chance in the amusement park, even though they had never really interested me. There were various kinds, but the ring-toss game caught our eye because we saw several people winning, one after the other. I let him try it; he had no luck. I tried it myself; every toss missed. I tried again; it was virtually hexed. I had soon gotten so caught up in the game that he started tugging at my sleeve, but I wouldn't give up. He watched our monthly allowance dwindling and was quite capable of gauging the consequences, but he said nothing. He didn't even say he'd like to try it again himself. I believe he understood that I couldn't bear the shame in front of him for my inexplicably bad marksmanship, and that I had to make up for it with a series of lucky tosses. He stared paralyzed, pulling himself together now and then; he looked like one of the automaton figures in the Tunnel of Fun. I tossed and tossed; I kept tossing more and more poorly. The two shames blended, flowing into one. It seemed like a brief time, but it must have been long, for suddenly all our money for May was gone.

Had it involved me alone, I wouldn't have taken it so badly. But it also concerned my brother, for whose life I was responsible, for whom I had to be a surrogate father, so to speak, whom I gave the loftiest advice, whom I tried to fill with high ideals. In the Chemical Laboratory, where I had just started to work, I would think of things that I felt I had to tell him in the evening, things that would impress him so deeply that he would never forget them. I believed—precisely because of my brotherly love for him, which had become my predominant emotion—that every sentence carried responsibility, that a single false thing I told him would make him go a crooked way, that he could thereby waste his life—and now I had wasted the whole month of May, and no one must find out about it, least of all the Sussin family with whom we were living—I was scared they would give us notice.

Luckily, no one we knew had watched my fall from grace, and Georg instantly understood how important silence was. We comforted each other with manly resolves. We used to eat lunch regularly right near the Carl Theater, at the Benveniste Restaurant, where Grandfather had introduced us. But we didn't have to eat there. We would make do with a yogurt and a piece of bread. For supper, a piece of bread would suffice. How I was going to come up with money—at least for this food—was something I didn't tell him: I didn't know myself.

This little misfortune that I had caused was, I believe, what made us become close—even closer than the nightly question-and-answer game. We led our exceedingly chary life for one month. I don't know how we could have managed without the breakfast that Frau Sussin brought us every morning. We waited, absolutely famished, for the café au lait and two rolls each. We woke up earlier, washed earlier, and were already seated at the square table when she entered the room with the tray. We quelled any jittery movements that would have betrayed our eagerness; we sat there stiffly as though having to memorize something together. She set great store by a few morning phrases. We always had to tell her how we'd slept, and it was lucky that she spared us her own accounts of how she'd slept.

But every morning, she most emphatically mentioned her brother, who was in a Belgrade prison. "An idealist!" That was how she began, plunging right in, never mentioning him without first calling him "An idealist!" She didn't share his political convictions, of course; but she was proud of him, for he was friendly with Henri Barbusse and Romain Rolland. He was ill; he had suffered from tuberculosis at an early age; prison was poison for him; good and copious food would have been especially important. When she carried breakfast in to us, the steaming coffee, she thought of his deprivation, and so naturally she spoke about him. "He started very early, in school. At his age," she pointed at Georg, "he was an idealist. He gave speeches at school and was punished. Even though his teachers were on his side, they had to punish him." She didn't approve of his stubbornness but she never uttered a word of reproof. She and her unmarried sister, who lived with the Sussins, had heard any number of things about their brother's convictions. Serbian royalists cared as little for his views as good Austrians. And so the sisters had once and for all made it a habit to understand nothing about politics and to leave them to men.

Moshe Pijade—that was their brother's name—had always considered himself a revolutionary and a writer. The fact that he had gotten somewhere in these capacities was vouchsafed by the names of his French friends. The prison, and especially her brother's illness and hunger, greatly preoccupied Frau Sussin. The breakfast she carried into our room was something she would have wanted to give him; and so it was the least she could do to remember him every morning. True, she thus delayed us in our ravenousness; but to make up for it, she strengthened us by talking about her brother's hunger. He would never have owned up to being hungry. Even as a boy at home, he had never noticed he was hungry, for he had always been busy with his ideals. In this way, he had become a pillar for us. And every morning, we waited no less for Frau Sussin's story than for the café au lait with the good rolls. This was also the first time that Georg heard about tuberculosis, which subsequently became the content of his life.

We left the apartment together. Right in the courtyard, to the left, we saw Herr Fink, the tailor; he had been sitting at his sewing machine for a long time already. It was the first sound we heard upon awakening in the morning, as well as the last sound before falling asleep at night. Now we walked past the window of his shop and greeted him, the taciturn man with the painful cheekbones. When I saw him with the needles in his mouth, he looked as if he'd stuck a long needle through his cheek and couldn't talk. When he did say something after all, I was surprised; the needles he held in his lips, they too, were gone.

There, in the window of his shop, was his sewing machine, which he never left—a young man who never went out. By the time I got to know him better, it was summer; the window was open, the hum of the machine was audible in the courtyard, softly accompanying the laughter of his wife, whose black, voluptuous beauty filled the shop. If you wanted to see Fink about tailoring and you knocked at the door of the small room in which he lived with his family, you hesitated briefly before entering, in order to hear his wife's laughter a bit longer and to believe it. You knew very well that the joy with which the shop received you wasn't meant for you; it was the joy of her brimming body, which imparted its scent to everything. The scent and the laughter permeated one another, and there were also the occasional calls to Kamilla, the three-year-old daughter. This child preferred playing near the threshold, right behind the door—another reason why you opened it hesitatingly. And the first thing you heard amid the laughter was the sentence: "Kamilla, get out of the way, let the gentleman come in." She always said "the gentleman," even though I wasn't yet nineteen; and she also said it if I was inside and a woman was coming in. The instant she saw it was a woman, she briefly stopped laughing, but never altered her sentence; which didn't surprise me, for Herr Fink was a gentlemen's tailor. He would quickly look up, his needles in his mouth. A huge, dreadful needle had pierced both his cheeks—how could he have spoken? The laughter spoke in his stead.

Karl Kraus and Veza

It was natural that the rumors about both these people should reach me at the same time; they came from the same source, from which everything new for me came at that time. And had I been entirely on my own after arriving in Vienna or dependent on the university (which I was about to start), then I would have had a hard time with my new life. Every Saturday afternoon, I visited Alice Asriel and her son Hans at their home on Heinestrasse near the Prater Star, and here I found out enough things to last me for years: names that were completely new, and suspect, if only because I had never heard them before.

But the name I heard most often from the Asriels was Karl Kraus. He was, I heard, the strictest and greatest man living in Vienna today. No one found grace in his eyes. His lectures attacked everything that was bad and corrupt. He put out a magazine, I heard, written entirely by himself. Unsolicited manuscripts were undesirable; he refused contributions from anyone else; he never answered letters. Every word, every syllable in *Die Fackel* (*The Torch*) was written by him personally. It was like a court of law. *He* brought the charges and *he* passed judgment. There was no defense attorney; a lawyer was superfluous: Kraus was so fair that no one was accused unless he deserved it. Kraus never made a mistake; he couldn't make a mistake. Everything he produced was one hundred percent accurate; never had such accuracy existed in literature. He took personal care of every comma, and anyone trying to find a typographical error in *Die Fackel* could toil for weeks on end. It was wisest not to look for any. Kraus hated war, I was told, and during the Great War he had managed to print many antiwar pieces in *Die Fackel,* despite the censors. He had exposed corruption, fought against graft that everyone else had held their tongues about. It was a miracle he hadn't landed in prison. He had written an eight-hundred-page play, *The Last Days of Mankind,* containing everything that had happened in the war. When he read aloud from it, you were simply flabbergasted. No one stirred in the auditorium, you didn't dare breathe. He read all parts himself, profiteers and generals, the scoundrels and the poor wretches who were the victims of the war—they all sounded as genuine as if they were standing in front of you. Anyone who had heard Kraus didn't want to go to the theater again, the theater was so boring compared with him; he was a whole theater by himself, but better, and this wonder of the world, this monster, this genius bore the highly ordinary name of Karl Kraus.

I would have believed anything about him but his name or that a man with this name could have been capable of doing the things ascribed to him. While the Asriels belabored me with items about him—which both mother and son greatly enjoyed—they mocked my distrust, my offense at this plain name; they kept pointing out that it's not the name that matters but the person, otherwise we—she or I—with our euphonious names would be superior to a man like Karl Kraus. Could I possibly imagine anything so ridiculous, anything so absurd?

They pressed the red journal into my hands; and much as I liked its name, *Die Fackel, The Torch,* it was absolutely impossible for me to read it. I tripped over the sentences; I couldn't understand them. Anything I did understand sounded like a joke, and I didn't care for jokes. He also talked about local events and typographical errors, which struck me as terribly unimportant. "This is all such nonsense, how can you read it? I even find a newspaper more interesting. You can at least understand something. Here, you drudge away, and nothing comes of it!" I was honestly indignant at the Asriels, and I recalled my schoolmate's father in Frankfurt who, whenever I visited his home, read to me out of the local author Friedrich Stoltze and would then say at the end of a poem: "Anyone who doesn't like this deserves to be shot. This is the greatest poet who ever lived." I told the Asriels, not without scorn, about this poet of the Frankfurt dialect. I badgered them, I wouldn't let go, and I embarrassed them so greatly that they suddenly started telling me about the elegant ladies who attended every lecture given by Karl Kraus and were so carried away by him that they always sat in the first row so that he might notice their enthusiasm. But with these accounts, the Asriels missed the boat with me altogether: "Elegant ladies! In furs no doubt! Perfumed aesthetes! And he's not ashamed to read to such people!"

"But they're not like *that!* These are highly educated women! Why shouldn't he read to them? They understand every allusion. Before he even utters a sentence, they've already caught the drift. They've read all of English and French literature, not just German! They know their Shakespeare by heart, not to mention Goethe. You just can't imagine how educated they are!"

"How do you know? Have you ever talked to them? Do you talk to such people? Doesn't the smell of the perfume make you sick? I wouldn't spend one minute talking to someone like that. I just couldn't. Even if she were really beautiful, I'd turn my back on her and at most I'd say: 'Don't put Shakespeare on your lips. He'll be so disgusted he'll turn over in his grave. And leave Goethe in peace. *Faust* isn't for monkeys.' "

But now the Asriels felt they had gotten through to me, for both of them cried at once: "What about Veza! Do you know Veza? Have you ever heard of Veza?"

Now this was a name that surprised me. I liked it right off though I wouldn't admit it. The name reminded me of one of my stars, Vega in the constellation of Lyra, yet it sounded all the more beautiful because of the difference in one consonant. But I said gruffly: "What kind of a name is that again? No one's got a name like that. It *would* be an unusual name. But it doesn't exist."

"It does exist. We know her. She lives on Ferdinandstrasse with her mother. Ten minutes from here. A beautiful woman with a Spanish face. She's very fine and sensitive, and no one could ever say anything ugly in her presence. She's read more than all of us put together. She knows the longest English poems by heart, plus half of Shakespeare. And Molière and Flaubert and Tolstoy."

"How old is this paragon?"

"Twenty-seven."

"And she's read everything already?"

"Yes, and even more. But she reads intelligently. She knows why she likes it. She can explain it. You can't put anything over on her."

"And she sits in the front row to hear Karl Kraus?"

"Yes, at every lecture."

On April 17, 1924, the three-hundredth lecture of Karl Kraus took place. The Great Concert House Hall had been selected for the occasion. I was told that even this building would not be large enough to hold the multitude of fans. However, the Asriels ordered tickets in time and insisted on taking me along. Why always fight about *Die Fackel?* It was better to hear the great man in person for once. Then I could form my own verdict. Hans donned his most arrogant smirk; the thought that anybody, much less a brand-new high school graduate, fresh out of Frankfurt, could possibly resist Karl Kraus in person made not only Hans smirk: his nimble, delicate mother couldn't help smiling as she repeatedly assured me how greatly she envied me for this first experience with Karl Kraus.

She prepared me with a few well-turned bits of advice: I shouldn't be frightened by the wild applause of the audience: these weren't the usual operetta Viennese who assembled here, no Heuriger winos, but also no decadent clique of aesthetes à la Hofmannsthal. This was the genuine intellectual Vienna, the best and the soundest in this apparently deteriorated city. I'd be amazed at how quickly this audience caught the subtlest allusion. These people were already laughing when he began a sentence, and by the time the sentence was over, the whole auditorium was roaring. He had trained his public carefully; he could do anything he wanted to with his people, and yet don't forget, these were all highly educated people, almost all of them academic professionals or at least students. She said she had never seen a stupid face among them; you could look all you liked, it was futile. Her greatest delight was to read the responses to the speaker's punchlines in the faces of the listeners. It was very difficult for her, she said, not to come along this time, but she greatly preferred the Middle Concert House Hall: you could miss nothing there, absolutely nothing. In the Great Hall—even though his voice carried very nicely—you did miss a few things, and she was so keen on every word of his that she didn't want to lose a single one. That was why she had given me her ticket this time, it was meant more as an honor to him to appear at this three-hundredth lecture, and so many people were thronging to attend, that her presence really didn't matter.

I knew in what straitened circumstances the Asriels lived— even though they never talked about it; there were so many more important, namely intellectual things that totally absorbed them. They insisted on my being their guest on this occasion, and that was why Frau Asriel decided not to be present at the triumphal affair.

I managed to guess one intention of the evening, which they concealed from me. And as soon as Hans and I had taken our seats way in back, I stealthily peered around the audience. Hans did the same, no less stealthily; we both concealed from one another whom we were looking for. It was the same person. I had forgotten that the lady with the unusual name always sat in the first row; and though I had never seen a picture of her, I hoped I would suddenly come upon her somewhere in our row. It seemed inconceivable to me that I couldn't recognize her on the basis of the description they had given me: the longest English poem that she knew by heart was Poe's "The Raven," they said, and she looked like a raven herself, a raven magically transformed into a Spanish woman. Hans was too agitated himself to interpret my agitation correctly, he stubbornly gazed forward, checking the front entrances into the auditorium. Suddenly, he gave a start, but not arrogantly now, rather embarrassedly, and he said: "There she is, she just came in."

"Where?" I said, without asking whom he meant. "Where?"

"In the first row, on the far left. I figured as much, the first row."

I could see very little from so far away; nevertheless, I recognized her raven hair and I was satisfied. I quelled the ironic comments I had prepared, and I saved them for later. Soon, Karl Kraus himself came out and was greeted by an applause the likes of which I had never experienced, not even at concerts. My eyes were still unpracticed, but he seemed to take little notice of the applause, he hesitated a bit, standing still. There was something vaguely crooked about his figure. When he sat down and began to read, I was overwhelmed by his voice, which had something unnaturally vibrating about it, like a decelerated crowing. But this impression quickly vanished, for his voice instantly changed and kept changing incessantly, and one was very soon amazed at the variety that he was capable of. The hush in which his voice was at first received was indeed reminiscent of a concert; but the prevailing expectation was altogether different. From the start, and throughout the performance, it was the quiet before a storm. His very first punchline, really just an allusion, was anticipated by a laughter that terrified me. It sounded enthusiastic and fanatic, satisfied and ominous at once; it came before he had actually made his point. But even then, I couldn't have understood it, for it bore on something local, something that not only was connected to Vienna, but also had become an intimate matter between Kraus and his listeners, who yearned for it. It wasn't individuals who were laughing, it was many people together. If I focused on someone cater-corner in front of me in order to understand the distortions of his laughter, the causes of which I couldn't grasp, the same laughter boomed behind me and a few seats away from me on all sides. And only then did I notice that Hans, who was sitting next to me and whom I had meanwhile forgotten, was laughing, too, in exactly the same way. It was always many people, and it was always a hungry laughter. It soon dawned on me that the people had come to a repast and not to celebrate Karl Kraus.

I don't know what he said on this evening of my earliest encounter with him. A hundred lectures that I heard later have piled up on top of that evening. Perhaps I didn't know even then, because the audience, which frightened me, absorbed me so thoroughly. I couldn't see Kraus too well: a face narrowing down to the chin, a face so mobile that it couldn't be pinpointed, penetrating and exotic, like the face of an animal, but a new, a different face, an unfamiliar one. I was flabbergasted by the gradations that this voice was capable of; the auditorium was enormous, yet a quivering in his voice was imparted to the entire space. Chairs and people seemed to yield under this quivering; I wouldn't have been surprised if the chairs had bent. The dynamics of such a mobbed auditorium under the impact of that voice—an impact persisting even when the voice grew silent—can no more be depicted than the Wild Hunt. But I believe that the impact was closest to this legendary event. Imagine the army of the Wild Hunt in a concert hall, trapped, locked up, and forced to sit still, and then repeatedly summoned to its true nature. This image doesn't bring us much closer to reality;

but I couldn't hit on a more accurate image, and thus I have to forgo transmitting a notion of Karl Kraus in his actuality.

Nevertheless, during intermission, I left the auditorium, and Hans introduced me to the woman who was to be chief witness to the effect I had just experienced. But she was quite calm and self-controlled, everything seemed easier to endure in the first row. She looked very exotic, a precious object, a creature one would never have expected in Vienna, but rather on a Persian miniature. Her high, arched eyebrows, her long, black lashes, with which she played like a virtuoso, now quickly, now slowly—it all confused me. I kept looking at her lashes instead of into her eyes, and I was surprised at the small mouth.

She didn't ask me how I liked the performance; she said she didn't want to embarrass me. "It's the first time you're here." She sounded as if she were the hostess, as if the hall were her home and she were handing everything to the audience from her seat in the first row. She knew the people, she knew who always came, and she noticed, without compromising herself, that I was new here. I felt as if she were the one who had invited me, and I thanked her for her hospitality, which consisted in her taking notice of me. My companion, whose forte was not tact, said: "A great day for him," and jerked his shoulder in my direction.

"One can't tell as yet," she said. "For the moment, it's confusing."

I didn't sense this as mockery, even though each of her sentences had a mocking undertone; I was happy to hear her say something so precisely attuned to my frame of mind. But this very sympathy confused me, just like the lashes, which were now performing lofty motions, as though they had important things to conceal. So I said the plainest and most undemanding thing that could be said in these circumstances: "It sure is confusing."

This may have sounded surly; but not to her, for she asked: "Are you Swiss?"

There was nothing I would have rather been. During my three years in Frankfurt, my passion for Switzerland had reached a boiling point. I knew her mother was a Sephardi, née Calderon, whose third husband was a very old man named Altaras; and so she must have recognized my name as being Ladino. Why did she inquire about the thing I would have most liked to be? I had told no one about the old pain of that separation; and I made sure not to expose myself to the Asriels, who, for all their satirical arrogance, or perhaps precisely because of Karl Kraus, plumed themselves on being Viennese. Thus, the beautiful Raven Lady couldn't have learned about my unhappiness from anyone, and her first direct question struck me to the quick. It moved me more deeply than the lecture, which—as she had accurately said—was confusing, for the moment. I answered: "No, unfortunately," meaning that unfortunately I wasn't Swiss. I thereby put myself completely in her hands. The word *unfortunately* betrayed more than anyone knew about me at that time. She seemed to understand, all mockery vanished from her features, and she said: "I'd love to be British." Hans, as was his wont, pounced upon her with a flood of chitchat, from which I could glean only that one could be very familiar with Shakespeare without having to be English, and what did the English today have in common with Shakespeare anyhow? But she paid as little attention to him as I, even though, as I soon saw, she missed nothing of what he said.

"You ought to hear Karl Kraus reading Shakespeare. Have you been to England?"

"Yes, as a child, I went to school there for two years. It was my first school."

"I often visit relatives there. You have to tell me about your childhood in England. Come and drop in on me soon!"

All preciousness was gone, even the coquettish way she paid homage to the lecture. She spoke about something that was close to her and important, and she compared it with something important to me, which she had touched quickly and lightly and yet not offensively. As we stepped back into the auditorium, and Hans, in the brief time remaining, quickly asked me two or three times what I thought of her, I pretended not to understand, and it was only when I sensed that he was about to pronounce her name that I said, in order to forestall him: "Veza?" But by now Karl Kraus had reappeared and the tempest broke loose and her name went under in the tempest.

The Buddhist

I don't believe I saw her again right after the lecture; and even if I did see her, it wouldn't have meant much, for now Hans's sluices were open all the way. A shallow flood of chitchat poured over me, lacking everything of the public speaker's impact: the self-assured passion, the wrath, the scorn. Everything Hans said washed past you as though it were addressed to someone near you, but who wasn't even there. "Naturally," and "of course," were his most frequent words, added to strengthen every sentence, but actually weakening them. He sensed how lightweight his statements were and tried to strengthen them by making them more general. But his generality was just as feeble as he was; his misfortune was that you believed nothing he said. Not that he was considered a liar; he was too weak to make anything up. But instead of *one* word, he used fifty, and nothing of what he meant was left over in this dilution. He repeated a question so often and so swiftly that you couldn't squeeze an answer in edgewise. He said "How come?" "I don't like that," "I know," interjecting them into his endless explanations, perhaps in order to give them more emphasis.

He had been unusually thin as a child, and now he was so skinny that there were no clothes that didn't look baggy on him. He seemed most assured when he swam; that's why he always talked about it. He was tolerated by the Felons (we'll hear more about them later) when they went swimming in Kuchelau, but he wasn't really part of them. He was part of no group; he was always on the periphery. It was his mother who attracted young boys in order to hear their verbal jousts, and she made sure that her son restrained himself on such occasions, out of hospitality, so to speak, and in order that things might be interesting. But he listened carefully, took in everything—I might almost say—greedily; and no sooner were the real jousters gone than the tournament was repeated as an epilogue, between him and some more intimate family friend, who remained longer, since he felt he had claims on the mother. Thus, every dispute and every topic were thoroughly rehashed until all that was left of spontaneous life and charm was an insipid aftertaste.

Hans wasn't yet aware of his problems in dealing with other people. So many young people came to their home, more and more duels took place—spurred on by Frau Asriel's admiring glances—nothing eluded her and nothing lasted too long for her. The duelers remained as long as they pleased, but they were never held back; they came and left whenever they felt like it. It was because of this freedom, which she knew how to deal with, and which was vitally necessary to her, that Frau Asriel's home was never deserted. However, Hans, who lived on intellectual imitation and consisted of nothing else, owed it to his mother that there was always something to imitate and that the torrent of what was called "stimuli" never dried up. He didn't notice that people never invited him to their homes, for Frau Asriel was welcome wherever things weren't too middle class, and, as a matter of course, she took along her intelligent son (for she did consider him intelligent).

April 17 had really turned out to be a big day for me: one and the same day had brought into my life the two people who were to rule my life for a long time. And then came a period of dissembling, which lasted nearly a year. I would have liked to see the raven woman again, but I didn't want to let on that I did. She had invited me to visit her, and the Asriels, mother and son, kept talking about this invitation, asking me whether I didn't feel like taking her up on it. Since I didn't really respond to the invitation, indeed acted almost negatively, they assumed I was too shy and they tried to encourage me with the prospect of their presence. They said they visited her often; they would soon be going again and would simply take me along. But that was exactly what intimidated me. I was used to Hans's chitchat and didn't take it too seriously—but the thought of it there of all places was highly unpleasant, as was the realization that Alice Asriel would interrogate me afterwards about what I thought of this and that. I couldn't possibly have talked about England in front of them, and I would have been unable to say anything about Switzerland in their presence. Yet it was the prospect of talking about Switzerland that attracted me the most.

Alice didn't want to miss out on this pleasure, and every Saturday, when I went to the Asriels, they would sooner or later ask me, amiably but insistently: "When are we visiting Veza?" I even found it unpleasant to hear them pronounce her name, which I regarded as too beautiful to come from anyone's lips. I excused myself by pretending I disliked her; I avoided her name and ascribed not very respectful attributes to her.

It was at Alice's that I met Fredl Waldinger, with whom I had wonderful conversations for several years; I couldn't have wished for a better interlocutor. We disagreed about nearly everything, but we never grew irritable or fought. He never let himself be bulldozed or violated: his calm cheerful resistance opposed my vehement manner, which had been molded by stormy experiences. The first time I met him, he was just back from Palestine, where he had spent six months on a kibbutz. He liked to sing Yiddish songs, which he knew a lot of; he had a nice voice and sang them well. You didn't have to ask him to sing; it was so natural to him that he would start singing in the middle of a conversation. He cited songs: they were his quotations.

Other boys whom I met in this circle indulged in the arrogance of higher literature: if not Karl Kraus, then Otto Weininger or Schopenhauer. Pessimistic or misogynous utterances were especially popular, even though none of these boys was a misogynist or misanthrope. Each of them had his girlfriend and got along with her, and both he and she and the friends, forming a group called the Felons (one of them was named Felo), went swimming in Kuchelau, a group of strong, healthy optimists. However, the severe, witty, scornful statements were viewed by these young people as the cream of intellect. You were not allowed to articulate these gems in anything but their correct wording; and much of the mutual respect consisted in taking the linguistic form of such things as earnestly as was demanded by the real master of all such circles, Karl Kraus. Fredl Waldinger was loosely associated with the Felons. He liked to go swimming with them; but he was no totally relentless fan of Karl Kraus's, since other things meant no less to him and some even more.

His eldest brother, Ernst Waldinger, had already published poems. Returning heavily wounded from the war, Ernst had married a niece of Freud's. He was friendly with the Austrian poet Josef Weinheber, a friendship based on artistic convictions. Both men were devoted to classical models; rigorous form was very important to them. "The Gem Cutter," a poem by Ernst Waldinger, could be called programmatic; it provided the title for one of his books of verse. Fredl Waldinger owed part of his inner freedom to this brother, whom he respected. He didn't show more than respect: he wasn't the sort to be proud of external things. Money impressed him as little as fame; but he would never have dreamt of scorning a poet merely because he had published books and was gradually making a name for himself. When I met Fredl, Josef Weinheber's *Boat in the Bay* had just come out. Fredl had the book on him and read aloud from it; he already knew several of the poems by heart. I liked the fact that he was serious about poetry; my home was filled with disdain of poets, who were generally put down as "poetasters." However, Fredl's quotations, as I have said, usually came from songs, Yiddish folk songs.

When singing, he raised his right hand halfway, opening it upward like a cup; it was as if he were offering you something for which he apologized. He seemed humble and yet self-assured; he reminded you of an errant monk, but one who comes to give people something instead of begging from them. He never sang loud; any immoderateness seemed foreign to him; his rustic grace won the hearts of listeners. He was aware that he sang his songs well, and he enjoyed his ability as other singers do. But far more important than any self-complaisance was the attitude he was testifying to: his love of country life, the tilling of soil, the clear, devoted, and yet demanding activity of his hands. He liked to talk about his friendships with Arabs; he made no distinction between them and the Jews in Palestine; any arrogance based on differences in culture and education was alien to him. He was strong and healthy: it would have been easy for him to fight with other men his age. But I have never known anyone as peaceful as Fredl; he was so peaceful that he never competed with others. It made no difference to him whether he was the first or the last; he never got involved in hierarchies and didn't even appear to notice that there *was* such a thing.

With him, Buddhism entered my life; he had come to it through poetry. *The Songs of Monks and Nuns*, translated into German by Carl Eugen Neumann, had cast a spell on him. He would recite many of the poems from memory, in a rhythmic singsong that was fascinatingly exotic. In this milieu, where everything focused on intellectual discussion as a contest between two young men, where an opinion obtained as long as it was defended wittily and cogently—in this milieu, which made no scholarly demands, which chiefly emphasized the fluency, agility, and variability of *speech*—in this milieu, Fredl's singsong, always the same, never loud or hostile, yet never losing itself, must have seemed like an inexhaustible, slightly monotonous well.

However, Fredl knew more about Buddhism than the singsong of these poems, even though they seemed strangely familiar to him. Fredl also knew Buddhist teachings. He was well acquainted with the Pali canon (to the extent that Neumann had translated it). The Dīgha-nikāya and the Majjhimanikāya, the Book of Fragments, the Path of Truth—he had assimilated anything of these works that was published, and he articulated it in the same singsong as the poems whenever the two of us had a conversation.

I was still filled with public experiences of the Frankfurt period. Evenings, I had gone to meetings, listened to speakers; and the ensuing discussions in the street had deeply agitated me. The most diverse sorts of people—professionals, proletarians, young, old—spoke away at one another, vehement, obstinate, unflappable, as though no other idea were possible; and yet the man each was talking to was just as stubbornly convinced of the opposite. Since it was night, an unusual time for me to be in the street, these disputes seemed like something unending, as though they went on forever, as though it were no longer possible to sleep, for each man's conviction was too important to him.

However, there was a very particular experience I had in these Frankfurt years, a *daytime* experience: the crowd. Early on, about one year after arriving in Frankfurt, I had watched a workers' demonstration on the *Zeil*. They were protesting the murder of Rathenau. I stood on the sidewalk; other people must have been standing near me, watching too, but I don't remember them. I can still see the large, powerful figures marching behind the Adler Works sign. They marched in serried ranks and cast defiant glances around. Their shouts struck me as though addressed to me personally. More and more of them came. There was something consistent about them, not so much in their appearance as in their conduct.

There was no end of them. I sensed a powerful conviction emanating from them; it grew more and more powerful. I would have liked to be part of them; I wasn't a worker, but I took their shouts personally as though I *were* one. I can't tell whether the people standing next to me felt the same way; I can't see them, nor do I recall anyone leaving the sidewalk and joining the procession; people may have been discouraged by the signs identifying specific groups of marchers.

The memory of this first demonstration that I consciously witnessed was powerful. It was the physical attraction that I couldn't forget. I was so anxious to belong to the march, but it wasn't deliberation or reflection and certainly not skepticism that kept me from taking the final leap. Later on, when I gave in and did find myself in a crowd, I felt as if this were what is known in physics as gravitation. But of course, this was no real explanation for that absolutely astonishing process. For one was not something lifeless, either beforehand, when isolated, or afterwards, in the crowd. And the thing that happened to you in the crowd, a total alteration of consciousness, was both drastic and enigmatic. I wanted to know what it was all about. The riddle wouldn't stop haunting me; it has stuck to me for the better part of my life. And if I did ultimately hit upon a few things, I was still as puzzled as ever.

In Vienna, I met young people of my age whom I could talk to, who made me curious when they spoke about their central experiences, but were also willing to listen when I came out with my own. The most patient person was Fredl Waldinger; he could afford to be patient, for he was immune to contagion: my account of my experience with a crowd, as I called it then, made him cheery, but he didn't seem to be mocking me. He realized I was coping with a state of intoxication, an intensification of possibilities for experience, an increase of the person, who leaves his confines, comes to other persons leaving their confines, and forms a higher unity with them. He doubted that this higher unity existed, and, most of all, he doubted the value of intoxicated intensifications. With the help of Buddha, he had seen the worthlessness of a life that doesn't free itself from its involvements. His goal was the gradual snuffing of life, Nirvana, which seemed like death to me. And although he offered many very interesting arguments denying that Nirvana and death were the same, the negative accent on life, which he had gotten from Buddhism, remained undeniable.

Our positions solidified in the course of these talks. Our mutual influence consisted particularly in our becoming both more thorough and more careful. He assimilated more and more of the Buddhist religious texts, not just limiting himself to Neumann's translations, although these remained closest to his heart. He delved into Indian philosophy, using English-language sources, which he translated into German with Veza's help. I tried to learn more about crowds, which I spoke about. I would have investigated this crowd process anyway, it was so deeply on my mind, having become the enigma of enigmas for me. But perhaps, if it hadn't been for Fredl, I might not have started in so early with the Indian religions, which repelled me because of the multiple deaths in their doctrine of reincarnation. In our conversations, I knew that the richly elaborate doctrine that Fredl advocated was one of the most profound and most important that mankind has developed. And I was painfully aware that all I could pit against it was the somewhat meager description of a single experience, which he termed "pseudomystical." He could resort to so many explications, interpretations, cause-and-effect series when he spoke about his things—and I was unable to come up with even one single explanation for my one single experience, which I was so zealous about. I obstinately harped on my experience, precisely because it had been so inexplicable; and my obstinacy must have struck Fredl as narrow-minded, perhaps even absurd. Indeed it was. And were I to talk about the stubborn streaks in my character, I'd have to say that they operate in regard to overwhelming experiences that I cannot explain. No one has ever succeeded in explaining something away for me; and neither have I.

The Final Danube Voyage. The Message

In July 1924, after my first semester at the University of Vienna, I went to Bulgaria for the summer. My father's sisters had asked me to stay with them in Sofia. I didn't plan to visit Ruschuk, where I had spent my earliest childhood. There was no one left there to invite me; in the course of time, all members of my family had moved to Sofia, which, being the capital, had gained in importance, gradually developing into a big city. This vacation was meant not for a return to my native town, but for visiting as many family members as possible. However, the highlight was to be the trip itself, the voyage on the Danube.

Buco, my father's eldest brother, was living in Vienna. He had to go to Bulgaria on business, so we traveled together. This voyage was very different from the ones I recalled from my childhood, when we had spent a good deal of our time in the cabins, and Mother had deloused us with a hard comb every day; the ships were filthy, and you always caught lice on them. This time, there were no lice. I shared a cabin with my uncle, a jokester; he was the same uncle who used to mock me with his solemn blessing when I was an infant. We spent most of our time on deck. He needed people to tell his stories to. He began with a few friends he met, but soon he had gathered a whole circle; and, without batting an eyelash, merely winking now and then, he spouted his jokes. He had a huge repertoire, but I had heard it so often that it was exhausted for me. He couldn't take a serious conversation for long. In the cabin, however, he felt put upon to give me, his nephew, who had just begun university, some advice on living. His advice bored me even more than his jokes; it was as annoying as his continual attempts at arousing laughter and applause were familiar to me.

He had no notion of what was really going on inside me; his advice could have been given to any nephew. I was fed up with the *usefulness* of chemistry. I had no older relative who wasn't delighted at my choice of study: they all hoped I would open up a territory that was closed to them. None of them had gotten any further than business college, and they now gradually realized that, aside from the operations of buying and selling, in which they were abundantly experienced, they urgently required special scientific and technical knowledge, of which none of them had even a smattering. I was to become the family expert on chemistry, and my knowledge would expand the area of their business enterprises. In the cabin, my uncle always talked about this expectation whenever we went to bed; it was like an evening prayer, albeit a rather brief one. The blessing with which he made a fool of me in my childhood, always disappointing me all over again; the blessing, which I took so seriously that I placed myself expectantly under his opened hand each time, simply yearning for the beautiful words that began: *"Io ti bendigo";* the blessing, which I had stopped wanting long ago, which had turned into my grandfather's curse and my father's sudden death—that blessing was now meant seriously: *I* was supposed to bring good fortune to the family and increase their prosperity with new, modern, "European" knowledge. My uncle soon broke off, however, because he had two or three jokes to tell before finally going to sleep. In the morning, he was anxious to get out early to his fans on deck.

The ship was full: countless people sat or lay on deck; it was fun winding along from group to group, listening to them. There were Bulgarian students going home for the holidays; there were people who were already professionally active; a group of physicians who had freshened up their knowledge in "Europe." One physician had a gigantic black beard; he looked familiar. No wonder: he had brought me into the world. It was Dr. Menachemoff from Ruschuk, our family doctor, whose name always cropped up among us, whom everyone liked, and whom I hadn't seen since before my sixth birthday. I took him no more seriously than anything or anyone in that supposedly "barbaric" Balkan period. And now—we quickly got into a conversation—I was astonished to see how much he knew, how much he was interested in. He had kept up with the progress of science, and not just in his own field. He answered critically, went into everything, didn't automatically reject what I said merely because I was nineteen. The word *money* never *once* popped up in our conversations.

He said he had thought of me occasionally and had always been sure that, after my father's sudden death, which no one could properly explain, I could *only* study medicine, for that death was an enigma that would have to haunt me till the end of my life. Although unsolvable, he said, it was an enormous incentive, a special kind of source; and if I went into medicine, he said, it would be impossible for me not to discover new and important things. He had attended me after my dreadful scalding [see *The Tongue Set Free*], when my father had saved my life by returning from England. I thus owed him my life doubly, said the doctor. I had been unable to save his life a year and a half later, in Manchester, and I now owed him this debt, too, and was obligated to pay it by saving other lives. The doctor said this simply, without rhetoric or bombast; yet from his lips, the word *life* sounded like not only something precious but something *rare;* which was peculiar, considering the countless people crowded on deck.

I was ashamed of myself, especially of my hypocrisy in justifying to myself my absurd study of chemistry. But I didn't say anything to him: it would have been too ignoble. I told him I wanted to know everything that was to be known. He interrupted me and pointed at the stars—it was already night—and he asked: "Do you know the names of the stars?" We now took turns showing one another the individual constellations. I showed him Lyra with Vega, for he had asked me first; then, he showed me Cygnus with Deneb, for he had to demonstrate that he knew about the stars, too, when he asked me. Thus we showed one another the entire nocturnal sky, neither of us knowing what the other would hit on next. Soon, omitting no constellation, we exhausted the nightly heavens. I had never sung such a duet with anyone. He said: "Do you know how many people have died in the meantime?" He meant the short time in which we had been naming the stars. I said nothing; he offered no figure. "You don't know them. It doesn't matter to you. A doctor knows them. It does matter to him."

When I had bumped into him, at twilight, he had been sitting in a group of people who were conversing animatedly, while, not far from them, a group of students were ardently bellowing Bulgarian songs. My uncle had told me in Vienna that Dr. Menachemoff would be on the boat; he'd be delighted to see me again after such a long time—thirteen years. I had given him no further thought, and now I was suddenly standing in front of the black beard. How deeply I had hated a black beard just like this one during the intervening years! Perhaps it was a remnant of that old emotion that had drawn me near this beard. I knew it was him: this was a physician's beard. I stared at him with mixed feelings. He broke off in midsentence (he was involved in a conversation) and said: "It's you, I knew it was you. But I didn't recognize you. How could I have? You weren't even six the last time I saw you."

He lived in the old days much more than I did. I had left Ruschuk behind with some arrogance; those had been the days before I knew how to read. I expected nothing of the people who lived there and suddenly crossed my path in "Europe." He, however, who had been there since I'd left, had kept an eye on his patients, and he expected special things of those who had left Ruschuk as little children. He knew that my grandfather had cursed my father when we moved to England; it had been the talk of the town; but it went against the doctor's scientific pride to believe in the effect of the curse. My father's death so soon afterwards was a mystery to him, and since it hadn't been solved in time, he considered it natural that I would devote my life to solving such or similar enigmas.

"Can you remember your pains when you were ill?" he said. His thoughts had all returned to my scalding. "Your entire skin was gone. Only your head hadn't submerged in the water. It was Danube water. Perhaps you don't know that. And now we're peacefully sailing on the same Danube."

"But it's not the same," I said. "It's always a different one. I don't remember the pains, but I do remember my father coming back."

"It was a miracle," said Dr. Menachemoff. "His return saved your life. That's how one becomes a great physician. If this happens to a man in his infancy, he becomes a doctor. It's impossible for him to become anything else. That's why your mother moved to Vienna with you little children right after your father's death. She knew you'd find all the great teachers there that you need. Where would we be without the Vienna Medical School! Your mother was always an intelligent woman. I hear she's rather sickly. You'll take care of her. She'll have the best doctor in her own family, her very own son. Make sure you finish soon. Specialize, but not too narrowly."

And now he gave me detailed advice on my studies. He ignored all my—timid—objections when it came to this matter. We spoke about a lot of things. He would answer *anything else,* and he always thought a long time before speaking. He was flexible and wise, interested and concerned; and only gradually did I realize that there was something he hadn't grasped and would never grasp. He couldn't believe that I wouldn't be a physician; after one semester, many things were still open. I was so ashamed that I gave up trying to tell him the truth of the matter, and I avoided this embarrassing point. Perhaps, I began to waver. When he inquired about my brothers, I, as usual, spoke only about the youngest, as proudly as if I had fathered him myself, crowing about his talent. The doctor wanted to know what *he* was going to study, and I felt relieved that I could say "medicine," for this was settled. "Two brothers—two doctors!" he said and laughed. "Why not the third one, too?" But this was only a joke, and I didn't have to explain why the middle brother wasn't suited for medicine.

In any case, Dr. Menachemoff was clear about *my* vocation. We bumped into each other on deck a few more times. He introduced me to some of his colleagues, explaining simply: "A future luminary of the Vienna Medical School." It didn't sound boastful; it sounded like something natural. It became harder and harder for me to tell him the cruel and unmistakable truth. Since he talked so much about my father, since he had been present when my father returned and saved my life, I couldn't bring myself to disappoint him.

It was a wonderful voyage. I saw countless people and talked to many of them. A group of German geologists, inspecting the formations at the Iron Gates, discussed them, using expressions I didn't understand. An American historian was trying to explain Trajan's campaigns to his family. (He was en route to Byzantium, the real object of his research.) But only his wife would listen to him; his two daughters, beautiful girls, preferred talking to students. Speaking English, we grew a little friendly; they complained about their father, who always lived in the past; they were still young, they said, they were alive now. They said this with such conviction that you believed them. Peasants brought baskets of fruits and vegetables on board. A longshoreman carried a whole piano on his back; he ran up the plank and put it down. He was small and bull-necked and bursting with muscles; but even today, I still don't understand how he managed to carry his load all by himself.

At Lom Palanka, Buco and I disembarked. We were supposed to spend the night here and take the morning train for Sofia via the Balkans. Dr. Menachemoff, who was returning to Ruschuk, stayed on the steamer. When I took leave with a very uncertain conscience, he said: "Don't forget what I expect of you." Then he added: "And don't let anyone talk you out of it, do you hear? Anyone!" These were his strongest words so far; they sounded like a commandment. And I breathed a sigh of relief.

Throughout our bedbug night in Lom, I didn't sleep a wink. I kept thinking about the meaning of his last words. He must have understood after all that I had defected. He had dissembled. I had been ashamed of my deception, for I had given up the idea of explaining the truth to him plainly and irrefutably. But he had dissembled as well. He acted as if he didn't realize what had happened. That same night, I went over to Buco, who couldn't sleep in his bedbug room either, and I asked him: "What did you say to Dr. Menachemoff? Did you tell him what I was studying?"

"Yes. Chemistry. What *should* I have told him?"

So the doctor had really known and had been trying to bring me back to the straight and narrow path. He was the only one who did what my father would have done: give me the freedom of making my own choice. He had witnessed what had developed between my father and me, and he had preserved it, he alone. He had come to the boat carrying me back to that country, and he had transmitted the message to which, in the eyes of the world, he had no right. He had done so cunningly, by ignoring what had happened. He had cared only about the purity of the message, its unadulterated wording. He had paid no heed to my state of mind when the message reached me.

The Orator

During my first three weeks in Sofia, I lived with Rachel, my father's youngest sister. She was the nicest of all his brothers and sisters, a beautiful, upright woman, tall and stately, warmhearted and cheerful. She had two faces. You could see them, whether she was laughing, or was convinced of something that she supported with spirit and warmth; and it was always something unegotistical, a faith, a conviction. She had an elderly, thoughtful husband, who was respected for his sense of justice; they had three sons, the youngest eight years old and, like me, named after our grandfather. Their home was a lively place, full of noise and mirth; people yelled to each other through all the rooms; no one could hide; anyone seeking peace and quiet ran outdoors, finding tranquility there rather than at home. However, the center of gravity in the home, the husband and father, remained an enigma. He almost never spoke; all you could get out of him was an ineluctable verdict. What then came was a "Yes" or "No," a very brief sentence, and so calm that it was painstaking to listen. When he was about to speak, the place grew still, though no one ordered the family to keep quiet. For one moment, which was so short that it seemed eerie, the place was really silent; and then, soft and barely audible, in few and slightly gray words, came the verdict, the decision. Right after that, all hell broke loose again. It was hard to say which was noisier: the racket made by the boys or the loud demands, admonitions, questions from the mother.

Such a hustle and bustle was new to me. Everything about these boys focused on physical activity; they had no interest in books; but they were mad about sports. They were strong, active boys, who could never keep still; they were always trading belligerent punches. Their father, who was altogether different, seemed to want to encourage this excessively physical life. I kept expecting a *"Ya basta!"* (That's enough) from him; I looked over at him in the midst of the worst tumult. He did notice it, he missed nothing, and he knew what I expected; but he held his tongue. The hubbub continued, stopping briefly only when all three boys went out at the same time.

This encouragement of sheer vital energy was based on conviction and method. The family was about to emigrate. They were planning to leave the city and the country during the next few weeks, with several other families. Palestine, they said, was their promised destination; they were among the first; they were regarded as pioneers, and were keenly aware of this. The entire Sephardic community in Sofia, or rather not only in Sofia, but throughout Bulgaria, had converted to Zionism. They weren't badly off in Bulgaria: there were no persecutions of Jews, no ghettoes, nor was there any oppressive poverty. But there were orators, whose sparks had ignited, and they kept preaching the return to the promised land. The effect of these speeches was remarkable in more ways than one. They were aimed at the separatistic arrogance of the Sephardim: they preached that all Jews were equal, that any separatism was despicable, and by no means could the Sephardim be credited with special achievements for mankind during the most recent period in history. On the contrary, the Sephardim were trapped in a spiritual torpor; it was time they awoke and discarded their useless crotchet, their arrogance.

One of the fieriest speakers, a man who was supposedly working true miracles, was a cousin of mine, Bernhard Arditti. He was the eldest son of that legalistically possessed Josef Arditti in Ruschuk (who accused everyone in the family of being thieves and reveled in litigation) and beautiful Bellina (who had stepped out of a Titian painting and spent day and night thinking about presents to gladden everyone's heart). Bernhard had become a lawyer, but his practice meant nothing to him; his father's pettifogging might have destroyed his interest. He had converted to Zionism while very young, discovering his oratorical powers, which he put in the service of the cause. When I came to Sofia, everyone was talking about him. Thousands gathered to hear him; the largest synagogue could barely hold his listeners. People congratulated me on having such a cousin and pitied me because

I wouldn't be hearing him myself: in the few weeks of my visit, no lecture was scheduled. Everybody was moved by him, everybody was won over. I met very many people, there was no exception; it was as if an enormous tidal wave had grabbed them and carried them out to sea, making them part of the ocean. I never found a single opponent to his cause.

He spoke Ladino to them and scourged them for their arrogance, which was based on this language. I was amazed to discover that it was possible to use this language, which I regarded as a stunted language for children and the kitchen; it was possible to speak about universal matters, to fill people with such passion that they earnestly considered dropping everything, leaving a country in which they had been settled for generations, a country which took them seriously and respected them, in which they were certainly well off—in order to move to an unknown land that had been promised them thousands of years ago, but didn't even belong to them at this point.

I had come to Sofia at a critical moment. No wonder they couldn't have a bed for me under these circumstances. One of the sons had to sleep out in order to make room for me. Thus, the generosity they welcomed me with was all the more remarkable. They moved things around, they packed; the normal hubbub that obviously prevailed here was joined by an unusual kind of house-moving. I heard the names of other families who were going through the same thing. A whole group of them was emigrating together; it was the first major action of this kind, and people hardly talked about anything else.

When I went out to sightsee or just to escape the noise, I often ran into Bernhard, the cousin whose speeches had begun all this or at least given the decisive thrust to the ultimate action. He was a thickset, corpulent man with bushy eyebrows, some ten years my senior, always in youthful motion, and never talking about anything private (the antipode of his father). His German words were as round and sure as though they were his native language; everything he said seemed immovable, and yet it remained white-hot and flowing, like lava that never cooled. If I voiced objections merely to stand my ground, he wiped them away with superior wit, laughing magnanimously and by no means offensively, as if apologizing for being practiced in political debate.

What I liked about him was the fact that material things didn't matter to him. Since his law practice didn't interest him and was more of a burden, he never concerned himself with profitable affairs. Walking alongside him through the broad, clean streets of Sofia, you wondered only what he was doing for his livelihood. It was obvious that he needed his own kind of nourishment: he lived on what fulfilled him. Perhaps his words were so effective because he never twisted or distorted them to his daily advantage. People believed him because he wanted nothing for himself; he believed himself because he wasted no thought on property.

I confided in him that I had no intention of becoming a chemist. I was only pretending to study in order to prepare myself for other things.

"Why pretend?" he said. "You've got an intelligent mother."

"She's gotten under the influence of ordinary people. When she was ill in Arosa, she met people who are 'in the thick of life,' as the phrase goes—successful people. Now she wants me to 'stand in the thick of life,' but in their way, and not in mine."

"Careful!" he said, suddenly looking at me very earnestly, as though seeing me as a *person* for the first time. "Careful! Or you're doomed. I know that kind. My own father wanted me to continue all his litigation for him."

That was all he said; the matter was too private to interest him any further. But he was plainly on my side; and it was only when I told him I wanted to write in German and no other language that he shook his head: "What for? Learn Hebrew! That's our language. Do you believe there's a more beautiful language?"

I liked getting together with him; he had succeeded in escaping money. He earned little, and yet no one was as respected as he. Among all the devoted slaves of business, including most of my family, none berated him. He knew how to fill them with hope, which they needed more than wealth or ordinary good fortune. I sensed that he wanted to win me over, but not brutally, not with a speech in a mass assembly, but man to man, as though he felt I could be as useful to the movement as he. I asked him what his state of mind was when he gave a speech, whether he always knew who he was, whether he didn't fear losing himself in the enthusiastic crowd.

"Never! Never!" he said, terribly resolute. "The more enthusiastic they become, the more I feel I'm myself. You've got the people in hand like soft dough and you can do anything you want with them. You could get them to start fires, to ignite their own houses. There are no limits to this sort of power. Try it for yourself! You only have to *want* it! *You* won't abuse this kind of power! You'll use it for a good cause, just as I do for our cause."

"I've experienced a crowd," I said, "in Frankfurt. I was like dough myself. I can't forget it. I'd like to know what it's all about. I'd like to understand it."

"There's nothing to understand. It's the same everywhere. You're either a drop dissolving in the crowd or someone who knows how to give the crowd a direction. You have no other choice."

He found it pointless to wonder *what* this crowd really was. He took it for granted, as something one could evoke in order to achieve certain effects. But did everyone who knew how to do it have a right to do it?

"No, not everyone!" he said decisively. "Only the man who does it for the true cause."

"How can he know whether it's the true cause?"

"He can feel it," he said, "here!" He thumped his chest

powerfully several times. "The man who doesn't feel it can't do it!"

"Then all a person has to do is believe in his cause. But what about his enemy, who may believe in the very opposite!"

I spoke hesitantly, tentatively. I didn't want to criticize or embarrass him. Nor could I have done so, he was far too self-confident. I only wanted to get at something that I felt vaguely, that had been on my mind since my experiences in Frankfurt and that I couldn't quite grasp. I had been *moved* by the crowd, after all; it was an intoxication; you were lost, you forgot yourself, you felt tremendously remote and yet fulfilled; whatever you felt, you didn't feel it for yourself; it was the most selfless thing you knew; and since selfishness was shown, talked, and *threatened* on all sides, you needed this experience of thunderous unselfishness like the blast of the trumpet at the Last Judgment, and you made sure not to belittle or denigrate this experience. At the same time, however, you felt you had no control over yourself, you weren't free, something uncanny was happening to you, it was half delirium, half paralysis. How could all this happen together? What was it?

Yet by no means did I expect Bernhard the orator to answer my still unarticulated question now, at this special high point of his effectiveness. I resisted him, although I approved of him. It wouldn't have sufficed for me to become his follower. There were many people whose follower one could become, and they advocated all sorts of things. Basically (but I didn't say this to myself), I viewed him as someone who knew how to excite people into a crowd.

I came home to Rachel, and the place was full of the agitation in which his speeches had been keeping these people, like so many others, for years. I witnessed this mood of departure for three weeks. I experienced its peak intensity when they started out at the railroad station. Hundreds of people had gathered to see off their near and dear. The emigrants, all the families occupying the train, were inundated with flowers and good wishes; people sang, people blessed, people wept. It was as if the station had been constructed specially for this leavetaking, and as though it had grown just big enough to hold this wealth of emotions. Children were held out from the windows of the compartments; old people, particularly women, already half shrunken, stood on the platform, blinded by tears, unable to see whether these were the right children, waving at the wrong ones. They were all grandchildren, they were what mattered, the grandchildren were leaving, the old were staying, that's what the departure looked like—not quite correctly. A tremendous expectation filled the station hall, and perhaps the grandchildren were there for the sake of this expectation and this moment.

The orator, who had also come, was staying behind. "I still have things to do," he said. "I can't leave yet. I have to give courage to those who are still afraid." He kept to himself at the station, didn't push forward; he looked as if he'd much rather have stayed incognito, in a cloak of invisibility. Now and then, people greeted him and pointed him out; this seemed to irritate him. But then someone insisted that he say a few words; and with the very first sentence, he was a different person; fiery and self-assured, he blossomed under his own words, he found the good wishes that they needed for their enterprise, and he gave them these good wishes.

Rachel's apartment was empty and deserted now, so I moved in with Sophie, my father's eldest sister. After the tumult of the past few weeks, everything now seemed dull and low-key, as though the people here distrusted any undertaking that went beyond everyday life. They did share the conviction of the emigrants, but they didn't speak about it; they saved excitement for festive occasions and just did what they had always done. This home was ruled by repetition, the routine of my early childhood, which now meant nothing to me. After all, we had escaped it by moving to England; and the dreadful thing that had happened in Manchester, my father's death, blocked the road to my childhood. I listened to Sophie's domestic talk; she knew all about diets and enemas, a caring woman; but she never told any stories. I listened to her sober husband, a man of few words, her more sober eldest son, who said just as little with many words, and, my greatest disappointment, her daughter Laurica, my childhood playmate, whom I had wanted to kill with an ax when I was five [see *The Tongue Set Free*].

Something was wrong with her size: I remembered her as *tall*, high above me; now, she was smaller than I, delicate, coquettish, intent on marriage and a husband. What had become of her dangerous character, her envied copybooks? She knew nothing about them now; she had forgotten how to read; she couldn't recollect the ax I had threatened her with, or her own shrieks. She hadn't pushed me into the hot water: I had fallen in myself; I hadn't lain in bed for several weeks: "You got a little scalded." And when I, thinking she had forgotten only the things concerning herself, reminded her of Grandfather's curse, she let out a ringing laugh, like a chambermaid in an opera. "A father cursing his son—oh, c'mon—there's no such thing, you made that up, those are fairy tales. I don't like fairy tales." And when I threw up at her that I had witnessed countless scenes between Grandfather and Mother in Vienna, scenes about the curse, that Grandfather had stormed out of the house without saying goodbye, and Mother had then collapsed, weeping for hours and hours, Laurica snippily wiped it all away: "You just imagined it."

No matter what I said, it was useless: nothing terrible had happened, nothing terrible was happening. And so—reluctantly—I came out with the fact that I had bumped into Dr. Menachemoff on the Danube steamer. We had spent hours talking, I said, and he recalled everything. He could remember it as clearly as if it were yesterday. Now he had been her family's doctor in Ruschuk, she knew him better than I because she had lived there until they moved to Sofia. But she had an answer for this, too: "People get like that in the provinces. Those are old-fashioned people. They concoct all these things. They have nothing else to think about. They believe all kinds of stuff and nonsense. You fell into the water yourself. You weren't so sick. Your father didn't come from Manchester. It's too far away. Besides, traveling wasn't so cheap in those days. Your father never came back to Ruschuk. When could Grandfather have cursed him? Dr. Menachemoff knows nothing. Only the family knows things like that."

"What about your mother?" The day before, her mother had talked about pulling me out of the water, stripping my clothes off, and about all my skin coming off in the process. "Mother keeps forgetting everything, now," said Laurica. "She's getting senile. But one mustn't tell her that."

I was furious at how stubborn and obtuse she was. Nothing existed for her but her one determination: to get a man at last and marry. She was twenty-three and afraid that people already considered her an old maid. She assailed me, begging me for the truth: I should tell her whether a man could still find her attractive. At nineteen, I ought to know these feelings. Did I feel like kissing her? Did her hairdo today make a man feel more like kissing her than the hairdo yesterday? Did I find her skinny? She was gracile, she said, but not skinny. Could I dance? Dancing was the best way to attract a man. A girlfriend of hers had gotten engaged while dancing. But afterwards, the man had said it didn't count, it had only been because they were dancing. Did I think the same thing could happen to her, Laurica?

I thought nothing, I had no answer to any of her questions, and the faster they rained down upon me, the more mulish I became. I didn't have such feelings, I said, though I was nineteen. I just didn't know whether a woman attracted me. How can one tell? They were all stupid, and what could you talk to them about? They were all like her, I went on, and remembered nothing. How can a man be attracted to someone who forgets everything? Her hairdo was always the same, I said. She *was* skinny; why shouldn't a woman be skinny? I couldn't dance. I had tried to dance once, in Frankfurt, and had always kept stepping on the girl's feet. A man who gets engaged while dancing is an idiot. Any man who gets engaged is an idiot.

I drove her crazy, and thereby made her see reason. In order to get an answer out of me, she began to remember. Nothing much came of it, but she did still see the raised ax, and she said she had dreamt of it over and over again; the last time was when her girlfriend's engagement was broken.

Cramped Quarters

In early September, we moved into Frau Olga Ring's apartment in Vienna. Olga Ring was a very beautiful woman with a Roman profile, proud and fiery, never wanting special treatment. Her husband had died some time ago, their love for each other had become almost legendary in their circles, but Frau Olga hadn't let it deteriorate into a death cult, if only because she owed him nothing. She wasn't afraid to think of him, she never embellished his picture, and she remained the same. Many men courted her, she never wavered, and she kept her beauty until the late, dreadful end.

She spent most of the year with her married daughter in Belgrade. Her Vienna apartment, where nothing had changed—or rather, its furthest part, a shabby little room with one window—was tenanted by her son Johnnie, a bar pianist. In both his own and his mother's eyes, he was no failure; but in the eyes of the rest of the family, he *was*. He, too, was a beauty, the very image of his mother, and yet very different from her, for he had run to fat. People were surprised that he didn't dress up as a woman; he was often taken for one. He was a cunning flatterer; he took whatever you gave him; his arm was always outstretched, his hand always open. He felt he deserved everything and even more, for he was a good pianist. At his bar, he was the darling of the customers. He played both the current and the most recondite hits; once he had played something, he never forgot it, he was the living inventory of nocturnal sounds. During the day, he slept in his pad, which was just big enough for a bed. The rest of the apartment, appointed with middle-class heaviness, was sublet.

For a while, he had the job of collecting the rent for his mother and sending it to Belgrade after a few deductions. That was what he was supposed to do. But in fact, the deductions ate up the entire rent, and nothing was left for the mother. All she received were unpaid bills; and since she didn't know how to pay them—nothing but the apartment remained from the happy marriage—some better arrangement had to be found. Her niece, Veza, took charge of subletting the apartment and collecting the rent every month; she made sure that bills were paid, and the remainder was given to Johnnie only if he needed it. He always did need it, and, as before, not a penny was left over for Frau Olga. She never complained, for she worshipped her son. "My son the musician," she used to call him. And since everything she said was marked by her pride, some people, who didn't know him, tended to view him as a secret Schubert, despite his bar moniker, Johnnie.

We were happy to move into this apartment; although furnished, it was nevertheless our own place. The vision of Scheuchzerstrasse, where we had lived in Zurich, hovered before us. And while this wasn't Zurich, my paradise, it was nevertheless Vienna, Mother's Vienna. We had left Scheuchzerstrasse five years earlier; in between came the Villa Yalta in Zurich for me, the forest sanatorium in Arosa for her, and later the rooming house and the inflation in Frankfurt. It was astonishing that after all those things, we could look forward to living together without tension. We all talked about it, each in his own way, as if a new era of health, study, and peace were commencing.

But there was one fly in the ointment, and this fly was Johnnie Ring. Our living and dining room bordered on his pad. And when the finally united family was dining, the door would open, Johnnie's corpulent figure appeared, wrapped in an old bathrobe and nothing else, and, with a "Hi, there!", he whisked past us in slippers, en route to the toilet. He had stipulated this right, but we had forgotten to restrict it to the periods between meals, for we liked to remain undisturbed at mealtimes. Thus he always showed up punctually, as soon as we had dipped our spoons into the soup. Perhaps our voices had awoken him and reminded him of his need; but perhaps he was also curious and wanted to find out what was on our menu. For he didn't come back through very soon; he made sure the entrée was already on our plates when he rustled back into his room. It really sounded like rustling, although he wasn't wrapped in silk; the noise came from the way he moved and from a series of certainly one dozen "Hi there excuse me hi there how are you excuse me hi how's everything excuse me how are you all excuse me." He had to pass behind Mother, squeezing between the sideboard and her chair in a skillful pirouette, managing not to graze her even once. She waited for the touch of his greasy bathrobe, let out a deep sigh of relief when the danger was past and he had vanished behind his door, and she then always said the same thing: "Thank goodness. He would have ruined my appetite." We knew the vastness of her disgust, without divining the cause; but what amazed all three of us was the polite way she responded to his words. The choice of her greeting—"Good *morning*, Herr Ring!"—was certainly ironic; but there was no hint of irony in her intonation: it sounded innocuous, friendly, even cordial. Nor was her sigh of relief after his passage ever loud enough to be heard behind the closed door of his room; and the conversation at the table then went on as if he had never appeared in the first place.

At other times, especially evening, he involved Mother in a conversation which she couldn't get out of. He began by praising her three well-bred boys. "One just can't believe it, dear Frau Canetti. They're as pretty as princes!"

"They're not pretty, Herr Ring," she retorted indignantly. "That's unimportant for a man."

"Oh, don't say that, dear lady; it helps in life! If they're pretty, they'll get ahead much more easily. I could tell you stories! Young Tisza hangs out in our bar. I don't have to tell you who the Tiszas were. They're still the Tiszas in Hungary today. A charming person, this young Tisza! A beauty, not just handsome, and a heartbreaker! He's got the world at his feet. I'll play anything he wants, and he says thank you every time; he says thank you for each number specially. 'Wonderful!' he says and looks at me. 'You played that wonderfully, dear Johnnie!' I anticipate his every wish. I'd go through fire for him. I'd share my last bathrobe with him! And why is he like that? Breeding, dear lady, breeding is responsible for everything. Good manners are half a heart. It all depends on the mother. Yes, indeed, to have such a mother! I wonder if your three angels realize how lucky they are to have such a mother! It took me a long time to say thank you to my mother. I don't wish to compare myself to your angels, dear Frau Canetti!"

"Why do you always say 'angels,' Herr Ring? Why don't you just say 'brats'? I won't be offended. They're not stupid, that's true, but that's no merit; I went to enough trouble educating them."

"You see, dear lady, you see, now you admit it yourself. *You* went to the trouble! You, you alone! Without you, without your self-sacrificing efforts, they might really have turned into brats."

Self-sacrificing—that was the word he caught her with. Had he known what part the word *sacrifice*, in all its derivations, played with her, he would have used it more often. At an early time, she had already begun to talk about how she had sacrificed her life for us; it was the only thing she had preserved from her religion. As the faith in God's presence gradually waned in her, as God was there for her less and less and almost disappeared, the meaning of sacrifice grew in her eyes. It was not only a duty, it was the highest human achievement to sacrifice oneself; but not at God's command; he was too far away to care; it was sacrifice in and of itself, sacrifice at one's own behest, that's what mattered. Although bearing this concentrated name, sacrifice was something compounded and extensive, something stretching over hours, days, and years—life compounded of all the hours in which you had *not* lived—that was sacrifice.

Once Johnnie had caught her, he could talk away at her all he liked. She couldn't let him go. It was *he* who finally left, to walk his German shepherd, Nero; or else the doorbell rang, and Johnnie had company. A young man appeared and vanished into the pad with Johnnie and Nero, remaining for several hours, until it was time for Johnnie to go to the bar and play the piano. We couldn't hear a sound from his room. Nero, accustomed to sleeping there, never barked. We could never tell whether Johnnie and the young man conversed. My mother would never have lowered herself to eavesdrop at the door; she simply assumed they never talked. The room, into which she never glanced (she avoided it like the plague), was tiny: there wasn't space for much more than a bed. And she just couldn't understand how two people, one of them the opulent Johnnie, and a huge dog could stand that tiny space for hours at a time. She never mentioned it, but I could sense when she was thinking about it. What really worried her, however, was that I might think about it—which never occurred to me; it didn't interest me in the slightest. Once she said: "I believe the young man sleeps under the bed. He always looks so pale and tired. Maybe he has no room of his own, and Johnnie feels sorry for him and lets him sleep under the bed for a couple of hours."

"Why not *on* the bed?" I asked, in all innocence. "Do you think Johnny is too fat, and there's no room for both of them?"

"*Under* the bed, I said." She glared at me. "What kind of odd things are you thinking?" I wasn't thinking any odd things, but she tried to anticipate them in any case, pushing my thoughts into the space under the bed, so that there was only enough room for the dog on the bed. This seemed harmless to her. She would have been greatly surprised if she could have read my mind: the events in the tiny room didn't interest me, for my thoughts were occupied with something else, connected with my mother, something that struck me as obscene, even though I wouldn't have used this word back then.

Every morning, a very pregnant woman, Frau Lischka, came to clean up. She remained after lunch to do the dishes and then went home. She came chiefly for the heavy chores: laundry, beating the carpets. "I don't need her for the lighter work," said Mother, "I could do that myself." No one wanted to hire her in that condition: people were afraid her pregnancy was so advanced that she couldn't work well. But she had assured us she did do a good job; we should just try her out. Mother felt sorry for her and allowed her to come. It was risky, said Mother. How unpleasant if she suddenly got ill, or if the expected came over her—out of consideration for our youth, Mother didn't get any more precise, sparing us the details. The woman had sworn it wouldn't be for another two months, and until then she could do everything right. It turned out she was telling the truth; she was amazingly hardworking. "Nonpregnant women could take an example from her," said Mother.

One day, when I came home for lunch, I peered down to the courtyard from the staircase: Frau Lischka was standing there, beating a rug. She had a hard time keeping her belly out of the way, and every time she struck the rug, she performed a strangely twisting motion. She looked as if she were turning away from the rug in disapproval, as if she disliked it so much that she didn't care to see it for anything in the world. Her face was crimson; from up where I was, one could have mistaken the color for anger. The sweat dripped down her crimson face, and she shouted something that I didn't understand. Since there was no one she could have been talking to, I assumed she was spurring herself on to keep beating.

I entered the apartment in dismay and asked Mother whether she had seen Frau Lischka down in the courtyard. She was coming right up, was the answer. Today she was getting something to eat: on days when she beat the rugs, she got something to eat. Contractually, said Mother, she wasn't at all obligated to do this (she used the word *contractually*), but she felt sorry for the woman. The woman had told her she was accustomed to not eating all day long: she fixed herself something in the evening, at home. Mother just couldn't stand the thought of this, and on days when the woman beat the rugs, she gave her a meal. The woman always looked forward to it, said Mother, and that was why she beat away so powerfully. She was bathed in sweat, said Mother, when she arrived upstairs with the rugs; you couldn't stand it in the kitchen because of the stench; that was why Mother herself served the meal in the dining room on those days, leaving Frau Lischka in the kitchen with her hunger. She gave her a gigantic plate, she said. None of us three, not even Georg, could eat that much. All the food vanished. Perhaps she packed some away and took it home in her grocery bag. The woman refused to eat before her, saying it wasn't proper. We discussed it at the table. I asked why she didn't always get something to eat. When she did the laundry, she did get something, too, said Mother, only not as much. But on days when the work was lighter, no—she wasn't contractually obliged to give her anything, and besides, Frau Lischka was grateful for whatever she got, more grateful, in any event, than I.

Gratitude was a frequent topic. If I was furious about something and criticized Mother, she promptly came out with my ingratitude. A calm discussion between us was impossible. I was ruthless when voicing my thoughts, but I voiced them only when I was angry about something; hence they always sounded offensive. She defended herself as best she could. When she felt cornered, she resorted to her sacrificing herself to us for twelve years and reproached me for showing no gratitude.

Her thoughts focused on the overcrowded tiny room and the danger threatening us three boys from those doings, whereby she spoke openly only about laziness, about the poor example of a grown man lying in bed all day or wandering around half naked in a greasy bathrobe; but secretly, she thought of all kinds of vices that I had no inkling of. *My* thoughts went to Frau Lischka in the kitchen. She was grateful for getting something to eat now and then, and I never ran into her without her joyfully asserting, "You've got a good mother," and corroborating it by vehemently waggling her head. She constantly served to bolster our egos: Mother had a good heart, for she gave her meals "noncontractually," and I was decent, for I felt guilty about her working in her condition. We plunged into a tournament of self-righteousness, two indefatigable knights. With the energy we applied to these jousts, we could have beaten the rugs of all the tenants in the building, with enough to spare for the laundry. But, as we were both convinced, it was the principle of the thing: gratitude for her, justice for me.

Thus distrust had moved into the apartment with us. For Mother, it wasn't good that this secret existed in the apartment—Johnnie's overcrowded pad. While the highly pregnant woman, drudging away in the courtyard or the kitchen, filled *me* with horror. I was always scared she would collapse, we would hear screams, run into the kitchen, and find her lying in her blood. The screams would be those of her newborn baby, and Frau Lischka would be dead.

The Gift

The year on Radetzkystrasse, where we lived in such crowded conditions, was the most oppressive year I can remember.

No sooner had I entered the apartment than I felt under observation. Nothing I did or said was right. Everything was so near, the little room in which I slept and which contained my books lay between the dining room and the bedroom that Mother shared with my brothers. It was impossible for me to slip into my room unseen. Greetings and explanations in the living room formed the start of every homecoming. I was questioned, and although my mother never accused me of anything, her questions did betray mistrust. Had I been to the laboratory or had I killed the time at lectures?

I had let myself in for such questions by being so open. I especially told her about lectures whose topics were almost generally accessible. European History since the French Revolution was closer to most people than Physiology of Plants or Physical Chemistry. My failure to talk about these latter subjects did not in any way spell a lack of interest on my part. But all that counted was what I said; this alone was valid; I was charged on the basis of my own words: the Congress of Vienna interested me more than sulfuric acid! "You're spreading yourself too thin," she said. "You'll never get anywhere at this rate!"

"I *have* to attend these lectures," I said, "otherwise I'll suffocate. I can't give up everything I'm interested in just because I'm studying something that's not in my line."

"But why isn't it in your line? You're preparing to practice no profession. You're afraid that chemistry might suddenly interest you. This *is* a profession of the future, after all—and you're blocking yourself off and barricading yourself against it. Just don't get your hands dirty! The only clean things are books. You go to all sorts of lectures, just so you can read more books about the topics. It'll never end. Do you still not realize what you're like? It began in your childhood. For every book in which you learn something new, you need ten others to find out more about it. A lecture that interests you is a burden. The subject will interest you more and more. The philosophy of the pre-Socratics! Fine, you have to take a test in that. You've got no choice. You take notes, you've filled up whole copybooks. But why all the books? Do you think I don't know about all the titles you've got on your list? We can't afford it. Even if we could afford it, it would be bad for you. It would keep luring you further and further away and divert you from your true studies. You said Gomperz is important in this field. Didn't you say that his father was famous for his *Greek Thinkers*?"

"Yes," I interrupted, "in three volumes. I'd like that, I'd like to get it."

"All I have to do is mention your professor's father, and a three-volume scholarly opus gets on the list. You don't honestly believe I'm going to give it to you, do you? The son should be enough for you. Just take notes and study out of your copybooks."

"That's too slow for me. It crawls and crawls, you just can't imagine. I'd like to get into it more deeply. I can't wait until Gomperz reaches Pythagoras. I want to find out something now about Empedocles and Heraclitus."

"You read so many ancient authors in Frankfurt. Evidently, they were the wrong ones. Those books were always lying around; they were so ugly, and they all looked alike. Why weren't the Greek philosophers among them? You were already interested back then in things you wouldn't need later on."

"I didn't like the philosophers then. I was put off by Plato's theory of ideas, which turns the world into a semblance. And I could never stand Aristotle. He's omniscient for the sake of categorizing. With him, you feel as if you were locked up in countless drawers. If I'd known the pre-Socratics back then, I would have devoured every word they wrote. But no one told me about them. Everything began with Socrates. It was as if no one had thought about anything before him. And do you know, I never really liked Socrates. Maybe I avoided the great philosophers because they were his disciples."

"Should I tell you why you didn't like him?"

I would rather not have learned it from her. She had a highly personal opinion even about things she didn't really know very much about. And though I knew that what she said couldn't be correct, it struck me every time, settling like mildew on the things I loved. I sensed she was trying to spoil things for me merely because they tore me too far away. My enthusiasm for so many things was something she found ridiculous at my age and *unmanly*. This was the word of censure that I heard most from her during the year on Radetzkystrasse.

"You don't like Socrates because he's so sensible: he always starts with everyday things, he has something solid, he likes to talk about craftsmen."

"But he didn't work very hard. He *talked* all day long."

"That's not good enough for you silent souls! I know just how you feel!" There it was again, the old scorn that I had gotten to know so early, when I had been learning German from her. "Or is it that you only want to keep talking yourself, and you're scared of people like Socrates who very carefully test everything that's said and won't let anyone get away with anything?"

She was as apodictic as a pre-Socratic, and who knows whether my preference for the pre-Socratics, whom I was just getting acquainted with, wasn't connected with *her* manner, which I had made all my own. With what self-assurance she always voiced her opinions! Can one even call them "opinions"? Every sentence she uttered had the force of dogma: everything was certain. She never had doubts, at least not about herself. Perhaps it was better like this; for had she felt doubts, they would have been as forceful as her assertions, and she would have doubted herself left, right, and center, till death and destruction.

I felt the narrow confines and pushed out in every direction. I returned to the narrowness, and the resistance I felt gave me strength for pushing out again. At night, I felt alone. My brothers, who seconded her, emphasizing her criticism of me with escapades of their own, were already asleep; she herself had gone to bed. I was free at last. I sat at the tiny table in my tiny room, interrupting whatever I was reading or writing with tender glances at the spines of my books. Their numbers weren't increasing by leaps and bounds as in Frankfurt. But the influx never quite dried up. There were occasions on which I received presents, and who would have dared to give me anything but a book.

There was chemistry, physics, botany, plus general zoology, which I wanted to study at night; and when I did so, it wasn't regarded as a waste of light. However, the textbooks didn't stay open for long. The lecture notebooks, in which one lagged behind the lectures, were soon replaced by the real, the true notebooks, in which I jotted down every exuberance, as well as my sorrows. Before going to sleep, Mother saw the light under the door of my little room; the relationship we had had on Scheuchzerstrasse in Zurich was reversed. She could imagine what I was doing at the little table; but since I was staying up for the sake of my studies, which she approved of once and for all, she had to accept my lucubrations and undertook nothing against them.

She had reasons, she felt, to supervise my activities during this period. She had no real trust in chemistry. It didn't attract me enough, nor could it interest me in the long run. The study of medicine lasted too long, and so I had given up the idea, out of consideration for my mother's material worries, even though I thought they were unfounded. She accepted this renunciation and praised the sacrifice she saw in it. She had sacrificed her own life to us, and her periodic weaknesses and illnesses proved how earnest and difficult this sacrifice was. So now it was time that I, as the eldest son, made a sacrifice. I renounced medicine, which I pictured as an unselfish calling, a service to mankind, and I chose a vocation that was nothing less than unselfish. Chemistry, as she could hear on all sides, belonged to the future. It offered promising jobs in industry; it was useful, oh, so useful; anyone who settled in this field would earn a good living, a very good living; and the fact that I gave myself up, or wanted to give myself up to this usefulness, seemed like a sacrifice, which she recognized. However, I had to stick to it through four years, and about this she had serious doubts. I had resolved to study chemistry only on one condition: namely, that Georg, whom I loved more than anyone else in the world ever since our months together on Praterstrasse, could study medicine in my stead. I had already filled him with my own enthusiasm for it, and there was nothing he desired more than someday to do what I had renounced for his sake.

Her doubts were justified. I had my own version of the matter. It was *not* a sacrifice, for I wasn't really studying chemistry in order to become a well-paid chemist someday. My bias against professions that one pursued in order to make a good living and not because of an inner calling was insuperable. I calmed Mother's fears by letting her believe that I would someday become a chemist in a factory. But I never brought it up; it was a tacit assumption on her part, which I tolerated. It might have been called a truce: I never said that any profession that was not a calling was not worth pursuing, and that a profession didn't count if it wasn't more useful for others than for oneself. In return, she never depicted the chemical future. She hadn't forgotten what had happened in the war, just a few years earlier, when poison gas was used. And I don't believe it was easy for her to get over this aspect of chemistry; for she remained an enemy of war even in the period of her sobering, her narrowing. Hence, we both kept silent about the hideous future that loomed before me as a consequence of my "sacrifice." The main thing was that I went to the laboratory every day, letting the regular hours there accustom me to a job that required its own discipline and that fed neither a voracious hunger for knowledge nor poetic proclamations.

She had no idea how greatly I deceived her about the nature of this enterprise. Not for an instant did I seriously plan ever to work as a chemist. I did go to the laboratory: I spent the bulk of each day there; I did what I had to do there, no worse than the others. I devised my own grounds to justify this occupation to myself. I still desired to find out *everything* and to acquire everything worth knowing in the world. I still had the intact faith that this goal was desirable and also possible. I saw no limits anywhere—whether in the receptivity of a human brain or in the monstrous character of a creature made up of nothing but what he has absorbed and the intention to keep on absorbing. Nor had I as yet discovered that any knowledge I pounced on could be inaccessible to me. True, I had had one or two bad teachers, who had transmitted nothing, absolutely nothing, even filling us with dislike for their subject in the bargain. One such man was my chemistry teacher in Frankfurt. Not much more than the formulas for water and sulfuric acid had remained with me from his class, and I had been disgusted at his movements during the few experiments he performed for us. It was as though a disguised sloth were sitting in front of us, handling the apparatuses slower and slower from hour to hour. Thus, instead of a smattering of chemistry, I was left with a gap in my knowledge. I now had to fill this gap, which was so huge that I could allow myself to study chemistry for this purpose.

There are no boundaries to self-deception, and I well remember how often I recited this reason to myself when my mother insisted that I shouldn't do too much on the side, that I had to restrict myself to chemistry. The very subject I knew least about would become my most thorough area. *That* was the sacrifice I made to inexcusable ignorance; and medicine, which I had renounced, was a *present* I had given my brother, to prove my love to him. He was a part of me; together, we would then have won the totality of knowledge; and thus nothing would ever separate us again.

Samson's Blinding

Among the reproaches I often got to hear in those twelve months, there was one that preyed on my mind: I was told that I didn't know what life was like, that I was blinded, that I didn't even *want* to know. I was told that I had blinders on and was determined never to see without them, I was told that I looked only for things I knew from books. I was told that whether I confined myself too narrowly to *one* kind of book or whether I gleaned the wrong things from them, any attempt to talk to me about the way things really were was doomed to failure.

"You want everything to be highly moral or not at all. The word *freedom,* which you're always spouting, is a joke. No one could be less free than you. It's impossible for you to deal with an event *impartially,* without rolling up all your biases in front of it, until it's no longer visible. That might not be so bad at your age, if it weren't for your obstinate resistance, your defiance, and your resolute determination to leave matters as they stand and never alter a thing. For all your big words, you haven't the foggiest notion about development, gradual maturity, improvement, and especially a person's usefulness to others. Your basic problem is that you've been blinded. You may have learned something too from Michael Kohlhaas.* Only you're not an interesting case, for he at least had to do something. What do you do?"

It was true that I didn't want to learn what the world was like. I had the feeling that by gaining insight into something

*The hero of Kleist's tale about a man blindly determined to obtain justice.—TRANSLATOR

objectionable, I would make myself its accomplice. I didn't want to learn about it, if learning meant having to take the same path. It was *imitative* learning that I resisted. This was why I wore blinders, and she was right. The instant I noticed that something was *recommended* to me purely because it was customary in the world, I got mulish and appeared not to understand what was wanted of me. But reality did come close to me in other ways, a lot closer than she and perhaps even I guessed at that time.

For one road to reality is by way of *pictures*. I don't believe there's any better road. You adhere to something that doesn't change, thus exhausting the everchanging. Pictures are nets: what appears in them is the holdable catch. Some things slip through the meshes and some go rotten. But you keep on trying, you carry the nets around with you, cast them out, and they grow stronger from their catches. However, it's important that these pictures exist *outside* a person, too; inside a human being, even they are subject to change. There has to be a place where he can find them intact, not he alone, a place where everyone who feels uncertain can find them. Whenever a man feels the precariousness of his experience, he turns to a picture. Here, experience holds still, he can look into its face. He thus calms down by knowing reality, which is his own, although merely depicted here. Apparently, it would be there even without him; but these appearances are deceiving; the pictures need *his* experience in order to awake. That is why pictures slumber for generations: no one can see them with the experience that awakes them.

A man feels strong if he finds pictures that his experience needs. There are several such pictures—there can't be all too many, for their significance is that they hold reality gathered; if scattered, reality would have to spray and ooze away. But there shouldn't be just one painting that violates the owner, haunting him forever and prohibiting him from changing. There are several pictures that a man needs for his own life, and if he finds them early, then not too much of him is lost.

It was lucky for me that I was in Vienna when I needed such pictures most. I was threatened with false reality, the reality of soberness, rigidness, usefulness, narrowness; and to counteract this false reality, I needed to find the other reality, which was vast enough to take command of those harshnesses and not knuckle under to them.

I stumbled upon paintings of Breughel's. My acquaintance with them didn't begin where the most splendid Breughels were shown, at Vienna's Kunsthistorisches Museum. In between lectures at the Institute of Physics and Chemistry, I found time to drop in at the Liechtenstein Palace. From Boltzmannstrasse, I quickly bounded down the Strudlhof Staircase, and there I was, in that wonderful gallery, which no longer exists today; here I saw my first Breughels. It didn't matter to me that they were copies—I'd like to meet the unflappable man, the man without senses or nerves, who when suddenly confronted with *these* paintings asks whether they're copies or originals. For all I cared, they could have been copies of copies of copies, for they were *The Six Blind Men* and *The Triumph of Death*. Any blind people I subsequently saw came from the first of these paintings.

The thought of blindness had haunted me ever since childhood, when I had been ill with measles and lost my eyesight for a few days. Now, I saw six blind men in a precipitous row, holding one another's sticks or shoulders. The first man, leading the rest, was already in the ditch. The second one, about to tumble in, was turning his full face toward the spectator: his empty eye sockets and the horrified open mouth with the bared teeth. Between him and the third man came the largest gap in the painting; both men were clutching the stick that linked them, but the third man had felt a jolt, an unsure motion, and was on tiptoe, slightly hesitant; his face, seen in profile—only one blind eye—revealed not his fear, but the start of a question. While behind him, the fourth man, still full of confidence, had his hand on the third man's shoulder and his face toward the sky; his mouth was wide open, as though he expected it to receive something from above, something denied to the eyes. His right hand held the stick for him alone, but he wasn't leaning on it. He was the greatest believer of the six, full of hope and confidence down to the red of his stockings. The two last men behind him followed him, devoted, each the satellite of the preceding man. Their mouths, too, were open, but not as wide; they were farthest from the ditch, expecting nothing, fearing nothing, and having no question. If their blind eyes were not so important, there would be something to say about the fingers of the six men: they hold and touch in a different way from the fingers of people who can see. Also, their groping feet tread the ground in a different way.

This one painting would have sufficed for a whole gallery; but then, I stumbled unexpectedly (I can still feel the shock today) upon *The Triumph of Death*. Hundreds of dead people, as skeletons, highly active skeletons, are busy pulling over an equal number of living people. The dead are people of every sort, crowds and individuals. Each figure's social class is evident, their action dreadfully strenuous, their energy many times greater than that of the living whom they tackle. And the spectator knows they *will* succeed, even though they haven't yet reached their goal. One sides with the living, one would like to help them resist; but it's confusing that the dead seem more alive than the living. The vitality—if one can use that term—of the dead has only one purpose: to pull the living over to the dead. They won't disperse, they won't undertake anything else; there is only this one thing they are after, while the living cling to life in so many ways. Each one is eager, no one gives in. I haven't found anyone *tired* of life in this painting. The dead wrest away from each person something he refuses to surrender voluntarily. The energy of this resistance, in hundreds of variations, flowed into me; and since then, I have often felt as if I were all these people fighting against death.

I understood that there was a crowd on each side. And

much as an individual may feel his death alone, the same is true of every other individual; which is why we should think of them all together.

It is true that death triumphs here. But the struggle doesn't seem like a battle that has been fought once and for all. It keeps on being fought, again and again; and whatever the outcome here, by no means will it necessarily always be the same. It was Breughel's *Triumph of Death* that first gave me confidence for my struggle. Each of his other paintings, which I saw in the Kunsthistorisches Museum, added one more lasting piece of reality. I stood in front of each canvas hundreds of times. I am as familiar with them as with the people closest to me. One of the books that I planned to write and that I reproach myself for never completing was to contain all my experiences with Breughel.

However, these weren't the earliest paintings I sought out. In Frankfurt, in order to reach the Städelsches Museum, one had to cross the Main River. You saw the river and the city, and you drew a breath; it gave you courage for the fearful things awaiting you. It was Rembrandt's huge painting *The Blinding of Samson* that terrified me, tormented me, and kept me on a string. I saw it as though it were taking place before my eyes; and since this was the moment when Samson lost his eyesight, I bore witness in the most horrible way. I had always been timid about blind people and never looked at them too long, even though they fascinated me. Since they couldn't see me, I felt guilty toward them. However, this canvas depicted not the condition, not blindness, but the blinding itself.

Samson lies there, bare-chested, his shirt pulled down, his right foot slanting aloft, the toes twisting in wild pain. A warrior in armor and helmet bends over him, having thrust the dagger into the right eye. Blood splashes on the victim's forehead; his hair is shorn. A second warrior lies under Samson, having shoved the victim's head toward the dagger. A further myrmidon occupies the left part of the canvas.

He stands there with spread legs, leaning toward Samson, both hands clutching a halberd aimed at Samson's tightly closed left eye. The halberd looms through half the canvas, a threat of the blinding about to be repeated. Samson has two eyes like any normal person; we see only one eye of the myrmidon holding the halberd and gazing at Samson's blood-smeared face and the execution of the order.

Full light falls upon Samson from outside the group, in which everything takes place. It is impossible to look away: this blinding is not yet blindness; it will *become* blindness, and it expects neither leniency nor quarter. This blinding wants to be seen; and everyone who sees it knows what blinding is and one sees it everywhere. In this painting, there is one pair of eyes that focus on the blinding and never abandon it: the eyes of Delilah, who hurries off in triumph, holding the scissors in one hand and Samson's hair in the other. Does she fear the man whose hair she holds? Is she trying to escape from the one eye, so long as he has it? She peers back at him, hatred and murderous anxiety in her face, on which as much light falls as on the face of the man being blinded. Her lips are parted; she has just cried: "The Philistines be upon thee, Samson."

Does he understand what she's saying? He understands the word *Philistines*, the name of her people, whom he fought and killed. Between the maiming and the maiming, she gazes at him; she won't grant him the other eye, she won't cry "Mercy!" and hurl herself in front of the knife, she won't cover him with his hair, which she holds—his former strength. What is she peering back at? At the blinded eye and the eye about to be blinded. She waits for the sword that strikes again. She is the will that makes it happen. The armored lansquenets, the halberdiers, are her handymen. She has taken away Samson's strength; she holds his strength, but still fears him and will hate him as long as she remembers this blinding, and, in order to hate him, will always remember it.

I often stood in front of this painting, and from it I learned what hatred is. I had felt hatred when very young, much too young, at five, when I had tried to kill Laurica with an ax. But you don't know what you have felt: you have to see it in front of you, in others, in order to recognize it and know it. Something you recognize and know becomes *real* only if you have experienced it previously. It lies dormant in you, and you can't name it; then all at once, it is there, as a painting; and something happening to others creates itself in you as a memory: now, it is real.

Early Honor of the Intellect

The young people I associated with had one thing in common, no matter how varied they may have been otherwise: all they were interested in was intellectual matters. They knew about everything in newspapers, but they grew excited when it came to books. Their attention focused on just a few books; it would have been despicable not to know about these. But still, it cannot be said that they parroted some general or leading opinion. They read such books themselves; they read passages from them aloud to one another; they quoted them from memory. Criticism was not only permitted, it was desired; they tried to find vulnerable points that compromised the public reputation of a book, and they heatedly thrashed out these points, setting great store by logic, snappy comebacks, and wit. Except for everything ordained by Karl Kraus, nothing was definite; they loved rattling away at things that found acceptance too easily and too quickly.

The particularly important books were those allowing great scope for discussion. The heyday of Spengler's impact, which I had witnessed at the boardinghouse table in Frankfurt, seemed past. Or had his effect in Vienna not been so decisive? However, a pessimistic note was unmistakable here, too. Otto Weininger's *Sex and Character*, though published twenty years earlier, cropped up in every discussion. All the pacifist books of my wartime days in Zurich had been superseded by Karl Kraus's *The Last Days of Mankind*. The literature of decadence didn't count at all. Hermann Bahr was a has-been: he had played too many parts; none was now taken seriously. Particularly decisive for a writer's prestige was his conduct *during* the war. Thus, Schnitzler's name remained intact; he was no longer urgent, but he was never scorned, for unlike the others, he had never lent himself to war propaganda. Nor was it a propitious time for Old Austria. The monarchy, having crumbled, was discredited; the only monarchists left, I was told, were among the "candle women" (the old women who spent their days in churches, lighting candles). The dismemberment of Austria, the amazing survival of Vienna—now an oversized capital—as a "hydrocephalic" head, was on everyone's mind. But by no means did they relinquish the intellectual claim that is part of a metropolis. They were interested in everything in the world, as if the world might value what they thought, and they clung to the specific proclivities of Vienna, such as had developed through generations, especially music. Whether musical or not, they attended concerts, standing room. The cult of Gustav Mahler, a composer still unknown to the world at large, had reached its first high point here; his greatness was undisputed.

There was hardly a conversation in which Freud's name did not pop up, a name no less compressed for me than that of Karl Kraus; yet the name Freud was more alluring because of its dark diphthong and the *d* at the end, as well as its literal meaning, "joy." A whole series of monosyllabic names was circulating; they would have sufficed for the most disparate needs. But Freud had become very special; some of his coinages had become everyday terms. He was still haughtily rejected by the leading figures at the university. Freudian slips, however, had become a sort of parlor game. In order to use this buzz word frequently, slips were produced in spates. During any conversation, no matter how animated and spontaneous it may have sounded, there arrived a moment when you could read on your interlocutor's lips: here comes a Freudian slip. And it was already out; you could already start analyzing it, uncovering the processes that had led to it, and thereby you could talk about your private life in tireless detail, without seeming overbearingly intimate, for you were involved in shedding light on a process of universal, even scientific, interest.

Nevertheless, as I soon realized, this portion of Freudianism was the most plausible. When slips were being discussed, I never got the feeling that something was being twisted to make a point, to fit into a never changing and hence soon boring pattern. Also, each person had his own way of devising Freudian slips. Clever things came out, and sometimes there was even a genuine slip, which you could tell was unplanned.

Now, Oedipus complexes were an altogether different affair. People had fistfights over them, everybody wanted his own, or else you threw them at other people's heads. Anyone present at these social functions could bank on one thing: if he didn't bring up his Oedipus complex himself, then it was hurled at him by someone else, after a ruthlessly penetrating glare. In some way or other, everybody (even posthumous sons) got his Oedipus; and eventually, the whole company sat there in guilt, everyone a potential mother-lover and father-killer, hazily wreathed with mythical names—all of us secret kings of Thebes.

I had my doubts about the matter, perhaps because I had known murderous jealousy since early˘ childhood and was quite aware of its highly disparate motives. But even if one of the countless advocates of this Freudian theory had succeeded in convincing me of its universal validity, I would never have accepted this name for the phenomenon. I knew who Oedipus was, I had read Sophocles, I refused to be deprived of the enormity of this fate. By the time I arrived in Vienna, the Oedipus complex had turned into a hackneyed prattle that no one failed to drone out; even the haughtiest scorner of mobs wasn't too good for an "Oedipus."

Admittedly, however, they were still under the impact of the recent war. No one could forget the murderous cruelty they had witnessed. Many who had taken an active part in it were now home again. They knew what things they had been capable of doing—on orders—and they eagerly grabbed at all the explanations that psychoanalysis offered for homicidal tendencies. The banality of their collective compulsion was mirrored in the banality of the explanation. It was odd to see how *harmless* everyone became as soon as he got his Oedipus. When multiplied thousands of times, the most dreadful destiny crumbles into a particle of dust. Myth reaches into a human being, throttling him and rattling him. The "law of nature," to which myth is reduced, is nothing more than a little pipe for him to dance to.

The young people I associated with hadn't been to war. But they all attended Karl Kraus's lectures and knew *The Last Days of Mankind*—one could say: by heart. This was their chance to catch up with the war that had overshadowed their youth, and there can hardly be a more concentrated and more legitimate method for getting acquainted with war. It thus constantly remained before their eyes; and since they didn't wish to forget, since they hadn't been forced to escape the war, it haunted them incessantly. They did not investigate the dynamics of human beings as a crowd, in which people had devotedly and willingly gone into the war, remaining trapped in it—albeit in a different way—years after it was lost. Nothing had been said about this crowd, no theory of these phenomena existed as yet. Freud's comments about them were, as I soon found out myself, completely inadequate. So people contented themselves with the psychology of individual processes, such as Freud offered in unshakable self-assurance. Whenever I came out with anything concerning the enigma of the crowd, which I had been mulling over since Frankfurt, they found my remarks not worth discussing; there were no intellectual formulas for what I said. Anything that couldn't be reduced to a formula did not exist, it was a figment of the imagination, it had no substance; otherwise, it would have appeared in some way or other in Freud or Kraus.

The lacuna I felt here could not be filled for the time being. It wasn't long before the "illumination" came, during my first winter in Vienna (1924–1925): the "illumination" that determined the entire rest of my life. I have to call it an "illumination," for this experience was connected with a special light; it came upon me very suddenly, as a violent feeling of expansion. I was walking down a street in Vienna, with a quick and unusual energetic motion, which lasted as long as the "illumination" itself. I have never forgotten what happened that night. The illumination has remained present to me as a single instant; now, fifty-five years later, I still view it as something *unexhausted*. While its intellectual content may be so simple and small that its effect is inexplicable, I nevertheless drew strength from it as from a revelation—the strength to devote thirty-five years of my life, twenty of them full years, to the explanation of what a crowd really is, how power comes into being from a crowd and how it feeds back upon it. At the time, I was unaware of how much the manner of my enterprise owed to the fact that there was someone like Freud in Vienna, that people talked about him in such a way as if every individual could, by himself, of his own accord and at his own resolve, find explanations for things. Since Freud's ideas did not suffice for me, failing to explain the phenomenon that was most important to me, I was sincerely, if naïvely, convinced that I was undertaking something different, something totally independent of him. It was clear to me that I needed him as an adversary. But the fact that he served as a kind of model for me—this was something that no one could have made me see at that time.

The illumination, which I recall so clearly, took place on Alserstrasse. It was night; in the sky, I noticed the red reflection of the city, and I craned my neck to look up at it. I paid no attention to where I was walking. I tripped several times, and in such an instant of stumbling, while craning my neck, gazing at the red sky, which I didn't really like, it suddenly flashed through my mind: I realized that there is such a thing as a crowd instinct, which is always in conflict with the personality instinct, and that the struggle between the two of them can explain the course of human history. This couldn't have been a new idea; but it was new to me, for it struck me with tremendous force. Everything now happening in the world could, it seemed to me, be traced back to that struggle. The fact that there was such a thing as a crowd was something I had experienced in Frankfurt. And now I had experienced it again in Vienna. The fact that there was something that forces people to become a *crowd* seemed obvious and irrefutable to me. The fact that the crowd fell apart into individuals was no less evident; likewise, the fact that these individuals wanted to become a crowd again. I had no doubt about the existence of the tendency to become a crowd and to become an individual again. These tendencies seemed so strong and so blind that I regarded them as an instinct, and labeled them one. However, I didn't know what the crowd itself really was. This was an enigma I now planned to solve; it seemed like the most crucial enigma, or at least the most important enigma, in our world.

But how stale, how drained, how anemic my description now sounds. I said, "tremendous force," and that's exactly what it was. For the energy I was suddenly imbued with made me walk faster, almost run. I dashed along Alserstrasse, all the way to the Gürtel; I felt as if I'd gotten here in the twinkling of an eye. My ears were buzzing; the sky was still red, as though it would always be this color; I was still stumbling, but never falling; my stumbles were an integral part of my overall movement. I have never again experienced motion in this way; nor can I say that I would care to do so—it was too peculiar, too exotic, a lot swifter than is appropriate for me, an alien thing that came out of me, but that I didn't control.

Patriarchs

Everyone found Veza exotic. She drew attention wherever she went. An Andalusian who had never been in Seville, but spoke about it as though she had grown up there. You had encountered her in *The Arabian Nights*, the very first time you'd read any of the tales. She was a familiar figure in Persian miniatures. But despite this Oriental omnipresence, she was no dream personage; your conception of her was very definite; her image never melted, it never dissolved; it retained its sharp outline and its radiance.

Her beauty was breathtaking, and I threw up a resistance to it. As an inexperienced creature, barely out of boyhood, clumsy, unpolished, a Caliban next to her (albeit a very young one), awkward, insecure, gross, incapable in her presence of the one thing that may have been in my control, namely speech, I cast about for the most absurd insults before seeing her, insults to armor me against her; "precious" was the least; "saccharine," "courtly," a "princess"; able to use only half of language, the elegant half; alien to anything real, inconsiderate, rigorous, relentless. But I only had to recall that lecture on April 17 to disarm these accusations. The audience had cheered Karl Kraus not for his elegance, but for his rigor. And when I was introduced to her during intermission, she had seemed controlled and lofty, and was not about to flee the second part of the program. Since then, at every lecture (I now attended all of them), I had stealthily peered around for her and always found her. I had greeted her across the auditorium, never daring to approach her. And I was dismayed whenever she didn't notice me; mostly, however, she returned my greeting.

Even here, she drew attention, the most exotic creature in this audience. Since she always sat in the first row, Karl Kraus must have noticed her. I found myself wondering what he thought of her. She never clapped, it must have struck him. But the fact that she was always back again, in the same place, was a tribute that must have mattered even to him. During the first year, when I didn't dare visit her despite her invitation, I felt more and more irritated about her sitting in the front row. Failing to understand the nature of my irritation, I concocted the most peculiar things. I felt it was too loud up there: how could she stand the intensest parts? Some of the characters in *The Last Days of Mankind* made you feel so ashamed, you just had to sink into the ground. And what did she do when she had to cry, during Hauptmann's *The Weavers,* during *King Lear?* How could she endure his watching her cry? Or did she want him to watch her? Was she proud of this reaction? Was she paying homage to him by weeping in public? She was certainly not devoid of shame; she struck me as being extremely modest, more than anyone else; and then there she sat, showing Karl Kraus everything he did to her. She never went over to the platform after the reading; many people tried to crowd up there, she merely stood and watched. Shaken and shattered as I was every time, I, too, remained in the auditorium for a long while, standing and applauding until my hands ached. In this state of mind, I lost sight of her; I wouldn't have found her again but for her conspicuously parted, blue-black hair. After the reading, she did nothing that I could have regarded as unworthy. She stayed in the auditorium no longer than others; when he took his bows, she wasn't among the very last to leave.

Perhaps it was her concurrence that I sought, for the excitement after these readings persisted on and on; whether he read *The Weavers, Timon of Athens,* or *The Last Days of Mankind,* these were high points of existence. I lived from one such occasion to the next; anything occurring in between belonged to a profane world. I sat alone in the auditorium, speaking to no one, making sure I left the building alone. I observed Veza because I was avoiding her; I didn't realize how deeply I longed to be sitting next to her. This would have been quite impossible so long as she sat in the first row, visible to all. I was jealous of the god I was imbued with. Even though I didn't try to barricade myself against him anywhere, at any point, even though my every pore was open to him, I begrudged him the exotic creature with black, parted hair, sitting near him, laughing for him and weeping and bending under his tempest. I wanted to be next to her, but not up front, where she was; it could only be where the god didn't see her, where we could exchange glances to communicate what he did to us.

Although steadfast in my proud resolution not to visit her, I was jealous of her and failed to realize that I was gathering strength to abduct her from the god. At home, while thinking I would suffocate under my mother's animosity, which my conduct provoked, I pictured the moment when I would ring Veza's doorbell. I shoved that instant away from me like a solid object, but it came closer and closer. To remain strong, I imagined how the flood of Asriel chitchat would smash over me. "How was it? What did she say? I thought so! She doesn't like that. Of course not." I could already hear the warnings of my mother, who would be told everything "hot off the press." In an imaginary repartee, I anticipated the conversations that eventually did take place. While painstakingly avoiding any closer contact with Veza and unable to figure out what I could say to her that wasn't too gross or too ignorant, I devised all the nasty, hateful things I would get to hear about her at home.

Notwithstanding my self-inflicted prohibitions, I always knew I would go there; and every lecture I saw her at made this realization more intense. But when the time came, one free afternoon, more than a year had passed since the invitation.

No one learned that I was going; my feet found their own way to Ferdinandstrasse. I cudgeled my brain to come up with a plausible explanation that didn't sound immature or servile. She had said she wished she were English; what could be more obvious than asking her about English literature? I had recently heard *King Lear*, one of Karl Kraus's grandest readings; of all the Shakespeare plays, it was the one that absorbed me the most. I was haunted by the image of the old man on the heath. She must have known the play in English. There was something about *King Lear* that I couldn't cope with. This was what I wanted to talk to her about.

I rang, she herself opened, greeting me as though she'd been expecting me. I had seen her just a few days earlier at the reading in the Middle Concert Hall. By chance, as I thought, I had come near her, applauding, on my feet with the others. I behaved like a lunatic, waving my arms, shrieking "Bravo! Bravo! Karl Kraus!," clapping. I wouldn't stop, no one stopped, I dropped my hands only when they ached. And then I noticed someone next to me, in a trance like myself, but not clapping. It was Veza; I couldn't tell whether she had noticed me.

Letting me into her apartment, she took me through the dark corridor to her room, where a warm radiance welcomed me. I sat down amid books and paintings, but I didn't take any closer look at them, for she sat opposite me at the table and said: "You didn't notice me. I was at *Lear*."

I told her I had very much noticed her, and that was why I had come. Then I asked her why Lear has to die in the end. He was a very old man, granted, and had suffered terrible things. But I would gladly have gone away knowing he had overcome everything and was still there. He should always be there. If a different hero, a younger one, were to die in a play, I was ready to accept it, especially braggarts and fighters, the sort people called heroes; I didn't mind their dying, for their prestige was based on their causing the deaths of so many other people. But Lear, who had grown so old, ought to grow even older. We should never learn about his death. So many other people had died in this play. But someone should survive, and this someone was Lear.

"But why he of all people? Doesn't he deserve to have peace and quiet at last?"

"Death is a punishment. He deserves to live."

"The eldest? Should the eldest live even longer? While young people have preceded him into death and been deceived of their lives?"

"*More* dies with the eldest. All his years die. There is a lot more that perishes with him."

"Then you'd like people who are as old as the Biblical patriarchs?"

"Yes! Yes! Don't you?"

"No. I could show you one. He lives two rooms away. Perhaps he'll make his presence known while you're here."

"You mean your stepfather. I've heard about him."

"You couldn't have heard anything about him that approaches the truth. The only ones who know the truth are we, my mother and I."

It came too quickly for her, she didn't want to tell me about him right away. She had managed to protect her room, her atmosphere from him. Had I had an inkling of what it cost her, I would have avoided this subject of old people who ought to keep on living because they have grown so old. I had come to her blind, as it were, from *Lear,* and thankful that we had experienced something wonderful together. I had to talk about it. I was in Lear's debt, for he had driven me to her. Without him, I would surely have waited longer before coming; and now, here I sat, filled with him; how could I not have paid homage to him. I knew how much Shakespeare of all authors meant to her, and I was convinced there was nothing she would rather speak about. I didn't get to ask about her trips to England, and she didn't think about my childhood there. Originally, she had invited me over so that I might tell her about it. Now, I had struck her sorest point;

for both of them, her mother and herself, life with this step-father was a torment. He was almost ninety, and here I came and seemed to be saying if a man was that old, it was best that he keep on living.

I hurt her so deeply at my first visit that it was very nearly my last. She pulled herself together, because she was so visibly frightened; she felt as if she had to justify herself, and she told me—it was difficult enough for her—how she made herself at home in this hell.

The apartment in which Veza lived with her mother consisted of three fairly large rooms in a row, their windows facing Ferdinandstrasse. This apartment was in the mezzanine, not very high; it was easy to catch their attention from the street. A hallway led from the apartment door past the main rooms, which were left of the hallway; the kitchen and the other rooms were to its right. Behind the kitchen lay a small, dark maid's room, so out of the way that no one thought about it.

The first of the three left-hand rooms was the parents' bedroom; Veza's stepfather, a haggard old man of almost ninety, lay in bed or sat in a bathrobe, upright, in front of the fire in the corner. Next came the dining room, used mostly for company. The third room was Veza's room, which she had furnished to her own taste, in colors she liked, with books and paintings, unsettled and yet serious. It was a room that you entered with a sigh of relief and were sorry to leave, a room so different from the rest of the apartment that you thought you were dreaming when you stood at its threshold—a severe threshold to a blossoming place. Very few people were allowed to cross into it.

The occupant of this room reigned over the others with an unbelievable control. It was no reign of terror; everything occurred soundlessly; a raising of the eyebrows sufficed to drive intruders away from the threshold. Her chief enemy was her stepfather, Mento Altaras. In earlier days, before I came on the scene, the struggle had still been waged openly, the demarcation lines had not been drawn, and it was still uncertain whether peace would ever be concluded. Back then, the stepfather would suddenly slam open the door and bang his cane repeatedly and ominously on the threshold. The skinny, haggard man stood there in his bathrobe, his narrow, somber, emaciated head resembling that of Dante, whose name he had never heard. Momentarily pausing in his banging, he spouted dreadful Ladino curses and threats, and, alternately banging and cursing, he stood at the threshold until his wish, for meat or wine, had been fulfilled.

As an adolescent girl, the stepdaughter had tried to help herself by locking both her doors—to the dining room and to the hall—from the inside. Then, as she grew older and more attractive, the keys used to vanish; and when the locksmith brought new ones, these vanished, too. The mother would go out, the maid wasn't always around, and when the old man craved something, he had the strength of three despite his age and could have overcome his wife, his stepdaughter, and the maid. They had every reason to be scared. The mother and the daughter couldn't stand the thought of separating for good. In order to remain in her mother's apartment, Veza devised a tactic for taming the old man. Her tactic demanded a strength, insight, and persistence that were unheard of in an eighteen-year-old girl. What happened was that the old man would receive nothing if he left his room. He could knock, rage, curse, threaten, all to no avail. He got neither wine nor meat until he was back in his room; if he asked for them then, they were instantly brought. It was a Pavlovian method, thought up by the stepdaughter, who knew nothing about Pavlov. It took the old man several months to give in to his fate. He saw that he received juicier and juicier beefsteaks, older and older wines by skipping his assaults. If ever he did lose his temper again and appeared at the forbidden threshold, cursing and raging, he was punished and got nothing to eat or drink before evening.

He had spent most of his life in Sarajevo, where, as a child, he had peddled hot corn on the cob in the streets. People talked about these beginnings. That was back in the middle of the past century, and his origins had become the most important part of his legend, its commencement. You learned nothing about his later life. There was an enormous leap. Before retiring from his business in old age, he had become one of the richest men in Sarajevo and Bosnia. He owned countless houses (forty-seven was the number that you always kept hearing) and huge forests. His sons, who took over his business, lived in grand style; it was no surprise that they wanted to get the old man out of Sarajevo. He insisted that they live frugally and quietly and not flaunt their wealth. He was renowned for both his avarice and his harshness: he refused to donate to charities, which was considered scandalous. He showed up unannounced at the great festivities given by his sons and drove the guests out with a cane. They managed to get the widower, who was over seventy, to remarry in Vienna. A very beautiful widow, much younger than he, Rachel Calderon, was the bait he couldn't resist. The sons breathed a sigh of relief the instant he was in Vienna. The eldest son—and this was unusual back then—bought himself a private airplane, which greatly enhanced his prestige in their home town. From time to time, he came to Vienna, bringing his father cash—thick packets of banknotes; the father demanded the money in this form.

During the first few years in Vienna, the old man still went out, refusing to let anyone accompany him. He donned worn-out trousers and a baggy, threadbare overcoat, and, in his left hand, he carried a raggedy hat, which looked as if it came from a garbage can. He kept the hat in a secret place and refused to let it be cleaned. No one understood why he took it along, since he never put it on.

One day, the maid came home all atremble and said she had just seen the master at a midtown street corner, the hat had lain open in front of him, and a passerby had tossed in a coin. No sooner was he back than his wife confronted him about it. He grew so furious that they were afraid he would kill her with the cane, with which he never parted. She was a gentle, terribly kind person and normally stayed out of his way; but this time, she wouldn't let up. She grabbed the hat and threw it away. Without the hat, he wouldn't go begging anymore. However, he continued to wear the worn-out trousers and the threadbare coat whenever he left the house. The maid was dispatched to observe him and followed him all the long way to Naschmarkt. She was so scared of him that she lost the trail. He returned with a bag of pears, holding them up triumphantly to his wife and his stepdaughter: he crowed that he had gotten them for free, from a market woman; and truly, he could look so famished and down-at-the-heels that even hard-boiled hawkers at Naschmarkt felt sorry for him and handed him fruit that wasn't even rotten.

At home, he had other worries: he had to hide the thick packets of banknotes somewhere in the bedroom, so that they'd always be at hand. The mattresses on both beds were bursting with them, a subcarpet of paper money had accumulated between the rug and the floor; of his many shoes, he could only wear one pair: the others were chock full of cash. His dresser contained a good dozen pairs of socks, which no one was allowed to touch, and whose contents he frequently checked. Only two pairs, which he wore alternately, were used by him. His wife received a weekly amount of household money, carefully counted out; it had been established by his son in an agreement with her. The stepfather had tried to cheat her out of part of it, but this affected his wine and meat, of which he devoured enormous quantities; so he then paid the stipulated amount.

He ate so much that they feared for his health. Nor did he stick to the usual meals. At breakfast, he already asked for meat and wine, and for the midmorning snack, long before lunch, he asked for the same. He wanted nothing else. When his wife tried to satisfy his appetite with side dishes, rice and vegetables, to keep him from devouring so much meat, he scornfully sent the food back. And when she tried again, he angrily dumped it on the carpet, ate only the meat in one gulp, and demanded more, saying they had given him far too little. There was no coping with his raging hunger, which concentrated on this one bloody food. The wife summoned a doctor, sedate, experienced, himself a native of Sarajevo, informed about the old man, speaking his language, and able to converse with him fluently. Nevertheless, the old man refused to be examined. He said there was nothing wrong with him, he had always been skinny, his only medicine was meat and wine, and if he didn't get as much of them as he wanted, he would go into the streets and *beg* for them. He had noticed that nothing horrified his family so deeply as his lust to beg. They took his threat as seriously as he meant it. The doctor warned him that if he kept on eating like that, he'd be dead within two years; to which the old man replied with a terrible curse. He wanted meat, nothing else. He had never eaten anything else, he said; he had no intention of becoming an ox at the age of eighty. That was that, *ya basta!*

Two years later, instead of him, it was the doctor who died. The old man was always delighted when people died. But this time his joy kept him awake for several nights, and he celebrated with meat and wine. The next doctor they tried it with, a man in his late forties, sturdy and very much of a meat-eater himself, had even less luck. The old man turned his back on him, refused to say a word, and dismissed him without cursing him. The doctor died like his predecessor; but this time it took longer. The old man took no notice of his death. Survival had now become second nature for him; meat and wine were nourishment enough, and he needed no more doctors as victims. One more attempt was made when his wife fell ill and lamented *her* complaint to the doctor. She said she wasn't getting enough sleep: her husband would wake up in the middle of the night and ask for his feed. Since he was going out less, it had become worse. The physician, a daredevil—perhaps he didn't know about his predecessors' fate—insisted on having a look at the old man, who was devouring his bloody beefsteak in the next bed, unconcerned about his sick wife. The doctor grabbed the plate and scolded him: What did he think he was doing? This was mortally dangerous! Did he realize he was going blind? The old man got scared for the first time; but the reason for his fright didn't come out until later.

Nothing changed about his food intake; but he totally gave up going out; now and then, he locked himself up in his bedroom for an hour or two—something he had never done before. He wouldn't respond to any knocks. They heard him poking around in the fire, and since they knew he liked the fire, they assumed he was sitting in front of it lost in thought; he would surely respond as soon as he got hungry for the usual. This always happened. But one day, the stepdaughter, accustomed to the hide-and-seek game with her own keys, took the key for the door between the dining room and the bedroom and suddenly opened it when she heard him poking around the fire. She found him clutching a packet of banknotes, which he was tossing into the fire before her very eyes. A few packets lay next to him on the floor, others had already turned to ashes in the fire. "Leave me," he said. "I don't have time. I'm not done." And he pointed to the unburned packets on the floor. He was burning his money so as not to leave it to anyone; but enough was still left, the room was brimming with packets of banknotes.

It was the first symptom of senility: old Altaras was burning money. This third physician—who hadn't even been summoned for him, whom he received disinterestedly, as though it were no concern of his, to whom he wanted to show, by means of his usual food, his indifference to his wife and her complaints—this physician had impressed and frightened him with his grossness. Perhaps, he now felt doubts that things could always go like this; in any case, the threat about his eyes had confused him. He gazed at money and fire as often as possible; and more than anything, he loved it when one was consumed by the other.

Having been found out, he didn't lock himself in anymore; he sat down openly to his occupation. It would have taken the strength of several men to hinder him. The helpless wife was at her wit's end. She brooded about it for a while and then wrote to the eldest son, in Sarajevo, who, for all his generosity, was so indignant at this willful destruction of money that he instantly came to Vienna and hauled the old man over the coals. Neither mother nor daughter ever found out what he threatened him with. It must have been something that he feared more than the rare announcements of the doctor—perhaps he was told he would be legally dispossessed and thrown into a sanatorium, where there would be an end to the usual quantities of meat and wine. At any rate, the threat worked. He kept whatever was left of the banknotes in his hiding places, but he burned them no more and had to put up with the family's entering the bedroom regularly to check up on him.

Veza was marked by saving her own atmosphere from the banging cane, the threats and curses of this sinister man; she had succeeded in doing so at the age of eighteen. It now seldom happened that he appeared at her threshold. He would tear her door open at most every few weeks, and stand there, tall and haggard, in front of her visitors, but always at a distance; and they were more astonished than frightened. He did clutch the cane, but he didn't bang it, he didn't curse, he didn't threaten. He came for help. It was fear that now drove him to the forbidden door. He said: "They've stolen my money. It's burning." No one could endure him, and so he spent a lot of time alone, and the anxieties that overcame him were always connected with money. Since he could no longer burn it, he was being robbed: the flames leaped into his room to obtain forcibly what was no longer sacrificed to them voluntarily.

He never came when Veza was alone, but only when he

heard voices from her room. His hearing was still good, he always heard when she had company: the ringing of the doorbell, the footsteps past his room, the lively voices in the hall and then in her room, speaking a language he didn't understand—seeing nothing of all this, he got scared that a secret attack on his money was being plotted. Thus I witnessed his appearance two or three times during my early visits. I was struck by his resemblance to Dante.

It was as if the Italian poet had risen from the grave. We were just talking about the *Divine Comedy*, when suddenly the door flew open, and he stood there, as though draped in white sheets, raising his cane not in defense but in lament: "*Mi arrobaron las paras*—They've stolen my money!" No, not Dante. A figure from hell.

The Blowup

On July 24, 1925, one day before my twentieth birthday, the blowup came. I have never spoken about it since then, and it is difficult for me to describe it.

Hans Asriel and I had planned a hike through the Karwendel Mountains. We wanted to live very modestly, sleeping in huts. It wouldn't have cost very much. Hans, who worked for Herr Brosig, a manufacturer of leather goods, had saved just barely enough from his tiny salary. He was extremely careful—he had to be: he lived in the most straitened circumstances with his mother and two siblings.

He calculated the entire hike budget; it was to last less than a week. After that, we might have settled in somewhere for another week, for I wanted to use this time for working, namely for starting a book on crowds. I would much rather have been all alone somewhere in the mountains. But I didn't say so, because I didn't want to hurt Hans's feelings. However, we were all the more thorough in preparing for our hike. Hans, very methodic, sat hunched over maps, calculating every stretch of road and every mountain peak. We spent the first few weeks of July discussing our project. At home, I reported on it during meals. Mother listened to everything and said neither yes nor no. But as our preparations grew more and more detailed, and we were absolutely abuzz with the name "Karwendel Mountains," it seemed unthinkable that she could have anything against our hike. Indeed, I almost felt as if she were participating mentally. Our goal was to be Pertisau on Lake Achen. Once, she even toyed with the idea of taking a vacation in Pertisau and waiting for us there. But this plan wasn't serious, and she promptly dropped it, while the detailed discussions between Hans and myself continued. Then, on the morning of July 24, Mother suddenly declared that I should forget about the hike, it was out of the question, she had no money for luxuries. She said I ought to be glad I could attend the university; wasn't I ashamed to make such demands when other people didn't even know what they could live on?

It was a hard blow, because it came so suddenly, after weeks of her benevolent, even interested, tolerance of our plans. After almost a year of pressure and friction in our apartment, it was imperative for me to get away and feel free. Lately, the pressure had grown worse and worse; after every embarrassing exchange of words, I took refuge in looking forward to the hike. The naked chalk rocks, which I had heard so much about, appeared to me in the most radiant light. And now, during a breakfast, the relentless guillotine blade crashed down, cutting off my breath and my hope.

I wanted to beat my hands on the walls, but I controlled myself to prevent any physical outburst in front of my brothers. Anything that did occur took place on paper, but not in my normal intelligible and reasonable sentences. Nor did I use my familiar notebooks. I grabbed a huge, almost new pad of writing paper and covered page after page with gigantic capital letters: "MONEY, MONEY, AND MONEY AGAIN." The same words, line after line, until the page was full. Then I tore it off and began the next page with "MONEY, MONEY, AND MONEY AGAIN." Since my handwriting was huge, such as it had never been, every page was soon filled; the torn-off pages lay scattered around me on the large table in the dining room. There were more and more of them, then they dropped to the floor. The rug around the large table was covered with them, I couldn't stop writing. The pad had a hundred sheets; I covered each single page with my writing. My brothers noticed that something unusual was going on, for I pronounced the words I wrote, not excessively loud, but clearly and audibly. "Money, money, and money again" sounded through the entire apartment. They cautiously approached me, picked the pages up from the floor and read the writing aloud: "Money, money, and money again." Then Nissim, the middle one, dashed over to Mother in the kitchen and said: "Elias has gone crazy. You've got to come!"

She didn't come; she said: "Tell him to stop immediately. Letter paper is so expensive!" But I ignored him and kept covering the pages at a furious speed. Perhaps I *had* gone crazy at that moment. But whatever it was, the word in which all oppression and baseness was concentrated for me had taken over and held me fully in its control. I heeded nothing—neither my jeering brothers (the younger one, Georg, jeered only halfheartedly: he was very frightened) nor my mother, who finally deigned to come in. She was either annoyed at the waste of paper or else no longer sure that I was "play-acting," as she initially phrased it. I paid as little attention to her as to my brothers. I would have ignored anyone. I was possessed with that one word, which was the essence of all inhumanity. I wrote, and the power of the word driving me did not diminish; I didn't hate *her,* I hated only this word; and so long as any paper was left, my hatred was inexhaustible. What impressed her most was the furious speed of this act of writing. It was my hand that raced over the sheets, but

I was breathless, as though *I* were racing. Never had I done anything at such a speed. "It was like an express train," she later said, "heavy and fully charged." There it was, the word that she couldn't speak often enough, that she knew tormented me so dreadfully. There it was, thousands of times over, insanely lavish in contrast to its character, evoked and reevoked, as if it could be spent in this way, as if one could thereby come to an end with it. It is not out of the question that she feared for both of us, me and her favorite word, which I was pouring out right and left.

I didn't notice her leaving the room, and I didn't notice her coming back. I wouldn't have noticed anything so long as the writing pad wasn't used up. All at once, Dr. Laub stood in our room, our family doctor, the old senior medical officer. Mother stood behind him, half concealed, her face averted. I knew it was her, but I couldn't look into her eyes. She was hiding behind him, and now I realized that there had been a loud knocking at the door. "What's wrong with the little boy?" he said in his elevated speech. His slowness, the pauses after each sentence, the emphatic stress on each word, the ineffable triviality of his weighty declarations, the seamless welding with the previous visit as if nothing had occurred in between (last time, it was jaundice; what was it now?)—everything together had its effect, bringing me back to my senses. Although I still had a few sheets left, I instantly stopped writing.

"What are we writing so diligently?" said Dr. Laub. It took him an eternity to get the sentence out. I fell off the express train in which I had been sweeping across the paper; and, in a tempo more like his own, I handed him the last page. He read it solemnly. He pronounced it, the word, as I had uttered it. But in his mouth, it didn't sound hateful, it sounded thoughtful, as if one ought to think it over tenfold before releasing such a precious word from one's lips. Since he lisped, it sounded thrifty, and even though I said that to myself, I remained calm. I was surprised that I didn't flare up anew. He read aloud *everything* that was written on this last page; and since it was more than half covered and he never read any faster, it took him quite a while. No "MONEY," not a single one, was lost. And when he was finished, I misinterpreted a movement of his; I thought he wanted a second page from me in order to keep reading aloud the *MONEY*s. But when I held out another page, he begged off, saying: "Fine. The time has come." Then he cleared his throat, placed his hand on my shoulder, and asked, as though honey were dripping from his mouth: "And now tell me: Why do we need money?" I don't know whether he was being wise or innocent, but his question made me talk. I told the entire Karwendel story chronologically. I said the project had been heard at home for weeks without the least objection; indeed, she had even added to the plans. And now suddenly she had quashed the whole project. Nothing had happened in the meantime to alter anything; it was absolutely arbitrary, like most of the things happening in our home. I wanted to get away from here, get away and go to the ends of the earth, where I would never have to hear that damn word.

"Aha," he said, motioning to the papers covering the floor. "That is why we wrote it down so often, so that we might know what we no longer wish to hear. But before we go to the ends of the earth, let us instead go to the Karwendel Mountains. It will do us good." At this prospect, my heart melted; he sounded as certain as if *he* were in charge of the money needed for this trip, as if it were in *his* keeping. The form of my attention changed, I began to pin my hopes on him. And I might think back to him with gratitude, if he hadn't promptly spoiled everything with his inexcusable wisdom. "There's more here than meets the eye," he declared. "The issue is not money. It is an Oedipus complex. A clear case. This has nothing to do with money." He examined me a bit and left me. The door to the vestibule remained open. I heard my mother's anxious question and his verdict: "Let him take the trip. Tomorrow would be best. This will be good for the Oedipus complex."

The matter was thus settled. Physicians were the supreme authority for my mother. In regard to herself, she liked to get opinions from several physicians. She could thereby pick out whatever suited her from all the verdicts together and never acted against any. For us, however, *one* doctor and *one* opinion sufficed, and we had to adhere. The trip was now settled, quibbling was out of the question. I was allowed to go to the mountains with Hans for two weeks. I spent two more days in the apartment. There were no more accusations. I was regarded as threatened; my mind was unstable. The written sheets had been picked up from the floor, carefully assembled, and put aside. Since so much paper had been wasted, those pages should at least be preserved as a symptom of my mental disturbance.

I felt no less oppressed during these last few days at home, but I now had the prospect of going far away. I managed to hold my tongue, which was anything but my wont, and she managed to do the same.

The Justification

On July 26, Hans and I went to Scharnitz. There, we began our hike through the Karwendel range. The bare, rugged chalk mountains made a deep impact on me; seeing them did me good in my condition. I didn't realize what a bad state I was in, but I felt as if I were leaving everything behind, all the superfluous things, especially the family, and starting out with nothing but naked stone, a knapsack containing very little but more than enough for two weeks. Perhaps I would have been better off without a knapsack. Nevertheless, my knapsack contained several important things: two notebooks and a book, for the further week of vacation. I wanted to settle in at some place I liked and begin the "work," as I called it with some pretension. The notebook was meant for comments and criticism on the book I had along, a book on crowds. This was to be the basis of my work, a delimitation against whatever ideas were circulating about the topic. After just cursory acquaintance with this book, I already knew how unsatisfying it was, and I had made up my mind to remove all "scribblings"—as I called them—from crowds, to have the crowd before me as a pure, untouched mountain, which I would be the first to climb without prejudices. In the second notebook, I planned to free myself from the pressure accumulated at home and to jot down anything that moved me about the new landscape and the people inhabiting it.

It was better to conceal these "grand" intentions during the hike. The tools for implementing them lay at the bottom of my knapsack. I pulled out neither the notebooks nor the book, and I didn't even tell Hans of their existence. On the other hand, I took in the mountains with great gulps, as though they could be breathed. Although we did climb to certain heights, it wasn't the views that mattered to me so much as the endless bareness, which we left behind us and which stretched out in front of us. Everything was stone, there was nothing but stone. Even the sky seemed like not altogether permissible relief. And whenever we came to water, I was secretly displeased that Hans pounced on it, instead of passing it by and doing without it.

He couldn't know what sort of a state I'd been in when starting out on this hike. He learned nothing about my difficulties at home. I was too proud to let on anything; and even if I had, he would scarcely have understood me. My mother enjoyed great prestige among the Asriels; she was considered an intelligent and original woman, with her own ideas and opinions beyond her middle-class background. Alice Asriel had no notion of the effect of the Arosa sanatorium on my mother; there, everything in her background had been revived. Alice saw Mother as she had been earlier:

the proud, young, self-willed widow of our first Viennese days. Alice considered her wealthy, as she herself had once been, and she didn't mind, because she sensed nothing of the narrowness that was linked to Mother's wealth. Perhaps Mother concealed from her how greatly she had changed. Her childhood friend was now living in straitened circumstances, and how could Mother talk to her about money without offering to help her? Thus, money, which had become the main topic between us, an everlasting droning and nagging, was taboo in her conversations with Alice. And Hans felt he had good reason to envy me for my "healthy" conditions at home.

We talked about everything else, incessantly; it was almost impossible to keep silent with Hans. His drive to compete with me forced him to interrupt my every sentence, finish it, and provide adjoining sentences that seemed unending. In order to say more than I, he spoke faster, denying himself time to reflect. I was thankful for the hike, which had been his idea, and which he had prepared. And so I played a peculiar game with him: as long as he left the mountains verbally untouched, I was willing to talk to him about anything. He noticed, when he came to peaks and possibilities of climbing, that I shifted the conversation to books, and he assumed that talking about mountains bored me. Since scarcely anything was to be seen but eternally consistent bare rock, longer discussions about the mountains would have really been fruitless. Thus, his words soon likewise avoided the mountains, which I had made it my job to leave intact. Not that I could have designated it as my job: I am simply trying to give an abbreviated description of what was going on inside me. I had to pile up bare fruitlessness in front of me, because I had committed myself to an assignment, the "work," which would remain fruitless for a long time. It was no mining operation, nothing was to be carried away, it had to maintain its overall ominous character and remain intact, without thereby becoming burdensome or hateful to me. I was to travel up and down, from end to end, touch the assignment at many points, but always in the knowledge that I still didn't know it.

Thus the *undiscussed* Karwendel range, which I entered right after my twentieth birthday, stood at the outset of the period that became the longest in my life and also the most important in content.

It is indeed amazing that for five or six days I spent every moment with a person who never stopped talking, whom I answered and discussed things with (I don't believe there was a moment of silence between us). Yet we never brought up the space through which we were moving, and I never touched on the thing that had become an agonizing pressure upon me in the course of the preceding year. Chitchat about books flowed glibly and meaninglessly from our lips. I did *mean* what I said, and Hans, so far as he found the strength in himself, meant what he said. But it was all nothing but interchangeable blabber. It could just as easily have been other books than those we were talking about. He was satisfied to be holding his own or even anticipating me; I was satisfied to be saying nothing about what I was filled with. Today, I couldn't repeat even one sentence, even one syllable of our blather. This was the real water during that hike through chalk; it oozed into the chalk and vanished without a trace.

It appears, however, that words can't be treated like that impunitively. For when we reached Pertisau on Lake Achen, there was a sudden and unexpected catastrophe. Hans stretched out in the sun by the lake. I, instead of doing the same, ambled up and down. His hands were folded under his head and his eyes were shut. It was hot, the sun was high. I thought he was asleep, so I paid no attention to him. I strolled along the shore of the lake, not far from him. The sand crunched under my heavy hiking boots; I wondered if the noise had woken him up and I glanced over at him. His eyes were wide open, he was staring at my movements with a hatred so powerful that I could feel it. I would never have thought him capable of strong emotions; this was the very thing I missed in him. I was amazed at this hatred and I didn't think that it was aimed at me or that it could have consequences. I remained at the railing by the water, so that I could keep an eye on him from the side. He was silent and staring motionlessly. And gradually it dawned on me: his hatred was so powerful that it prevented him from talking. His silence was as new for me as the feeling that dictated it. I undertook nothing against it, I respected it; all words between us were invalidated by their endless numbers.

His condition must have lasted for quite a while. He lay there as if paralyzed. But his eyes weren't paralyzed; their effect intensified so greatly, that the word *murder* crossed my mind. I walked a few paces toward my knapsack, which lay next to his on the ground. I picked up my knapsack and walked away before unbuckling it. He saw that the knapsacks were now separated; he shook off his rigidity, leaped up, and got his knapsack. He stood there, an open knife blade; he was already striding away, he was already on the road down to Jenbach, without having glanced at me.

He walked fast. I hesitated until he vanished from sight, then I started off, taking the same road as he. In Jenbach, I planned to catch the train to Innsbruck. Soon, I noticed how relieved I was to be alone, all alone. No word had passed between us—one single word could have led to others, but these would have been a hundred thousand words; the sheer thought of them nauseated me. Instead, he had kept *silent,* slicing everything in two. I didn't try to find a reason for his silence. Nor was I worried about him. He was determined to walk off, with no intention (contrary to his habit) of going into a detailed explanation of his behavior. Striding along, I reached back to my knapsack and felt the book and the notebooks. I hadn't shown them to him, hadn't even mentioned taking them along. He knew that after the hike, I wanted to settle down in some spot for a week in order—as I said—to work. We hadn't discussed whether he would stay in the same place during this week. Perhaps he expected a clear invitation to spend the second week with me. I never extended the invitation. In Pertisau, the hike was over. The Karwendel Mountains lay behind us; the road to Jenbach in the Inn Valley was short. That's where the railroad station was, that's where the train to Innsbruck would come and, going the opposite way, his train to Vienna.

And that's how it was. I saw him as I crossed the tracks in Jenbach. He stood not far from me, waiting on the platform, where the train to Vienna was announced. He seemed a bit indecisive, not at all so rigid; his knapsack dangled limply from his thin shoulders, and his alpenstock appeared to have lost its tip. He made no effort to approach me on my platform. Perhaps he did follow me, but in such a way that he was concealed by railroad cars. I sat in my train, and with no bad conscience whatsoever, I rode off toward Innsbruck, escaping the danger of a last-minute reconciliation. All I felt toward him was something like gratitude for not standing by *my* track, where a confrontation would have been difficult to avoid. Not until later did I realize that his personal misfortune was to create the distances separating him from people he was close to. He was a distance builder; this was his talent, and he built distances so well that it was impossible for others and for him to leap across them.

In Innsbruck, I took a train to Kematen, which lay at the entrance to the Sellrain Valley. There, I spent the night, descending into the valley the next day. I wanted to find a room in Gries and begin my week of solitude with the notebooks.

It was a rainy, almost stormy day when I set out. I walked through clouds of fog; the rain lashed my face. This was the first time that I hiked alone, and it was not a friendly start. I was soon drenched; my clothes stuck to my skin. I dashed along in order to escape the bad weather and I quickly became breathless. During the previous week in the radiant sun, everything had been too easy. It seemed right that I had to pay a price for being alone. The rain poured over my face;

I drank the drops. I could see only a few paces ahead of my feet. Sometimes, on a wayside farmhouse, I could make out a pious sentence, which greeted me in the storm. I was soaked from head to foot, and I made sure not to knock on the door of any of these neat, trim, word-adorned houses. It wasn't very long, perhaps two hours, before I reached the flat, higher level of the valley. In Gries, the main village, I soon found a room in the home of a farmer, who was also the village tailor. The welcome was friendly, my things dried out. Toward evening, the rain cleared up, fine weather was predicted for the next day, and I could make my preparations.

I told the farmer and his wife that I had to study during the ten days I planned to stay, and that I intended to devote every morning to work. I was given a card table, which I could set up in the tiny garden next to the house. I rose very early and, right after breakfast, sat down outside, with pencils, both notebooks, and the aforementioned book. It was a wonderfully clear, cool morning when I began. I wasn't surprised at the farmer and his wife for shaking their heads. I was surprised at myself for managing to open up this book out here, even though it repelled me from the very first word, and still repels me no less fifty-five years later: Freud's *Mass Psychology and Ego Analysis*.

The first thing I found in it, typical for Freud, was quotations by authors who had dealt with the same subject matter; most of these passages were from Le Bon. The very manner in which the topic was approached irritated me. Nearly all these writers had closed themselves off against masses, crowds; they found them alien or seemed to fear them; and when they set about investigating them, they gestured: Keep ten feet away from me! A crowd seemed something leprous to them, it was like a disease. They were supposed to find the symptoms and describe them. It was crucial for them, when confronted with a crowd, to keep their heads, not be seduced by the crowd, not melt into it.

Le Bon, the only one attempting a detailed account, recalled the early working-class movement and probably the Paris Commune as well. In his choice of readings, he was decisively influenced by Taine; he was enchanted with Taine's *History of the French Revolution,* especially the narrative of the massacres of September 1792. Freud was under the repulsive impact of a different sort of crowd. He had experienced the war enthusiasm in Vienna as a mature man of almost sixty. Understandably, he defended himself against this sort of crowd, which I, too, had known as a child. But he had no useful tools for his enterprise. Throughout his life, he had studied processes in individuals. As a physician, he attended patients whom he saw repeatedly during a lengthy treatment. His life unrolled in his medical office and in his study. He participated no more in the military than in a church. These two phenomena, army and church, resisted the concepts that he had previously developed and applied. He was too serious and too conscientious to overlook the significance of those two phenomena, and his late investigation was meant to tackle them. But what he lacked in personal experience he obtained from Le Bon's description, which was nourished by very different manifestations of a crowd.

The results struck even the unschooled reader of twenty as dissatisfying and incongruent. True, I had no experience in theory; but in practice, I knew the crowd from the inside. I had unresistingly fallen prey to a crowd in Frankfurt for the first time. Since then, I had never forgotten how *gladly* one falls prey to the crowd. This was what had so greatly astonished me. I saw crowds around me, but I also saw crowds within me, and no explanatory delimitation could help me. What I missed most in Freud's discussion was *recognition* of the phenomenon. This phenomenon struck me as no less elementary than the libido or hunger. I didn't set out to get rid of this phenomenon by tracing it back to special constellations of the libido. On the contrary, the point was to focus on it squarely, as something that had always existed, and that existed now more than ever, as a given phenomenon to be thoroughly investigated, namely to be first experienced and then described. To describe it without experiencing it was virtually misleading.

I had found nothing as yet. All that had happened was that I had planned to do something. But behind my resolution was a determination to commit a lifetime to it, as many years and decades as would prove necessary to carry out the task. To demonstrate how fundamental and ineluctable this phenomenon is, I spoke about a *crowd instinct*, which, I felt, was as much of a drive as the sexual drive. My first few comments on Freud's investigation were tentative and clumsy. They didn't evince much more than my dissatisfaction with the text, my resistance to it, my determination not to be talked into anything, much less have anything put over on me. For what I feared most was the *disappearance* of things whose existence I could not doubt because I had experienced them. Our conversations at home had made me aware of how blind one could be if one wanted to be blind. I began to understand that books were no different in this respect, that a reader has to be *alert;* that it is dangerous to get lazy, putting off criticism and accepting whatever you're told.

Thus, during the ten mornings in the Sellrain Valley, I learned how to be an alert reader. I regard this period, from August 1 to August 10, 1925, as the true beginning of my independent intellectual life. My rejection of Freud came at the start of my work on the book, which I didn't deliver to the public until thirty-five years later, in 1960.

During those August days, I also struggled for and attained my independence as a person. For the days were long, I was alone; after the five hours of work in the morning came the soliloquy of the afternoon. I explored the valley, climbed up to Praxmar, and then farther up to the passes leading into the neighboring valleys. Two or three times, I climbed the Rosskogel, the mountain immediately over Gries. I was happy about my effort and also about reaching goals that I had set; for these goals, unlike those big goals that I had placed far, far away, *were* attainable. I talked to myself a lot, probably to articulate the chaos of hatred, resentment, and confinement that had accumulated in me during the previous year. I wanted to put that chaos into words, organize it, and banish it from my mind. I confided it to the air around me, in which there was so much space as well as clarity and direction of the wind. It was blissful to have nasty words float off in the wind and disappear. They didn't sound ridiculous, because they didn't strike any ears. But I made sure not to be arbitrary; I released nothing that didn't yearn to take shape after being under pressure for so long. I replied to accusations that had insulted and frightened me; I was utterly truthful, heedless of any auditor whose feelings I would have had to spare. All the answers that formed in me were released, they were weighty and new, and they didn't adhere to ready-made forms.

The chief interlocutor for all my back talk was she who had become my irreconcilable enemy with the mission to tear out from my soil everything that she herself had planted in it. That was how I saw it, and it was good that I saw it like that; for how else could I have gathered the strength to put up a defense and not succumb? I was not being just; how could I have been? In this life-and-death struggle, I failed to see what I was to blame for; I failed to see that for years I had cultivated my opponent with my harshness and the cruel earnestness of my convictions. This was no time for justice, it was a time for freedom. And here, no one could twist my words or cut off my breath.

At nightfall, I sat down in the tavern and wrote down many of these things, in the second notebook, which was reserved for personal dealings.

I have since found this notebook and reread it. It was frightening to read it again after fifty-four years. What wildness, what great pathos! I found every sentence with which I had been threatened and insulted. None was forgotten, none omitted; the most embarrassing things that I had been unjustly charged with were included. But I also found the retort to everything and a passion going way beyond its goal, betraying homicidal strength that I hadn't realized I'd possessed.

If that had been all, if I hadn't then begun casting about on all sides, reaching for knowledge that could serve this passion, things would have ended badly and violently for me, and I wouldn't be here to justify that enormous ten-day anger.

In the evening, many people gathered at the tavern, farmers and outsiders, drinking, singing; but I managed not to get involved. I sat with a glass of wine in front of me, silently writing, a thin, bespectacled, unengaging student, who had every reason to make others forget his unattractive appearance by asking them questions and toasting. But I was busy with my justification. And though I took in everything with an alert eye, I never let on that I was doing so. I seemed so emphatically absorbed in my writing that eventually no one paid me any heed. Since I had the muscatel in front of me, my presence wasn't resented. I felt I mustn't get into any conversations. They would have shattered my soliloquy and weakened the strength of my justification. With these perfect strangers, I could not be myself. The hatred I was filled with would have seemed like madness to them. Nor was I in any mood to play a role.

Despite these unusual circumstances, I did make friends. These friends were children, and they showed up outside my window at 6 A.M. They were three boys, the youngest five, the eldest eight years old. On the first day, they had seen me sitting at my little table, writing, and this struck them as so unusual that they watched me for a time. Eventually, all of them in unison asked me what my name was. I liked them so much that I told them my first name, but it was too odd for them. They repeated it skeptically, shaking their heads. My name made me more alien to them than before. However, the eldest had a flash of genius and told the others: "It's a doggy name!" From that moment on, I was as dear to them as a dog. Every morning, they were my clock, waking me up with my name. When I withdrew to Freud and my notebook, they stood in a row for a long time, without disturbing me. Then they got bored and trotted away, in quest of other, better dogs.

In the afternoon, when I set out to do what I'd planned, they showed up, accompanying me part of the way. I asked them for the names of plants and animals in their dialect, about their fathers and mothers and relatives. They knew they weren't allowed to go too far from the village, and they suddenly halted as if on schedule. The thing they enjoyed most was waving. Once, when I forgot to wave back, they rebuked me the next morning. They were my company during these seemingly mute days. In my exalted condition, which was fed by the threats, curses, and promises of justification, no creature could have moved me more deeply than these children. And every morning, when they stood in a row to the side of my table—not too close in order not to disturb me—and watched me write, I felt them to be a kind of well-deserved boon.

Part Three

The School
of Hearing

Vienna 1926-1928

The Asylum

Toward mid-August, I returned to Vienna. I don't recall the first time I saw my mother again. The freedom I had won by "settling accounts" had a staggering effect on me. Without timidity or guilt feelings, I went to see the only person I felt drawn to, the only person I could speak to in my state. Whenever I dropped in on Veza and we talked about books and paintings that we loved, I never forgot with what strength and resolution she had won her freedom: the room in which everything looked as she wanted it to look, in which she could occupy herself with the things that suited her.

Her struggle had been a lot harder than mine: the age-old man, who was always there, even if no longer making his presence felt with his assaults, was an enemy to everyone. He cared only about himself. In order to escape his siege, one had to besiege him first, always observe him. And such actions were less consistent with Veza's character than the struggles with my mother were consistent with my character. After all, my struggles were true battles, between opponents who understood very well what they were accusing each other of.

And now, the asylum that Veza had created for herself became my asylum, too. I could go there at any time, my presence was never inconvenient, my visits were desired, but there was no obligation on either side. We always talked about something that excited us. I arrived filled with something, and I left no less filled. Whatever was on my mind would be transformed within two hours as in an alchemical process: it seemed purer and clearer, but no less urgent. It would pre-occupy me in a different, a surprising, fashion even during the next few days, until I had so many new questions that they served as the reason for the next visit.

Now I talked about everything that I had failed to talk about at my first visit, in May, because of my impetuous plea on behalf of unending life for King Lear. It wasn't that I complained about what was happening in my home. I was too proud to tell Veza the truth about that. Also, I clung to the image that people had of my mother, as though it had the power to change her back into her earlier self. She was only just forty and still considered beautiful; she was so well read that her literary knowledge had become legendary among those who knew about her. I don't believe that she read very many new things now. But since she forgot noth-ing, everything she had ever read was at her fingertips. And aside from things that she had to find out about from me, she always sounded elegant and clever. I was the only person to whom she let on to what extent her old character had died. Whenever things got very bad between us, she would claim that *I* had killed that old character.

During the early period of my visits to Veza, perhaps the first six months, I mentioned none of these things. Veza didn't mind that I never discussed my mother. She placed her very far above herself. And I only got an inkling of the capabili-ties that she ascribed to my mother when Veza once asked me, almost shyly, why my mother had never published any-thing. Veza was firmly convinced that my mother wrote books. And when I denied this (although flattered), she refused to believe me and hit on an explanation for the secrecy of her writing. "She thinks we're all chatterboxes. And she's right. We admire the great books and just talk about them all the time. She *writes* them and has such scorn for us that she speaks about them to no one. Someday we'll find out what pseudonym she publishes under. Then we'll all be so embarrassed that we never realized it."

I insisted it was impossible; I'd have noticed it if she wrote.

"She does it only when she's alone. During her sanatorium stays, when she withdraws from you boys. She's not really sick at those times. She's just after peace and quiet, so she can write. You'll be absolutely astonished when you read your mother's books!"

I caught myself wishing it were true, and I was quite certain it couldn't be true. Veza filled every person with faith in himself. Now, she had succeeded, albeit only halfway, to fill me with expectation about someone I had lost faith in. Veza didn't realize how greatly this splitting effect helped my defection. Mother missed no opportunity to hold up my ingratitude to me, and she painted her own future in somber colors: she would be without her eldest son, who would destroy himself by then or else reduce himself so woefully as to be no longer present for her. At such times, the mirage of her secret writing was now aroused in me: perhaps it *was* true, and she'd be able to comfort herself with that.

Far more important was the fact that during these visits with Veza everything was different from anything I had ever known before. The recent past dissolved; I had no history. False notions that had settled in were corrected, but without a struggle. I didn't feel compelled to hold on to anything merely because it was under attack.

Veza recited lots of poetry by heart without getting on anyone's nerves. There was one poem we had in common: Goethe's "Prometheus." She wanted to hear it from me. I read it to her. She didn't recite it along, which would have been easy for her to do; she really wanted to hear it. And when she then said, "You haven't taken anything away from it," I was absolutely delighted. It wasn't until later that I realized she had a longer poem in mind, for which she wanted to arouse my liking: Edgar Allan Poe's "The Raven." She was obsessed with it. It is a very long poem, she had memorized it when very young, and now she recited it to me in full. She wasn't put off by my astonishment at how obsessed she was (and yet she was exceedingly sensitive to everything going on in other people). I realized I mustn't interrupt her, when I itched to cry out, "Enough!," but I was afraid she'd never invite me over again if I gave in to this itch. Thus I listened to "The Raven" until the end and was then caught myself. The bird flew into my nerves; I began to twitch in the rhythm of the poem. And when she was done, and I was still twitching slightly, she said cheerily, "Now it's grabbed you, too. That's what happened to me. One should always read poems out loud, not just mutely to oneself."

The conversation soon turned to Karl Kraus, of course. She asked me why I avoided her at the lectures. She believed she knew the reason; and if it *was* the reason, then she had to respect it. I was, she said, so overcome that I couldn't talk to anyone. I wanted to take everything along unbroken and undiscussed. She, too, liked going to his readings by herself; however, she preferred talking about them afterwards to silence. After all, one didn't agree with everything that was said. She had the utmost veneration for Karl Kraus; but she wouldn't let him prescribe what one could or couldn't read. She showed me Heine's *French Conditions*. Had I read it? She said it was one of the most intelligent and most entertaining books she'd ever read. She had read the book three years ago, after going to Paris, and now she was reading it a second time.

I refused to take hold of the volume. There was no one Karl Kraus so utterly disapproved of as Heine. I didn't believe her: I thought she was playing a joke on me, and I was even terrified about the joke. But she insisted on showing me her independence. She held the title under my nose, read it aloud, leafed through the pages in front of me, and said: "Right?"

"But you haven't read it. It's bad enough you've got it lying around!"

"I've got all of Heine here. Look!" She opened the door of a bookcase, which contained the heart of her library, "the books I wouldn't want to live without." And there, although not at the top, was a complete edition of Heine. After this blow, which she had enjoyed dealing me, she showed me the books I expected: Goethe, Shakespeare, Molière, Byron's *Don Juan,* Victor Hugo's *Les Misérables, Tom Jones, Vanity Fair, Anna Karenina, Madame Bovary, The Idiot, The Brothers Karamazov,* and, one of her very favorite books, Hebbel's *Journals.* These weren't all, these were only what she picked out, the most important things. The novels meant a great deal to her; those she showed me were books she had read and reread over and over. And here, too, she proved her independence from Karl Kraus. "He's not interested in novels. He's not interested in paintings either. He's not interested in anything that could weaken his wrath. It's grand. But it can't be imitated. Wrath has to be *inside* a person; you can't borrow it."

These words sounded perfectly natural, and yet they shocked me. I saw her before me, in the front row at Karl Kraus's readings, sparkling and full of expectation. And yet she had been reading Heine, *French Conditions,* perhaps just recently. How did she dare sit in front of Kraus? Every sentence of his was a demand. If you couldn't meet the demand, you had no business being there. For a year and a half, I had gone to every reading, and I was filled with him as with a Bible. I did not doubt a single word he said. Never, under any circumstances, would I have acted against him. He was my conviction. He was my strength. Without him on my mind, I couldn't have endured the idiotic culinary arts in the laboratory for even one day. When he read from *The Last Days of Mankind,* he populated Vienna for me. I heard only his voices. Were there any others? It was only in him that you found justice—no, you didn't find justice, he *was* justice. One frown on his part, and I would have broken off with my best friend. One gesture, and I would have thrown myself into fire for him.

I said this to her, I had to say it, I said more, I said everything. A tremendous shamelessness came over me, forcing me to blurt out my secret slave emotions. She listened, she didn't interrupt, she heard me out. I grew more and more vehement; she was deadly serious when she suddenly—I don't know where she got it—held a Bible in her hand and said: "*This* is my Bible!"

I sensed that she wanted to justify me. She wasn't against the absoluteness with which I professed my god. But, although not really religious, she took the word *God* more seriously than I and gave no human being the right to become God. The Bible was the book that she read most frequently. She loved the stories, the psalms, the proverbs, the prophets. More than anything else, she loved the Song of Songs. She knew the Bible well, but never quoted it. She didn't bother anyone with it; but basically, she measured literature against it, and she also measured people's behavior against the demands of the Bible.

However, I am painting a colorless picture of her by listing the intellectual contents of her life. The titles of famous books strung together sound like concepts. One ought to take a *single* character and describe how that character gradually emerged from her lips, in order to give you some idea of what a flourishing and independent life that character led in Veza. None developed all at once; the character formed in the course of many conversations. And it was only after several visits that one had the feeling of really knowing a character that she cited. No more surprises were to be expected; her reactions were definite; one could rely on them. And the mystery of the character was totally absorbed in Veza's mystery.

Since the age of ten, I've felt as if I consisted of many characters. But it was a vague feeling. I couldn't have said which characters were speaking out of me, or why one replaced another. It was a river of many shapes, which never dried up, despite the specificity of newly acquired demands and convictions. I had the desire and the ability to leave myself at the mercy of this river; but I never *saw* it. Now, in Veza, I had met a person who had found characters in great literature and inserted them for her own multiplicity. She had implanted them in herself, they thrived in her. And whenever she wanted them, they were available. What astonished me were the clarity and definiteness, the fact that nothing mingled with anything accidental, anything that didn't belong. There was an awareness here, as if those characters were to be read off a higher tablet of the law. They were all inscribed, the pure characters, each sharply delimited and obvious and no less alive than oneself, determined by their veracity alone, not to be snuffed out by any damnation.

It was an exciting spectacle, watching Veza slowly move among her characters. They were her support against Karl Kraus. He could never have touched them; they were her freedom. *She* was never his slave. It was magnanimous of her to let me be when I came to her in fetters. However, there was something you felt a lot more acutely than her restrained wealth: her mystery.

Veza's mystery was in her smile. She was conscious of it and could evoke it. But once it had appeared, she was unable to revoke it. It persisted, and then it seemed to be her actual face whose beauty deceived so long as it didn't smile. Sometimes, she closed her eyes when smiling, her black lashes plunged deep, grazing her cheeks. At such times, she seemed to be contemplating herself from the inside, with her smile as a light. The way she appeared to herself was her mystery; yet, despite her silence, you didn't feel excluded. Her smile, a shimmering rainbow, reached from her to the observer. Nothing is more irresistible than the temptation to enter another person's inner space. If he is someone who knows how to place his words, his silence intensifies the temptation to the utmost. You set out to obtain his words and you hope you will find them in back of his smile, where they await the visitor.

Veza's restraint could not be overcome, for it was permeated with grief. She fed her grief incessantly; she was sensitive to every pain if it was someone else's pain. She suffered from another person's humiliation, as though experiencing it herself. She didn't stop at mere sympathy: she showered the humiliated with praise and gifts.

She bore such pains long after they had been alleviated. Her grief was abysmal: it contained and preserved everything that was unjust. Her pride was very great and could easily be wounded. But she granted the same vulnerability to anyone else and imagined herself surrounded by sensitive people who needed her protection and whom she never forgot.

The Peace Dove

It is astonishing what ten days of freedom can do for you. The days from August 1 to August 10, 1925, when I was all alone, when I staked off my borders against Freud, and also justified myself against my mother's accusations (without her finding out, so that I was satisfied—a stricter, harder, more valid satisfaction than if anyone else had also taken part in it); when I first spoke into the wind during the day and wrote those words down in the evening—this brief term of freedom, which nourished me for a lifetime, would always remain present for me, if only because I always referred to it, no matter what happened.

While I wrote down my accusation, in sentences so violent that they frighten me today, a face appeared to me, a face that I thought did not belong there, a face whose smile I had missed, which did not smile now, but spoke earnestly and steadfastly about a war that it had waged. It was Veza's face.

It spoke about *her* freedom. And the haggard old man, whom I had known initially only through her terrible words about him—words all the more terrible because they came unexpectedly from her lips—the haggard old man had *lost* the war against her. And hard as I tried to expunge his image in my astonishment, the words kept coming from Veza's lips, strengthening me in what I was doing. During those ten days, she participated in my struggle for freedom with her own struggle for freedom. After my return, I felt driven to her, beginning a never-to-be-exhausted conversation with her, going back again and again, having this conversation in place of the older one, which had degenerated into a power struggle and was now devastated—none of this could have astonished anyone. It consternated only the one person who lost out: my mother.

In September, she was back again, in a different atmosphere. We remained together on Radetzkystrasse for two more months. The fire that had heated us was out. My blowup in July had frightened her; the doctor's verdict had gone against her. She didn't attack me, she didn't tell me what to do. I didn't criticize her, because I could talk to Veza. I made no secret of my visits to Veza and spoke quite openly, without going into detail, about her literary proclivities. Perhaps I was too open when praising her taste, her judgment, and her excellent literary background. For the moment, my words were taken with no direct reaction. However, my mother was very annoyed about the disturbance of our meals. When Johnnie Ring was driven out of his room by his need to use the bathroom, squeezing behind her chair, she made a disgusted face and wouldn't return his greeting. On the way back, he began to stutter, embarrassed by her silence. His flatteries half stuck in his throat; she remained silent until he had closed the door to his room behind him.

But then she launched into a diatribe against Vienna, this cesspool of vice, where nothing was right anymore. People lay in bed till noon, or else they were aesthetes, only chattering about books. They went to museums and stood in front of paintings in broad daylight, shameless loafers. It all boiled down to the same thing, no one wanted to work; and then they were surprised at the unemployment when there were no men who stood in the thick of life. And if only it were merely a cesspool of sin. But Vienna had also become provincial. Nowhere in the world did anyone care what was going on in Vienna. All you had to do was say the name, and people made scoffing faces. Even Karl Kraus (whom she normally could not relate to) was cited as chief witness for the inferiority of Vienna. He knew what he was talking about, he knew it thoroughly, and the people he meant all ran to him and laughed at their own sins. Way back when, in the great days of the Burgtheater, everything had been different, Vienna had still been a city that counted. Perhaps it had been due to the Kaiser, after all. Say what you like about him, he *had* been a man with a sense of duty. Even at an advanced age, he sat over his documents day after day. But now? Did I know one single person here who didn't think first and foremost about his pleasure? And a mother was supposed to raise young people to become men in *such* a city? It was absolutely hopeless. Now in Paris, yes, in Paris, it would be totally different!

I had the feeling that this sudden hatred of Vienna was aimed at a specific person, whom she didn't name. I felt uneasy, although she very carefully spared me any accusations. It struck me as suspicious that she included museums in the catalogue of sins for the first time and attacked people for standing around in front of paintings. No one ever mentioned Veza without comparing her to a painting. And since the most diverse paintings were cited, a small museum had been assembled. During one of these angry attacks against Vienna, Veza's name might suddenly spring out. What would I do then? At the very first insult against *this* woman, I would leave the apartment, forever.

But before things reached that pass, Mother retreated to

Menton on the Riviera in early winter. From there, she wrote me pleading letters. She described her isolation among the people: they didn't like her at the hotel, people distrusted her, women feared her gazes, especially when they sat with their husbands in the dining room. These letters impressed me, for her descriptions contained something of her old strength. There were also detailed accounts of all sorts of physical complaints. Although I had known the often fictitious nature of these complaints since Arosa, I took them no less seriously. The ultimate high point of her letters, the culmination of everything, consisted of outbursts of hatred so blind and wild, that I began to fear for Veza's life.

For now her letters openly named Veza. She ascribed the basest motives to her, spewed the most uninhibited and disgusting things about her: Veza had recognized my weakest side, my love for books, and was shamelessly exploiting it by not talking to me about anything else. She said that Veza was a woman and had nothing to do: she could afford to lead an aesthete's life. If Veza wasn't sickened by it, then that was her business. But to pull in a young man preparing for the struggle of life was criminal. Veza was doing it out of sheer vanity, merely to have a new victim in her coils. For what could a laughably young creature like myself mean to a woman with her experience? I would have a terrible awakening when it was the next man's turn. I was so innocent and naïve, said my mother, that she could only be alarmed when thinking about me. She was determined to save me. We had to get out, get out of Vienna! In this cesspool of Johnnies and Vezas—it was no coincidence that Veza was his cousin—there was no place for us.

Mother said she was planning to move to Paris with my brothers, who would go to school there and later to the university. It was plain we could no longer live together. At twenty-one, I would have to go my own way. But there were enough cities—for instance, in Germany—where the atmosphere wasn't contaminated by aesthetes, and I could continue my studies. She no longer feared that I would drop out of chemistry: I had already endured two years of it. What she feared was Vienna, where I was sure to perish in one way or another. I should by no means imagine that Veza was the only one. Vienna had thousands like her, unscrupulous pleasure-seekers, who, to indulge their vanity, thought nothing of driving mothers and sons apart, and as soon as they got tired of the sons, they would dump them. She knew about countless cases of this sort. She had never spoken to me about these things so as not to mislead me about women. But now, it was time for me to know what the world was like—it was quite different from books.

As long as she was in Menton, until March, I replied to her letters. I knew she was all alone, and I was unsettled by her complaints about the distrust shown her on all sides. Her insulting comments about Veza, which made up half of each letter, struck me hard. I was afraid they could intensify into a physical attack, and I made a rather hopeless attempt to change her attitude. I told her about other things that were happening in Vienna, discussions with the woman working next to me in the laboratory, a Russian émigré, whom I liked very much. I told her about a dwarf who had come and, in his loud, resolute way, had dominated the entire room; about every single reading given by Karl Kraus—now, she had, after all, officially recognized him as the despiser of Vienna and could no longer turn away at the mention of his name. I made it quite clear, in every letter, that I was determined to remain in Vienna. I repelled her attacks against Veza and made an effort not to take them too seriously. A few times, not too often, I wrote indignant letters, as the deeply offended person that I actually was throughout this period. She would then relent and bridle her hatred for perhaps a week. But after two letters, she started in again, and I was no further than before.

Her condition worried me, but I was a lot more concerned about Veza. I knew how sensitive she was: she felt responsible for everything going on around her and for many other things, too. Were she to learn even a smidgen of what my mother felt and wrote about her, she would break with me and refuse to see me again under any circumstances. As long as I didn't breathe a word of it, everything went well. Every week, a letter from Menton upset me. I made sure not to see Veza on those days, so she wouldn't notice anything.

We had given up the apartment at the beginning of the year; my brothers moved in with a family, I rented a room. In March, Mother went to Paris, where close relatives and many good friends of hers were living. She looked around and then scheduled the move for summer. She announced she would arrive in Vienna at the end of May. She planned to stay one month in order to take care of everything. After six months, it was time we finally had a *talk*.

I was scared upon learning of this imminent arrival. Things were getting serious. I had to protect Veza from my mother at any cost; they were not to meet on any account. Nor was Veza to find out about my mother's hatred, which would have upset her and changed everything between us. I couldn't tell how I'd act toward my mother until she arrived. She wanted to stay in a rooming house near the Opera, not in Leopold-stadt, where Veza lived; so a chance encounter of the two women was not to be feared. I had time to prepare Veza. She was not to find out any more than was absolutely necessary, just enough to go along with my wish that she avoid my mother, that was all.

Thus, I owned up to Veza that Mother would like it if I left Vienna. She had been told it was better for me to transfer to one of the large German universities, study with a world-famous chemist, and try to have him as my doctoral advisor. Vienna didn't have such a high-ranking man at this time. My later career as a chemist was largely dependent on my dissertation. This didn't mean, Mother said, that I couldn't come back to Vienna later on; no one could tell anything about the future. Now Mother had, of course, noticed there was something keeping me in Vienna. I had written her that I didn't want to leave Vienna under any circumstances. She was now coming, determined to make a last-ditch attempt, and would do everything in her power to change my mind. She wouldn't succeed. I was totally indifferent to chemistry; I had no intention of becoming a chemist. Veza knew best what I wanted to be and what I intended to do, come what may.

Then, why was I so nervous, she asked. If I didn't want to leave, nobody could force me.

"That's not it," I said. "You don't know Mother. If she wants something, she'll do anything to get her way. She'll visit *you* and talk to *you* about it. She'll convince you it would be best for me if I left Vienna. She'll manage to talk *you* into getting me to leave. I could never forgive you for that. She'll drive us apart. I'm horribly scared that you're going to talk to her."

"Never. Never. Never. She'll never succeed!"

"But I *am* scared, and when she's here, I won't have a moment of peace. I just tremble at the thought of her coming. You've got the highest opinion of her intellectual gifts, her will power. You have no idea of what she can do. Neither do I. It comes to her on the spur of the moment, and suddenly you see how right she is, and you promise her anything and then—what's to become of us?"

"I won't see her. I promise. I swear it. Nothing can happen. Will *that* put your mind at ease?"

"Yes, yes, it will. But only then."

I told her not to accept a single call or letter from her; she had to avoid her, cleverly and warily. Mother would be living in the First Bezirk, anyhow. She wouldn't be hard to avoid. But if, contrary to our expectations, a letter did come to her from Mother, then Veza absolutely had to hand it over to me unopened. I became hopeful when I saw how quickly she believed me. She would not only hand me any letter of Mother's unopened, but, if I so wished, she wouldn't read it *after* me and never answer it.

Mother came. And in the very first conversation, I realized that she too was eager to avoid any confrontation. She wanted to maintain her image of the "enemy" repulsively intact. She felt her image would dissolve without a trace once she saw Veza in the flesh. From my letters, which she had reread one after the other in Paris, she concluded that I would not leave Vienna right away under any circumstances. She believed that I cared even more about Karl Kraus than about Veza. In Menton, where she had felt excluded because she didn't know anyone, she had taken it for granted that I saw Veza every day. In Paris, where she had her relatives and her many friends, she was no longer so certain. Her distrust had ramified, becoming more subtle: she read all sorts of things between the lines of my letters, things she had never noticed before. I had written to her about my neighbor in the laboratory, the one who reminded me of Dostoevsky. I had said it was sheer delight talking with her about him. I even liked going to the laboratory because of her. Now Mother was struck by the words "sheer delight," which she hadn't at all heeded when she'd gotten the letter in Menton. She thought of my standing in the laboratory all day long. During the tedious procedures that were part of quantitative analysis, there was endless time for talking.

"Do you ever see Eva," she now asked, "your Russian girl in the laboratory?"

"Yes, of course. We nearly always eat together. You know, once we start talking about Ivan Karamazov, whom she hates, we just can't stop. We go and eat together at Regina's and keep talking about him, then back down Währingerstrasse to the Institute, and we never stop talking for an instant, and then we stand in front of our flasks, and what do you think we talk about then?"

"Ivan Karamazov! That's just like you people! Naturally, she's all for Alyosha! I've begun to understand Ivan. For the past few years, I've come to consider him the most interesting of the brothers."

She was so happy about the existence of my colleague that she began to converse about literary characters, just like old times. She remembered my jaundice on Radetzkystrasse, over a year ago. It was the only part of that period that I looked back on fondly. I had been in bed for several weeks and read through all of Dostoevsky, all the red volumes, from start to finish.

"You ought to be grateful for your jaundice," she said, "otherwise you couldn't pass muster now with your Eva." The "your" gave me a jolt. It was as if she had placed her in my arms with her own two hands. (I really did like Eva; this had led to conflicts in me.) But, in a sudden fit of cunning, I let it pass. For I sensed how sharply Mother was observing me. I even said:

"Yes, that's true. It's a wonderful conversation. She *lives* in Dostoevsky and takes it all very seriously. There's no one else in the entire lab with whom she could talk about it."

No sooner were we talking about literature again than I liked my mother. Of course, there was no mistaking why she had given the conversation this turn. She was reconnoitering, she wanted to find out how important my attractive colleague was in relation to any other woman. Did she mean something to me? Might she eventually mean even more? Mother came back to Dostoevsky and asked whether Eva had anything in common with female characters in Dostoevsky. This sounded like a harbinger of a new worry, but I could set her mind at ease, for the very opposite was true. Eva was exceptionally intelligent; her real talent was for mathematics. She knew more about physical chemistry than any of the male students. She had—this contradicted her intellectual faculties—a very rich emotional life. However, her feelings *maintained* their direction; any reversal into the opposite—which Mother had been thinking of with her question—was alien to Eva.

"Are you sure?" said Mother. "A person can be terribly mistaken. Would you ever have thought in the past that you would hate me someday?"

I ignored this first hostile remark since her arrival in Vienna and stuck to the actual topic of our conversation.

"Of course, I'm sure," I said. "I spend so many hours with her, day after day. This has been going on for almost a year. Do you think there's anything we haven't talked about?"

"I thought you only talked about Dostoevsky."

"That's what we talk about mostly, it's our favorite subject. Can you imagine a better way of getting to know a person than discussing *everything* that happens in Dostoevsky?"

We both clung to this peace dove. Eva Reichmann would have been astonished had she known what part my mother assigned her. She wouldn't have cared to serve as a topic of conversation in this way; for all we were really after was to avoid the other topic. However, I said nothing about Eva that I didn't mean, and my words made her dearer and dearer to me. Even though my Mother harped on her so much, I didn't start disliking Eva. She was truly our peace dove. After my mother's six-month absence, after our unbelievable correspondence, I had expected a terrible fight. It was obvious that we were both releasing our dislike and fear.

"*Revenons à nos moutons*," my mother suddenly said. This was an idiom that she loved and that she had never *once* used during the last few years of our battles. "Now let me tell you my plans." She intended to move to Paris in the summer. This would be a strenuous time for her. In order to be able to cope with it, she wanted to go off to a spa, to Bad Gleichenberg as in the previous year: it had done her good. Would I like to take care of my brothers during this time? They had to have a real vacation, for things would be difficult for them right after that: getting used to their new French school, and in fairly high classes at that, not so far from the *bachot*, the *lycée* degree. All three boys could go to Salzkammergut. This would put her mind at ease; I would be doing her and my brothers a real favor.

I realized what she had in mind and I agreed without hesitating. Nothing could give me greater pleasure. I wouldn't be seeing my brothers again for perhaps a year. After all, I myself wanted to go on a holiday. We'd definitely find a nice place for us. She was flabbergasted. I sensed the question that was on the tip of her tongue. She didn't come out with it. I almost came out with it in her stead. We reached a sort of compromise. She said: "You don't have any other plans for the summer, do you?"

I said: "What kind of plans could I have for the summer?"

Thus this conversation could have ended, and it could have ended well for both of us. The only worry preying on my mind was that she might injure and endanger Veza. Now, Veza hadn't been mentioned even *once*. But what would happen in our ensuing conversations, during the next four weeks or more that Mother would be spending in Vienna? It was a long time. I wanted to be absolutely certain and forestall anything. I felt good after our conversation about my colleague. Had the devil gotten into me, or was I really afraid for Veza? I said: "You know, Eva, my colleague, asked me whether I was going to the mountains for the summer. I didn't tell her anything definite. Would you mind if she came to the same area? Not to the same place, of course; maybe an hour away. Then we could go on occasional outings together. She'd be sure to have a good influence on the boys. I'd only see her now and then, perhaps once or twice a week, and I'd devote the rest of my time to the boys."

Mother was wild about my suggestion. "Why shouldn't you see her more often? So you did have plans for the summer! I'm delighted you've told me. It could work out marvelously. She's really a fine person. You can't blame her for asking you first. In earlier days, it would have been unthinkable. But that's the way women *are* today."

"No, no," I said. "You're imagining things. There's really nothing going on between us."

"Anything's possible," said Mother. She wasn't being very tactful. I'd never experienced something like this with her. She would have done anything to get me away from Veza.

However, with my sudden idea I had hit on the one possibility of protecting Veza against my mother. I had to talk about other women. This time, I had been helped out by a colleague who happened to be working next to me in the laboratory. I really did like her, and it was indecent of me to feed my mother's fancy that Eva was or could become my girlfriend. Even if I told Eva about it, and, even if, helpful and understanding as she was, she agreed to go along with my ploy, there was nevertheless something embarrassing about the matter. But it had happened, and it made me realize that something else had to happen: I had to *invent* women and entertain Mother with stories about them. Never again must she find out anything about Veza and myself. Mother would be far away in Paris and Veza would be in Vienna, and I would have saved Veza from all the horrible things my mother could do to her.

Frau Weinreb and the Executioner

Frau Weinreb, in whose home on Haidgasse I had rented a nice, spacious room, was the widow of a journalist, who had died a very old gentleman. She had been a lot younger than he and had already survived him by many years. The apartment was filled with pictures of him, a grandfatherly gentleman with a benevolent beard. The wife, with her dark, canine face, always devotedly talking about her husband, as if he, albeit dead, were vastly superior to her both intellectually and morally, transferred a small part of this veneration to students. Each single one of them could become something like a Herr Dr. Weinreb; she never referred to her husband in any other way; he was always a Herr and a Doktor. In group pictures with his colleagues—in front of which I had to stand and tarry for a while—he stuck out not only because of his beard, but also because of his central position. She rarely said "my husband": even this long after his death, she still hadn't gotten over the honor of this marriage. And if ever those words did pass across her lips, she broke off in terror, as if she had indulged in blasphemy, hesitated a bit, and then, virtually intoxicated, added the full name plus title: "Herr Dr. Weinreb." She must have called him that for a long time before marrying him; and perhaps she had continued to call him that even during the marriage.

A friendly family had told me about this room, where their son had lived for a year. It had ended badly (more about this later). The shy young man, known for his gentleness, had gotten into an awkward situation and had even been hauled into court. I had been warned not against the widow, but against the two women who lived in the same apartment. I expected some sort of den of iniquity. But I wanted to live in this area, not too far from, but also not too near, Veza. And Haidgasse, a side street of Taborstrasse, was just right—it was no satellite of Praterstrasse (whose surroundings dominated my life), but it *was* close by.

When I came to look at the room, I was astonished at how clean and orderly the apartment was. It couldn't have been more bourgeois; everywhere the picture of the venerable old gentleman, and in front of every picture, the panegyrical widow. Not even the room I was to live in was free of him; nevertheless, he appeared more sparingly here, three or four times in all. She said she preferred renting to students. My predecessor had been a bank clerk. Of course, he was already earning a living and was independent of his mother, but it was a modest living, and without a university degree nothing much could come of him. However, Frau Weinreb was careful to say no more; he was mentioned because he had lived there before me, and the room had remained empty ever since. However, she sided neither with nor against him. Her guard, who had brought the charges against him, was in the adjoining kitchen. All doors were open, and Frau Weinreb said nothing without instantly breaking off and anxiously listening in the direction of the kitchen.

Very soon, during this opening visit, I sensed that she was under some pressure from which nothing could free her. Since every other sentence, at times every sentence, was about her deceased husband, I figured this pressure had something to do with her being a widow. Perhaps she hadn't taken as good care of the old man as he had wanted. This didn't strike me as probable: no other man had played a part in her life; I was certain of this. But she was always listening for a voice whose orders she depended on, and it was not the voice of the dead man.

The housekeeper she lived with had opened the apartment door for me, handed me over to her employer, and then vanished into the kitchen. This housekeeper was a strong, massive, middle-aged woman; she looked like what I pictured an executioner to be. She had very prominent cheekbones and a grim face, which seemed a lot more dangerous because it smiled. I wouldn't have been surprised if she had received me with a slap. Instead, she made a catlike face, but one that was proportionate to her size, and therefore eerie. She was the person I'd been warned against.

When Frau Dr. Weinreb swung wide open the door to the room that was for rent (she always walked as if she were about to tumble forward) and then stepped in right after me, she made sure that the door remained wide open behind her and called "coming, coming!" which struck me as absurd, sort of like a chambermaid telling her mistress "I'm coming, I'm coming!" And then she began to praise the merits of this room, and especially the pictures of her deceased husband. She uttered no sentence without waiting for confirmation or encouragement.

At first, I thought she expected these things from me; but I soon realized she was waiting for confirmation from outside. And since I hadn't seen anyone else in the apartment, I assumed that the person in question was the creepy woman who had let me in, and I couldn't get her out of my mind throughout my inspection of the room. However, she remained in the kitchen, never interfering in our discussion.

I wondered where the third woman was who was supposed to be living here, the person who had been the subject of my predecessor's trial. But she never appeared. Perhaps she no longer lived here. Perhaps she had moved, because of the scandal about her, which made it difficult to rent out the room again. I had heard a great deal, although nothing very definite, about her rustic beauty, her tremendous blond braids (when her hair was let down, I'd been told, it reached all the way to the ground), her seductive arts. Her name, which I liked, had lodged in my memory; I liked Czech names, and Ružena was one of my favorites. I had hoped that *she* would open the door; instead, her aunt, the executioner, stood there in front of me; and the slap I expected from the aunt was my just deserts for being curious about Ružena. Perhaps the grim reception was a warning. The affair had been in the newspapers, and it was obvious that people would come to see not the room, but Ružena.

However, it was quite all right with me that Ružena was nowhere in view. I liked the room, and I could rent it without fearing complications. Frau Weinreb was satisfied that I could move in immediately; she seemed relieved that I didn't ask for time to think it over. She said: "You'll feel fine in his atmosphere, he was an educated gentleman." I knew whom she meant, without her adding the name. She took me out, calling into the kitchen. "The young man is coming right back. He's getting his baggage." The housekeeper (whose name I have forgotten, since I nicknamed her the "Executioner" on the spot) appeared and said, still smiling: "He doesn't have to be afraid, no one'll bite him here." She stood in the doorway to the kitchen; huge and massive, she filled the space out completely as she leaned back with her arms against the doorposts, as though intending to leap out at you. I paid her no heed and went to get my things.

During the first few days that I spent in the new room, the apartment was very quiet. Early in the morning, I left for the

Chemical Laboratory; at lunchtime, I stayed near the university, usually eating at the self-service section of Regina's. In the evening, when the laboratory closed, Veza would pick me up. We would take a walk, or go to her place. It was very late, perhaps eleven, by the time I came back to Haidgasse. I always found my bed ready, but never knew who had prepared it for me. I never gave it a second thought; I must have taken it for granted that the housekeeper saw to it. At night, I never heard a sound. Frau Weinreb, who lived and slept in the adjacent room, moved soundlessly in soft felt slippers; I imagined her gliding on them from picture to picture, performing her devotions.

At the end of the week, I came home early one evening; I was invited to the theater and I wanted to change. I sensed that someone was in my room. I entered and froze. In front of my bed stood a peasant girl, leaning way over, her voluptuous white arms plunging into my featherbed, which she was puffing up. She didn't seem to hear me come in, for she bent even deeper, turning a simply enormous backside toward me and powerfully banging the featherbed over and over, almost as if trying to thrash it. Her radiant yellow hair was twisted into thick braids and bound upon her head, which just touched the high featherbed in her bent position. Her rustic attribute was the pleated skirt, which reached down to the floor. I couldn't overlook the skirt, it was right in front of my nose. She punched the featherbed a few more times, as though she had no inkling that I was behind her. Since I didn't see her face, I didn't want to be the first to speak. I cleared my throat in embarrassment. She decided to hear this, straightened up, and whirled around with such a full, swinging motion that she almost grazed me. There we stood, face to face, with perhaps just enough room between us for a sheet of paper, nothing more. She was taller than I and very beautiful, like a Northern Madonna. She held out her arms as if about to grab me in lieu of the featherbed; but then she slowly dropped them and blushed. I sensed that she was able to blush at will. A yeastlike smell emanated from her. I could feel her beauty. And had she been as naked as her arms, I would have lost my head, since I was so close to her; any other man would have lost his head, too. But I remained motionless and silent. She finally opened her very small lips and said in a chirping voice: "I am Ružena, sir." The name, which I had been carrying about for a while, had its effect. And the "sir" was not in vain; for I didn't deserve more than a "young sir," according to Viennese usage. Her way of addressing me made me an experienced man whom a woman would give in to without resistance. However, the squeaky voice completely wrecked the impact of her appearance and devotion. It sounded like a tiny chick trying to speak. And everything that had been there earlier, the powerful white arms belaboring the featherbed, the radiant braids, the towering mountain of her behind, which had something enigmatic about it, although it didn't lure me—everything dissolved in the lamentable sounds. And even the name, which had filled me with expectation, no longer existed; it could have been any name. Ružena's magic was utterly wiped out. It must have been a woeful creature that she could seduce with that voice.

This thought flashed through my mind even before I returned her greeting. And my response was so cold and indifferent that she, squeaking more quickly, apologized for being in my room. She said she didn't mean to be in the way, she was only making my bed; she had made it every evening, and hadn't realized I'd be coming home so early. I grew more and more disdainful, merely saying, "Yes, yes." And as she left, moving rather nimbly for her size, I recalled the entire story from the newspapers and also what I had learned by word of mouth.

The young man (my predecessor) had come home from the bank one evening and found her in front of the bed. She had involved him in a conversation and seduced him on the spot. He was very timid and inexperienced, and—a rare case in Vienna—he had never had a mistress. The aunt had recognized his helplessness and brought charges against him for breach of promise. He denied everything, and given the sort of man he was, the court would have believed his innocence. But Ružena was pregnant and he was sentenced to pay her a reparation. His helplessness made him the butt of universal mockery. Everyone felt he was innocent, but that was the very reason why the case created a sensation. The Viennese found it hilarious that this man of all people should be tried for seduction and breach of promise and found guilty.

Ružena made two or three more attempts with the bed in the evening. But she knew how unpromising the matter was. Her aunt had ferreted out long ago that I had a girlfriend, who sometimes called for me in the evening. And when the aunt saw that it was always the same girlfriend, she didn't put much stock in Ružena's making the bed. The few ensuing attempts were nothing more than routine. I soon forgot everything. And it was only a few weeks later, when I had a certain experience in the apartment, a very frightening experience, that I began to think about Ružena again.

One afternoon, coming home earlier than usual, I heard violent noises from the kitchen. A slashing as if on flesh, a squealing and squeaking, a pleading and begging, a whistling and whirring and slash, slash, slash! In between, a deep, very strict voice, whose words I could make out only when I recognized its owner. It sounded like a man's voice, but it belonged to the aunt: "Take that! And that! And that, and that, and that!" The whimpering and squealing rose higher and higher. It wouldn't stop, it actually increased. And the threats of the deep voice likewise grew stronger and quicker. I thought the noise would stop and I at first remained very quiet; but it didn't stop, it only got worse. I dashed into the kitchen. There, Ružena was kneeling in front of the table, her upper body naked. Next to her stood the aunt, holding a whip, which she was just raising, and she then struck Ružena's back with it, slash!

They were grouped in such a way that anyone entering the kitchen could see both of them right in the eye. There was nothing to overlook: Ružena's breasts and Ružena's back, the furious expression on the Executioner's hideous face, the whistling whip. But it didn't sound as awful as it had sounded in my room. For when I saw it and didn't merely hear it, I couldn't *believe* it, it was like a stage play, but a lot nearer and so well arranged that you couldn't help seeing it. I also knew it had to stop now, for I made sure to make myself noticeable, despite the noise. Instead of dropping the whip, the aunt held it up for a while. But Ružena made a mistake and squealed as though the whip had struck her again. The aunt yelled at her: "Aren't you ashamed! Naked." And then the aunt addressed me point-blank: "Bad girl! Won't obey aunt. Must be punished."

Ružena had stopped squealing. Having been ordered to feel ashamed, she squeezed both hands to her breasts, which welled up and became even more visible. Then she crawled behind the table as slowly as possible, a true floor monster, no less massive than the aunt, who was rooted in front of me. The aunt continued the parental scolding, which was supposed to explain the scene. "Must obey, child. Must learn has aunt only, no one in world. Bad child. Lost without aunt. But aunt looks! Aunt watches!"

These words didn't come out quickly, they were heavy, weighty. And after every sentence, the helpful whip twitched. But she didn't lash her victim now; the back of the culpable child, who was now cowering on the other side of the table, was out of reach. The child's nakedness was even more perceptible in her hiding place. She was certainly excitingly feminine; but the childish words aimed at the luxuriant creature reduced her to something idiotic. Her humility, which was part of the scene, perhaps the most important part to be demonstrated, disgusted me no less than the executioner behavior of the aunt. I left the kitchen as though I *believed* the scene: the disobedient child had received her punishment.

When I vanished from the kitchen without hinting at my embarrassment and returned to my room, *I* had become the idiot for the two of them. And this was what saved me from any further attacks.

Now, I had my peace and quiet, and I saw no more of them—whether in tandem or Ružena alone. I sometimes heard the aunt talking to Frau Weinreb in the next room. There was no whipping, but I was very surprised to hear the aunt talking in the same tone to the widow, as if to a child. However, it sounded more propitiatory than threatening. It was obvious that Frau Weinreb had done something she shouldn't have; but I couldn't imagine what, and I gave it no further thought. It wasn't pleasant to hear the Executioner's voice, separated from me by only a wall; and I was always prepared for an embarrassing outburst. But there was never a squealing or a whimpering; I only heard something that sounded like a solemn promise. Frau Weinreb had a deep, dark voice; I would have liked to go on hearing it; I was almost sorry when it stopped.

One night, I awoke and saw somebody in my room. Frau Weinreb in a bathrobe was standing in front of the picture of her husband; she gingerly took it from the wall and gazed behind it, as if searching for something. I saw her very clearly: the room was lit up by the street lights; the curtains weren't drawn. She glided along with her nose very close to the wall; she kept sniffing while gingerly clutching the picture with both hands. Then, just as slowly, she sniffed the back of the picture. It was so still in the room that the sniffing was audible. Her face, which I couldn't see because her back was turned, had always seemed canine to me. With a swift movement, she put the picture back and then glided along the adjacent wall to the next picture. This picture was much larger; it had a heavy frame; I wondered whether she was strong enough to hold it by herself. But I didn't leap out of bed to help her. I thought she was sleepwalking; I didn't want to frighten her. She took down this picture, too, and held it securely; but now, her sniffing on the wall behind it wasn't as soft, I could hear her strenuously panting and moaning. Then she stumbled, she looked as if she were dropping the picture, but she managed to set it down on the floor, its face against the wall, without letting go of it entirely. She straightened up again, and while her fingertips still touched the top of the frame, she continued to sniff the place of the picture on the wall. Upon finishing, she crouched down again and tackled the back of the painting. I thought she was sniffing again, it was the same noise that I had gotten used to in this brief time. But now, I was astonished to see that she was licking the back of the painting. She licked it sedulously. Her tongue hung way out, like a dog's. She had become a dog, and seemed glad. It took her quite a while to finish: the picture was big. She stood up, strenuously raised it, and, making no attempt to look at the front or even touch it, she hung the painting on its nail and glided silently and quickly to the next. In my room, there were four pictures of Herr Dr. Weinreb. She neglected none; she took care of all four. Luckily, the remaining two were the size of the first; so she could do her job standing; and since she didn't crouch on the floor again, she was content to sniff.

Then she left my room. I thought of the many pictures of her deceased husband in her room, and I assumed that this same procedure could easily take half the night. I wondered whether she hadn't come here on earlier nights, for the same purpose, without my noticing, because I had been fast asleep. I made up my mind to get used to sleeping more lightly, so that this wouldn't happen again. I wanted to be awake when she was here.

Backenroth

In my third semester, I moved from the old "smoky" Institute at the beginning of Währingerstrasse to the new

Chemical Institute at the corner of Boltzmanngasse. The qualitative analysis of the first two semesters was now followed by quantitative analysis under Professor Hermann Frei. Frei was a small, thin man, who, without tormenting others with it, consisted largely of a sense of order, thus being highly suitable for quantitative analysis. He had cautious, almost delicate, movements, liked showing how something could be performed in a very clean way, and, since analysis involved minimal amounts of matter, he seemed virtually weightless. His gratitude for goodness exceeded the normal measures. He had no talent for impressing his students with scientific sentences. His forte was the practical side, the concrete procedures of analysis; in this, he was deft, sure, and skillful; and for all his delicacy, there was something resolute about him.

Of his utterances, the most impressive were those evincing his devotion, and they were often repeated. He had been an assistant to Professor Lieben, who had furthered his career, and Frei sometimes quoted him, although only in the following emphatic and ceremonious way: "As my highly venerated teacher, Professor Dr. Adolf Lieben, used to say . . ." This chemist had left a good name behind. His fans had established a foundation bearing his name and devoted to the promotion of science and its adepts. On Professor Frei's tongue, Lieben became a mythical figure, merely by the way that Frei spoke his name, without saying very much about him. However, there was a figure of the past who meant a lot more to Frei, although he spoke of him more seldom and never mentioned him by name. It was a specific sentence, always the same, with which he referred to him. And such intense ardor filled his small, thin body at those moments that you marveled, even though there was no one anywhere in the Chemical Institute who shared Frei's faith.

"When my Kaiser comes, I will walk on my knees all the way to Schönbrunn!" Frei was the only person expecting and desiring the emperor's return. And if we recall that the old emperor, Franz Joseph, had still been alive just ten years earlier, it is surprising that no one, literally no one, even understood this wish. Everyone, both his assistants and his students, regarded those dogmatic words as a symptom of madness. And perhaps this was why the sentence was uttered with such vehemence and resolution. For notwithstanding his naïveté, Professor Frei had no illusions: he was utterly alone in his ardent wish for the return of the Kaiser. I wondered whom he meant when he said, "My Kaiser": the young one, with whom we associated nothing definite, or Kaiser Franz Joseph alive again.

Perhaps it was because of his highly venerated teacher, Professor Dr. Adolf Lieben, the scion of a prominent Jewish banking family, that Professor Frei didn't show the slightest animosity toward Jews. He was anxious to be just and treated every student according to his merits. His sense of justice went so far that he never pronounced the names of Galician Jews any differently from other names; whereas there were one or two assistants who found such names irresistibly funny. If Frei wasn't present, then it could happen that such a name was drawled and pleasurably melted on the tongue. There was one student, just imagine, named Josias Kohlberg, a smart, merry lad, whose mood was never ruined by any interrogative drawling of his name. He did his work deftly and ably, never sucked up to anyone, never cringed before anyone, and never felt the least desire to have anything but strictly professional dealings with any of the assistants. Alter Horowitz, who worked next to him, was his mournful antipode; his voice was muted, his movements were slow. While Kohlberg always reminded you of a soccer player, you pictured Alter Horowitz bent over a book, although I never once saw him with a book that he didn't need for chemical purposes.

These two students complemented each other nicely and were inseparable; they did everything together, like twins, and you might have thought they didn't need anyone else. But this was a mistake; for right near them, worked a third student who also came from their native Galicia: Backenroth. I never knew his first name, or else it has slipped my mind. He was the only *beautiful* person in our laboratory, tall and slender, with very bright, deeply radiant eyes and reddish hair. He seldom talked to anyone, for he knew almost no German, and he rarely looked into anyone's face. But if he *did* ever look at you, you were reminded of young Jesus as he is sometimes shown in paintings. I knew nothing about him and felt timid in his presence. I knew his voice; he spoke Yiddish or Polish to his two fellow Galicians. And when I noticed him talking, I automatically drew closer, in order to hear his voice, though I understood nothing. His voice was soft and strange and extremely tender, so that I wondered whether it was the twittering sounds of Polish that feigned so much tenderness. But his voice sounded no different when he spoke Yiddish. I told myself that this, too, was a tender language, and I was no wiser than before.

I noticed that Horowitz and Kohlberg spoke differently to him than to each other. Horowitz didn't let himself go in his melancholy and he sounded more businesslike than usual; Kohlberg made no jokes and almost seemed to be standing at attention and holding a soccer ball in front of Backenroth. It was clear that both of them looked up to him; but I never had the nerve to ask why they were so respectful or cautious. He was taller than they, but also more innocent and more sensitive; it was as if they had to initiate him into certain situations of life and protect him against these situations. Yet he never lost the light that radiated from him. A friendly colleague, with whom I discussed this matter and who wanted to escape this effect, which he too sensed, made an attempt at humor; he said the effect was nothing but the color of the hair, not really red, not really blond, but in between; that was why it shone like the rays of the sun. Incidentally, the assistants, too, were timid with Backenroth. Because of his language difficulties, they usually communicated with him via

Horowitz or Kohlberg. And it was strange to hear how different his name sounded in their mouths, withdrawn, nay, timid; whereas they spread themselves mockingly over *Horowitz* and *Kohlberg*.

Unmistakably, both of them, especially Kohlberg, were trying to shield Backenroth from insults, which *they* could defend themselves against, which *they* were accustomed to. He struck me as being protected by his ignorance of German, but also by something that I rather hesitantly call radiance. Hesitantly, because at that time, I was not biased in favor of any superiority or sublimity, whether profane or religious, and I tended to carp and cavil at such things. Yet I never entered the laboratory without making sure that Backenroth was at his place, in his white smock, busy with retorts and Bunsens, which scarcely suited him. When working in the laboratory, he looked almost disguised; I didn't trust this costume and waited for him to throw it off and emerge in his true shape. Yet I had no clear notion of his true shape. Only one thing was certain: in this very busy chemical milieu, where people were dissolving, boiling, distilling, weighing, he was out of place. He was a crystal, but not a hard, insensitive crystal. He was a feeling crystal, which no one should take hold of.

When I looked over at his place and saw him standing there, I felt calmed, but only temporarily. The very next day, I was uncertain again and feared his absence. My neighbor, Eva Reichmann, my Russian friend from Kiev, with whom I talked about everything, was the only person whom I could tell about my anxieties concerning Backenroth. I played with these fears a bit; I didn't take them quite seriously. And she, who was bewitchingly serious—everything concerning human beings was holy to her—rebuked me, saying: "You talk as if he were ill. But he's not at all ill. He's merely beautiful. Why are you so impressed by male beauty?"

"Male? Male? He's got the beauty of a saint. I don't know

what he's doing here. What does a saint have to do in a chemical laboratory? He's going to vanish suddenly."

We deliberated for a long time on how he would vanish. Would he dissolve into red mist and rise to the sun from which he had come? Or would he give up chemistry and transfer to a different faculty? Which one? Eva Reichmann would have liked to see him as a new Pythagoras. The connection of geometry with the stars and the music of the spheres struck her as the right thing for him. She knew a lot of Russian poems by heart, which she liked reciting to me, but didn't like translating. She was an excellent student, and had an easier time with physical chemistry than any of her male colleagues did. "This is the easiest part," she would say about mathematics. "As soon as mathematics comes into it, it's child's play."

She was tall and voluptuous; no fruit had a skin as seductive as her skin. While she emitted mathematical formulas with fascinating ease, as if they were part of conversation (not solemn, like poetry), one would have liked to stroke her cheeks. You didn't dare think about her breasts, which heaved stormily during our verbal clashes. Perhaps we were in love. But since everything took place in a Dostoevsky novel and not in our world, we never admitted our feelings for one another. Only today, fifty years later, do I realize that we each had all the symptoms of being in love. Our sentences entwined like hair, the embraces of our words went on for hours and hours, the tedious chemical procedures left us enough time. And just as lovers deprive the people near them of their specific weight by drawing them into their love talk and misuse them to heighten their own excitement, so too our minds orbited around Backenroth. We kept saying how worried we were that we might *lose* him; and thus the danger he was really in evanesced.

I asked Eva Reichmann whether she wanted to talk to him. She resolutely shook her head: "In what language?"

She had been brought up in Russian. She was twelve when her family, one of the wealthiest in Kiev, left the city. They moved to Czernowitz, where she attended a German school; but her German still sounded soft, like that of a Russian. Her family had lost most of their wealth, though by no means all. But she never spoke resentfully about the Russian Revolution. She used to say with profound conviction: "No one should be that rich." And though we were talking about inflation profiteers in Austria, one sensed that she was also thinking about the past wealth of her own family. She had never spoken Yiddish at home. I had the impression that this language was as alien to her as to me; she regarded it neither as something special, nor with the tenderness one feels toward a language that is about to vanish. Her fate was the great Russian literature: she was utterly obsessed by it; she thought and felt in terms of the characters in Russian novels. And though it would have been difficult to find a person with more natural and spontaneous feelings, everything assumed the forms that she knew from Russian books. She stubbornly resisted my suggestion to try Polish with Backenroth. I assumed that, with some goodwill, a Russian could understand Polish; but she refused—either because she really didn't understand Polish, or because, having taken in Dostoevsky with her mother's milk, she had also absorbed his prejudices against everything Polish. Whenever I tried pleading with her to make the attempt, she fought me with my own weapons: "Do you want me to speak a broken Polish to him? The Poles set great store by their language. I don't know their literature. But they have one. So do the Russians." This last sentence was brief, since she was fundamentally opposed to all chauvinism; that was why she didn't say anything more than "So do the Russians."

She avoided talking to Backenroth for lack of a common tongue. Sharing my "sublime" conception of him, she was slightly bothered when she heard him talking to Kohlberg or

Horowitz. She despised Kohlberg because he looked like a soccer player and was always whistling some ditty. She found Horowitz uninteresting because he looked "like any Jew." She took seriously those Jews who had totally assimilated to some language by way of the literature, but without becoming berserk nationalists. And since she consistently rejected national prejudices, she was left with only some against Jews who had bogged down on the road to this free mentality. She was not at all certain whether Backenroth had gotten this far. "Perhaps he's just a young Chassidic rebbe," she once said, to my dismay, "but doesn't realize it yet." It turned out that she was no lover of the Chassidim. "They're fanatics," she said. "They're devoted to their faith in miracles; they drink and hop around. They have no mathematics in their bodies." It never crossed her mind that mathematics was *her* faith in miracles. However, she nourished our conversation about Backenroth. This was the love talk that we *permitted* ourselves. For I belonged to another woman, whom she had seen calling for me at the laboratory. Eva Reichmann was far too proud to yield to an emotion for someone who let on that he was attached. So long as we talked about Backenroth, our feelings remained unnamed and the fear of his suddenly vanishing became a fear for the extinction of our feelings for each other.

One morning, he wasn't there; no one stood at his place. I assumed he'd be late and I said nothing. Then I noticed how fidgety Eva was; she avoided my eyes. "All three of them are out," she finally said. "Something must have happened." No one was standing at Kohlberg's or Horowitz's place either, and I had failed to notice; she didn't see him in such isolation as I did, she always saw him with the other two, the only people he talked with. Seeing him with them calmed her a bit; she didn't want to fully admit his isolation, which I feared.

"They're at some religious celebration," I said. I tried to see a favorable sign in the absence of all three and not just him alone. But she seemed distraught precisely because all three were out. "It's a bad sign," she said. "Something has happened to him, and the other two are with him."

"You think he's sick," I said, a bit annoyed, "but that wouldn't keep both of them away from the laboratory."

"Fine," she said, trying to assuage me. "If he *is* sick, then one will look in on him and the other will come here."

"No," I said, "the two of them never separate. Have you ever seen either of them doing anything without the other?"

"That's probably why they live together. Have you ever been to their room?"

"No, but I know they share a room. He lives very close to them, three doors away."

"You certainly *have* ferreted out a lot! Are you a detective?"

"I once followed them from the laboratory. Kohlberg and Horowitz walked him home. Then they said goodbye to him very formally, as if he were a stranger, and they walked back a few paces to their house. They didn't notice me."

"Why did you do that?"

"I wanted to find out whether he lives alone. Maybe I figured that when he was finally alone, I'd suddenly pop up next to him, sort of by accident, and say hello. I'd have acted very surprised, as though it really *were* an accident, and then we'd definitely have gotten into a conversation."

"But in what language?"

"That's not hard. I can communicate with people who don't know a word of German. I learned how from my grandfather."

She laughed: "You talk with your hands. That's not nice. It doesn't suit you."

"I wouldn't do it normally. But that's how we'd have broken the ice. Do you know how long I've been wanting to talk to him!"

"Perhaps I *should* have tried Russian. I didn't realize it was so important to you."

Thus we talked about nothing but him; and their places remained empty. The morning waned, and we made an effort to forget. I changed the subject and talked about a book I had started reading the day before: Poe's tales. She didn't know them, and I told her about one, "The Telltale Heart," which had really terrified me. But while I tried to free myself of this terror by repeating the story to her, I kept feeling my fear grow and grow with every glance at the empty place, until Fräulein Reichmann said, "I'm so scared I feel sick."

At that moment, Professor Frei appeared in the laboratory with his retinue (usually there were two, this time there were four people). He made a vague motion for us to come closer, waited a bit until most of the people in the laboratory were standing in front of him, and then he said, "Something very sad has happened. I have to tell you. Herr Backenroth poisoned himself with cyanide last night." He stood there a while. Then he shook his head, saying: "He seems to have been very lonely. Didn't any of you notice anything?" Professor Frei received no answer: the news was too horrifying; there was no one in the room who didn't feel guilty, and yet no one had done anything to him. That was it: no one had made any attempt.

As soon as the professor left the room with his train, Fräulein Reichmann lost control and sobbed heartrendingly, as if she had lost her brother. She had none, and now he had become her brother. I realized that something had happened between us as well; but compared with the death of the twenty-one-year-old, it had little significance. I also knew, just as she did, that we had exploited the strange presence of the young man for our conversation. He had stood between us month after month; we had grown hot with his beauty; he was our secret, which we kept from ourselves, but also from him. Neither of us had spoken to him, not she nor I; and what excuses we had devised to justify this silence to each other! Our friendship shattered on the guilt we felt. I never forgave myself, nor did I forgive her. When I hear her sentences again today in my memory, the sentences whose strange tone enchanted me, I feel anger, and I know that I failed to do the one thing that would have saved him: instead of toying with her, I should have talked her into loving him.

The Rivals

There was someone else in the laboratory who rarely spoke. But in his case, it wasn't due to ignorance of German. He came from the countryside, I believe from a village in Upper Austria, and he looked shy and hungry. The poor clothes he wore, always the same, hung baggily on him; perhaps they had been handed down to him from someone else. Or perhaps he had lost a lot of weight since living in the city, for he most certainly had nothing to eat. *His* hair didn't shine; it was a wan, weary red, which fitted his pale, sickly face. His name was Hund [dog], but what an odd dog that never opened its mouth. He never even returned anyone's "good morning." If he did take notice of the greeting, then he merely nodded morosely, usually glancing away. He never asked anyone for help, he never borrowed anything from anyone, and he never requested information. He'll collapse any moment, I thought to myself, whenever I looked in his direction. He was anything but skillful and spent a long time on his analyses. But his movements were so terse and meager that you couldn't tell what a difficult time he was having. He never eased into anything; he would merely pull himself together, and no sooner had he commenced than it was already done.

Once, he found a sandwich at his place, still wrapped; someone had put it there, unnoticed. I suspected Fräulein Reichmann, who had a soft heart. He opened the package, saw what it contained, wrapped the sandwich up again, and took it from one person to another. He showed it to everyone, saying hatefully: "Is this yours?" And then went to the next person. He left no one out; it was the only time he ever spoke to everybody in the laboratory, but all he said was the same three words. No one claimed the package. Upon reaching the last person and obtaining the last "No," he lifted the small package aloft and cried in an ominous voice: "Is anyone hungry? This is going into the wastebasket!" No one responded, if only so as not to be considered the perpetrator of the abortive deed. Hund furiously hurled the small package—he suddenly appeared to have excess energy—into the wastebasket. And when a few voices became audible, daring to say, "Too bad," he hissed: "Why don't you fish it out!" No one would have thought him capable of being so articulate, much less decisive. Hund thus gained respect, and the charitable gift had not been in vain.

A few days later, he entered the laboratory with a small package, which he put down in the place of that sandwich. For a while, he left it there unopened while he tackled some of his lengthy and futile procedures. I was not the only person to wonder about this package. I soon stopped conjecturing that he had gotten his own sandwich and was flaunting it; the package looked as if it contained something angular. Then he picked it up and came over to me, dangled it before my eyes, and said: "Photos! Look!" It sounded like an order, and that was quite all right. No one had expected him to show anything to anyone. And just as they had previously noticed that he did nothing that had anything to do with anyone else, they now all instantly realized that he was making an offer. They came over to my place and formed a semicircle around him. He waited quietly, as though this were something he frequently experienced, until they had all gathered. Then he opened the package and held out one picture after another: excellent photographs of all sorts of things—birds, landscapes, trees, people, objects.

Thus he transformed himself from a poor, starving devil into an obsessed photographer, spending all his money on his passion. *This* was why he was so badly dressed and *this* was why he was starving. He heard cries of praise, which he countered with more pictures; he had dozens of pictures; there must have been fifty or sixty this first time, and their contrasts were astonishing; a few of the pictures were alike, and then all at once there was something different. He thus held us in his power. And when one woman said: "Why, Herr Hund, you're an artist!" and meant it, he smiled and didn't contradict her. One could see the word *artist* sliding down his throat; no food and no drink would have been so delicious. When the demonstration was over, we were all sorry. The same woman said: "How do you find your subjects, Herr Hund?" Her question was serious, as serious as her earlier astonishment. And he replied, dignified, but terse: "It's practice." To which a lover of locutions spouted: "Practice makes perfect." But no one laughed.

Hund was a master, and he sacrificed everything to his art. Food didn't matter, so long as he could take photographs. And he even seemed uninterested in his studies. One or two months passed before he showed up with a new package. His colleagues instantly gathered around him. They willingly marveled. The pictures were as varied as the first time. And soon it was an established fact that Hund came into the laboratory only to surprise us, his public, with new photos from time to time.

Not long after this second demonstration by Hund, a newcomer entered the laboratory, drawing everyone's attention: Franz Sieghart, a dwarf. He was well proportioned, his body fine, but delicate. The table was too high for him, so he set up his apparatuses on the floor. With his deft little fingers, he finished sooner than the rest of us. And while boiling and distilling down below, he spoke to us incessantly, indefatigably, in a penetrating, somewhat croaking voice, trying to convince us that he had experienced everything that a "big person" knew and a few things more. He announced the visit of his brother, who was taller than any of us, six feet four, a captain in the Austrian army. They resembled one another like two peas in a pod, he said; no one could tell them apart.

When the brother came in his uniform, you wouldn't be able to guess which was the chemist and which the officer. We believed a great deal that Sieghart said; he always knew better; his words had an enviable persuasive power; but we were skeptical about his brother's existence.

"If he were five six," said Fräulein Reichmann, "but six four! I just don't believe it. And why should he visit us in uniform?" After just a few hours of fiddling around on the floor, Sieghart had succeeded in commanding everyone's respect; and it wasn't long before he impressed the assistants with the results of his first analysis. He was done with these rather tedious chores faster than was normal; his tempo was adjusted to the deftness of his fingers. But the early announcement of his brother's visit was a mistake. We waited and waited. Of course, no one was so tactless as to remind Sieghart; but he seemed to read his neighbors' thoughts; from time to time, he said something about his brother himself. "He can't come this week. Military life is strict. You people don't realize how well off you are! He's often regretted going into the army. But he won't admit it. He's so tall, though—what else could he have done!" His brother's difficulties with his height came up in all sorts of variations. Actually, Franz Sieghart felt sorry for him, but he did respect him and found words of reverence, because his brother had made it all the way up to captain, young as he was.

Eventually, however, it became boring, and people stopped listening. No sooner was the brother mentioned than people closed their ears. Sieghart, accustomed to making others listen, suddenly felt the blank wall around him and quickly changed the topic of his size. There wasn't just the brother, there were also girls. All the girls that Sieghart knew were, if not gigantic like the brother, then a natural size. But here, the point was variety and number rather than height. Not that he was crass or revealed intimate details about their appearance; he was the perfect gentleman, protecting each one of his girls. He never mentioned their names. But in order to distinguish among them and to let people know whom he was talking about, he numbered them, preceding a number with his statement about that particular girl. "My girlfriend no. 3 is standing me up. She has to work overtime at her office. I'll comfort myself and go to the movies with no. 4."

He said he had photos of all of them. He photographed every single one. This was what his girls liked most: being photographed by him. The first question at every rendezvous was: "Listen, will you take a few photos of me today?"

"Be patient, just be patient," he would then say. "There's a time and a place for everything. Each one will have her turn." They were especially keen on nude photos, he said. All of them decent pictures. But he could only show them, he said, if you didn't see the faces. He wouldn't be guilty of indiscretions. He would show us a few. Someday, he'd bring in a whole pile of photos. Nothing but nude photos of girls. But he was in no hurry. We would have to be patient. Once he got started, he said, people would badger him: "Sieghart, do you have any new nude photos?" However, he couldn't think about such things; he had other things on his mind besides his girls. And we would have to learn to bide our time. When the day came, he would ask the female colleagues to step aside; this was nothing for their chaste eyes. This was strictly for men. But mind you, he emphasized, he took only decent photos.

Sieghart knew how to heighten the curiosity in the room. He brought a well-tied shoebox into the laboratory and locked it up in his locker for the time being. But then he wasn't satisfied with the storage place; he took the box out, put it back in, thought about it, said, "It's better here," took it out again, and declared, "I have to be careful. I shouldn't tell you people. It's full of nude photos. I'm sure there's no thief among you." He kept finding new reasons to turn the box over and over in front of us. "No one's going to open it behind my back. I know the way I tied it up. I know it precisely. If even the slightest thing happens to it, I'll take the box home again, and I'll never show you the photos! Does everyone understand?" It sounded like a threat, and it *was* a threat, for now everyone believed in the content of the box. Fräulein Reichmann, who was prudish, could repeat all she liked: "You know, Herr Sieghart, no one's interested in your shoebox." Sieghart responded: "Oho!" and winked at every male in the room. A few winked back, and everyone knew why she longed to see the content of the box.

Sieghart kept us on tenterhooks for weeks. He had heard about the master photographer among us, Hund, and had us describe Hund's subjects in exact detail. He then made a face and declared: "Old-fashioned! It's all old-fashioned! There were photographers just like that in the old days. Mind you, I'm all in favor of nature. But anyone can do that. All you have to do is go outdoors and snap, snap, snap, you've got a dozen photos right off. That's what I call old-fashioned. It's so easy! But when it comes to my girls, I have to seek them out. You've got to find them first. Then I have to court them. Mind you, in the summer, it's not so hard when you're swimming. But in the winter, you've got to warm them up. Otherwise, she just says no, and that's that. I tell you, I'm experienced. No one turns me down. Every girl lets me photograph her. Now you people may think it's because I'm small, because they think of me as a child. Wrong! Far from it. I let them notice what they're up against with me. I'm just as much of a man for them as any other man. First, they have their triumph in front of the camera—you ought to see how *proud* they are!—and then they get a picture! One each, no more, *one* copy of each photograph, if it comes out well. I don't ask for a thing. But I have to think of the overhead. If a girl wants more copies, she has to pay. Some of them do want more copies, for their boyfriends. I earn a pretty penny on them, I tell you, there's nothing wrong with money."

This shed light on the great number of Sieghart's friendships. The "friendship" consisted of his being the girl's personal photographer. But he made sure that this point didn't get any clearer, and he had an original phrase for this purpose: "Please, not a soul will learn anything more definite from me. There *is* such a thing as discretion. For me, discretion is a matter of honor. My girlfriends know that. They know me as well as I know them!"

One morning, a uniformed giant stood in the doorway and asked for Franz Sieghart. So anxious were we to see the photos of girls that we had forgotten all about the brother, and we marveled at the tall captain, whose body ended in a very small head and who wore Franz Sieghart's face—like a mask. Someone pointed to where the dwarf was working. He was kneeling on the floor, gingerly inserting a Bunsen burner with a small flame under a retort of alcohol. Recognizing his brother's legs in the uniform, he sprang up and crowed: "Hi! Welcome. Chemistry Laboratory for Quantitative Analysis greets you. Let me introduce you to my colleagues. First, the ladies. C'mon, don't be coy. We know all about you!" The captain had blushed. "He's shy, you know," the dwarf declared. "Chasing after nude photos—that's not his cup of tea!"

This suggestive remark completely intimidated the brother. He was just trying to bow to one of our ladies when the dwarf mentioned the photos. The captain's body flew up straight, in midbow, his face brick-red—a red that our dwarf could never have become. Now the faces of the two brothers were easy to tell apart. "Don't worry," said the little one. "I'll spare you. He's so polite, you just can't imagine. Everything has to run smoothly, just like soldiers on review. Now, that was the Greek lady, and this is the Russian lady. And here, for a change, a Viennese girl, Fräulein Fröhlich [merry]. A credit to her name, always laughing, without anyone tickling her. But the Russian lady doesn't care for such jokes. No man would dare tickle her calves, not even I, although I'm the right size to do it." Fräulein Reichmann made a face and turned away. The captain shrugged lightly to express regret at his brother's impudence; and the dwarf had already noticed that the captain liked Fräulein Reichmann's restraint:

"She's a fine lady. Highly educated, an excellent family. But out of the question. What do you think? Every man would like to have a bite. You've got to control yourself. Pull yourself together, please. You're accustomed to doing so as an officer."

Then it was our turn. However, the dwarf kept his brother on a leash and wouldn't let go for long. Each of us was introduced. He found an accurate satirical formula for everyone. It turned out that the dwarf had observed us carefully. And though the manner of his introduction was mordant rather than considerate toward his colleagues, everything raced by, in rapid succession, so that we couldn't stop laughing. We were behind with our mirth, we were still laughing when he was two people ahead of us with his comments. It was considered lucky that Hund wasn't in the laboratory that day. From the very beginning, he had glared at Sieghart with undisguised hatred, even before the nude photos had come up. It was as if, at the very first sight of Sieghart, Hund had sensed the misfortune that would strike him because of the dwarf's zealous activities. Sieghart had never addressed Hund directly, although he had asked people what sort of photos his were, and he had never concealed his scorn for them. But now, Sieghart would have mentioned Hund by name and said something about him, for he introduced his brother to everyone, even Wundel, our village idiot, who led a rather underground existence. Thus, Sieghart couldn't have avoided saying something about Hund; and given Hund's obvious sensitivity, the outcome would have been terrible.

Actually, the entire presentation didn't last all that long. Sieghart seemed to have us in his pocket along with his brother. He pulled each of us out in turn; and as soon as that person had gotten his share, Sieghart put him aside again. The brother, however, came out of the frying pan into the fire. He received as much scorn as all of us together. I began to understand why he was in uniform. Fleeing the dwarf's domineering ways and eternal sarcasm, the brother had sought refuge in the army. There, orders were at least expected, and he didn't have to fear the little one's unpredictable flashes. I wondered why the captain had even bothered dropping in. He must have known what to expect from his brother. My question was answered right after he took leave of us.

"I told him to come and have a look at chemistry, if he's got the gumption. People aren't as well behaved here as in the army, you can talk while you're working. But *he* always thinks people should keep quiet during work. Everybody has to keep his mouth shut, like a recruit. Can you imagine how often I've badgered him to come! 'You're chicken, that's right, you're chicken,' I told him. 'You don't know real life. In the army, you're all protected, like historical landmarks. Nothing can happen to you. War is a thing of the past. There won't be any new wars ever.' Why do we need an army? We need it for cowards who are scared of life. He's six feet four and he's scared of chemistry! Blushes in front of every female. We've got five ladies in the room and he blushes five times. Why, I wouldn't be able to stop blushing at all with my eight numbers, that's how many there are now. Incidentally, I told him about our ladies. Especially the fine Russian lady. She's something for you, I said. She doesn't look right, she doesn't look left, but it's education, not cowardice! Well, he was scared long enough. But he finally did come, after all. And now you've seen the guy! Six feet four—you almost have to be ashamed of a brother that tall. What a scaredy-cat! He's scared of me! When we were children, he was so scared of me, he cried. Now, he doesn't show it so much. But he's still scared of me. Did any of you notice? He's *afraid* of me! What a scaredy-cat! The captain is afraid. What a laugh! I'm not afraid. He could learn something from me."

Sieghart's braggadocio was sometimes annoying because of its loud volume, but it didn't hurt his work. He progressed nimbly and skillfully with his analyses; but he also had sympathy for Wundel, the swindler, who looked like a village idiot, cautiously grinning as he stole through the room with the tiny glass jar of substance in his crooked hand, which was concealed in the right pocket of his smock. He zigzagged softly from person to person, never in the expected order, suddenly standing in front of you, his eyes pleading, close to your face, as he said: "Herr Colleague, do you know this? It smells like a forest." He held the open jar under your nose, you inhaled the smell deeply, looked at the substance, and said: "Yes, of course, I know that. I've made it." Or: "No, I don't know it." If the former were the case, Wundel wanted to know how you had made it. He asked to borrow your notebook with the weights and calculations, and you lent it to him briefly. Then he secretly wrote down the results and, full of confidence, tackled the experiments, knowing the outcome in advance.

Everyone knew he cheated, but no one gave him away. He arranged things in such a manner that no one knew everything about him. When he had set up his apparatuses and his retorts were bubbling, when he weighed his jar with pinched lips, one assumed he was doing his work and merely checking the results against the figures he had begged from various sources. Had we known that all his work processes were bogus from start to finish, that he never did more than offer a *semblance* of working, we would certainly have hesitated to support him so consistently. He never went to the same colleague twice, he zigzagged in such a way as to avoid those whom he had already used. And though you saw him sneaking to and fro every few weeks, you weren't always clear about the results of his discreet investigations. His real talent was a knack for tricking people into underestimating him. Such systematic cunning was the last thing you would have attributed to this grinning pancake. For that was just what his mask looked like. His eyes, like those of a mushroom gatherer, were always on the ground; his grin fitted them as badly as his high drawling voice.

Since he had to be quiet in his doings, he avoided Sieghart, who always spoke loudly. However, Wundel couldn't prevent Sieghart from soon recognizing him as a mushroom gatherer and greeting him as such. "We've met before, Herr Colleague!" Sieghart sonorously addressed him, and Wundel recoiled in terror. "And do you know where we met? It was a long time ago! And now, just you guess where! You can't remember? I remember everything. I've got the memory of an elephant."

Wundel flailed his arms helplessly as if trying to swim out of the laboratory. But it was no use. Sieghart grabbed hold of a low button on Wundel's smock and repeated several times: "Well, you still don't remember? Gathering mushrooms, of course. Where else? In the forest. I always see you gathering mushrooms. But you're always looking at the ground. You only have eyes for mushrooms. Oh, well, that's why you always get your basket filled with mushrooms. Me too, me too, because I'm so close to the ground. I don't even know who's got more mushrooms in his basket, you or I. But I also have a good look at the people. I'm a nosy bastard. It comes from my photography. What would you do now if I showed you a snapshot of you gathering mushrooms? I caught you." *Caught* wasn't a word that Wundel liked to hear; the dwarf's affable chitchat was agony for Wundel. He did his best to avoid him in the future by arranging his zigzags more carefully. He didn't always succeed. Sieghart had taken a great fancy to him. Once he apostrophized someone with the aid of a particular flash of inspiration, he would never let that person go again. And Wundel, truly a connoisseur of mushrooms, was one of the dwarf's favorite victims.

However, this was merely a skirmish. He actually liked Wundel. Perhaps he sensed his cunning. For if anyone disparaged Wundel as the "village idiot," Sieghart would resolutely declare: "Wundel? He's no village idiot. He knows what he's doing. He won't be caught napping."

But still, Sieghart did set his sights on someone whom he

wanted to wipe out merely because of this man's reputation as a photographer.

The promising shoebox had been stowed away in Sieghart's locker for some time now. He did take the box out from time to time, amply turning it over in his hands—occasionally, he even began to untie it (the box was covered with knots). But no sooner had a fellow student noticed and taken a step or two toward the box than Sieghart paused, as though suddenly inspired, and said: "No, I don't feel like it today. You people don't deserve it. This is something you really have to earn the right to see!" He offered no information on what one had to do to earn this privilege. Sieghart was waiting for something, no one knew what, and he contented himself with luring the fools in the laboratory and making their mouths water by undoing a knot or two. The box was soon knotted up again and stowed away. And comments like "Who cares! There's probably nothing in the box!" didn't put Sieghart off.

Then, one day, Hund showed up with a new package, a very thick one this time; and he plopped it down by his place at the table. This wasn't like him. He had learned from Sieghart. The dwarf impressed many people; his boastful ways were attracting followers in the laboratory. Hund waited a bit, but not as long as the previous time. Then, louder than usual, he said: "I've got photos! Who wants to see them!"

"Do I *ever* want to see them!" crowed the dwarf. He was the first to dash over to Hund and station himself at his side. "I'm waiting!" he said provocatively, while the others, far more slowly, clustered around Hund. This time, everyone who could leave his work came over. "I got the place," said the dwarf. It was meant to sound cheerful, but it sounded hateful. And equally hateful was Hund's retort: "Stand in front of me, otherwise you won't see anything because of your size."

"It's not the size that counts, it's the pictures. Boy, am I excited. When he's done, I'll open up my big box. Nothing but nude photos of young women. I hope you haven't started specializing in nudes, Herr Colleague; that would be regretful—or are we still sticking to nature? A kitten in a window or a silver poplar in the wind? A snow landscape in the mountains last winter? I'd like a dear little village church, surrounded by the graveyard, and a couple of pious crosses. After all, the dead won't be forgotten. Or do you have a rooster on a dungheap, whereby I don't mean to say that you want to show us any crap, Herr Colleague. Please don't misunderstand. I mean a real rooster on a real dungheap!"

"If you don't go away, I won't show anything," said Hund. "Go away from my place or I won't show anything."

"He won't show anything! How will we ever get over it! Yes, indeed, I have no choice now." The dwarf was shouting. "I have to make amends with the nude photos of my young ladies! Come over to my place, dear colleagues. You'll have a wonderful time. It's worth the trouble. Not this!"

Sieghart grabbed two of his colleagues by their arms and, pinching them mightily, he pulled them over to his place. The others followed. The thing that had been awaited for so long was finally here. Who cared about Hund's fighting chaffinches. Only one person remained with Hund, and another stopped halfway, turning back to him irresolutely.

"Go ahead!" said Hund. "Now, I won't show anything. Today, I had something special. Just go and look at his shit!"

With his elbow, Hund pushed away the only person who had remained true to him, perhaps out of pity. Hund didn't rest until he stood at his place again, as totally alone as always. Nor did he make any effort to disturb Sieghart's performance. He stood, silent and gloomy, in front of his package, on which he had placed his right hand as if to protect it against insolent invasion.

Sieghart, meanwhile, was untying his shoebox. He worked lightning-fast; the box was already open; he was already taking out a whole pile of photos, scattering them across the table as if they were nothing special.

"Please, help yourselves, gentlemen. Ladies for all seasons, anyone can have a lady here. There's several for everyone. No false modesty now! Everyone can put together his own harem. Now what's this? Doesn't anyone have the courage to reach into happiness? Do I have to take you by the hand? So cowardly, gentlemen? I would never have dreamt. Just imagine, I had all these ladies before me *en nature!* I had to plunge right in and snap the shutter. Why, just think what would have happened if I hadn't been resolute and snapped quickly! These young ladies wouldn't have undressed a second time! What would they have thought of me! And what do the young ladies think of you now if you don't plunge right in!"

He grabbed the hand of the student closest to him and pulled it into the heap of pictures, making a trembling motion with the hand, as though it were recoiling at the splendors it wanted to plunge into. The dwarf thrust a good dozen pictures into the student's hand and cried: "The next gentleman, please!" Now, the others came of their own accord, and soon all of them were gaping stupidly at the unclad girls, who were by no means seductive in offering themselves to our eyes. It struck all spectators as a bit risky. What would happen if an assistant or even the professor with his retinue walked in? Yet one couldn't call these pictures indecent; otherwise, some of the students wouldn't have had the nerve to take hold of them in front of the others. Only it was embarrassing that the female students were excluded. And every man felt guilty about Fräulein Reichmann, whose place wasn't so far away (she gazed into the air, acting as if she heard nothing).

Hund, however, was totally forgotten. The students didn't even realize he was still in the room. Suddenly, he stood there, in the midst of the students and pictures, he spat and shrieked: "Sluts, nothing but sluts!" Then he vanished. But the atmosphere was no longer the same. Sieghart felt insulted on behalf of his lady friends. "My lady friends didn't deserve this," he said, quickly gathering the photos together. "Had I known, I wouldn't have brought anything. If my lady friends find out, it will be over between us. I must ask the gentlemen to observe utmost discretion. You mustn't breathe a word of this outside the laboratory. No apology will suffice, even if we go to the ladies together and beg them in unison to forgive us, over and over again—it won't help. There'll be nothing but silence. I *can* rely on your discretion, can't I, gentlemen? Nothing has been unpacked here, and the insulting word was not uttered. I, too, will keep silent. I won't even tell my big brother."

A Red-Haired Mormon

I spent the summer of 1926 with my brothers in Sankt Agatha, a village between Goisern and Lake Hallstatt. We found an old, lovely hotel, the former smithy, with a spacious tavern. It wasn't suitable for adolescent boys. But right next to it, there was a much smaller, newer boardinghouse, the Agatha Smithy, run by an old lady named Frau Banz. The rooms were small and modest, as was the dining room, which didn't have more than three or four tables. We sat at one table with the owner, a sturdy woman, who looked stricter than what she seemed like when she spoke. For it turned out that she wasn't prejudiced against unmarried couples.

The other guests were a pair of lovers: a middle-aged stage director, dark and bushy, somewhat ravaged-looking, always joking; and his extremely young, slender girlfriend, who was a lot taller than he, ash-blond, not unattractive, and highly impressed by his incessant talk. He always explained everything; there was nothing he didn't know better. He liked getting into conversations with me, for I talked back to him. He listened to what I said, he even seemed to take it seriously. But then he very soon started in himself, swept away everything I had said, mocked, joked, hissed, playing lots of individual roles as in the theater—and he never ended without imperiously gazing into the eyes of Affi, his girlfriend. She took it for granted that *he* should say the last word, not I. While she never attempted to say anything, I did try a couple of times. No sooner had he beaten me to the ground than I unexpectedly sprang up and refuted what he had said, which in turn elicited *his* mordant rejoinder. However, Herr Brettschneider wasn't malicious; it was simply part of his un-disturbed ownership of Affi that she never heard any other male speak too long, not even an adolescent. Frau Banz lis-tened wordlessly; she took no side, never revealing with even the slightest twitch of her face whom she agreed with. And yet we knew that she followed every twist and turn of the conversation.

Herr Brettschneider and Affi lived in a small room next to mine; the walls were thin; I could hear every sound from over there: whistles, teasing, giggling, and often a satisfied grunting. Only it was never silent. Perhaps Herr Brettschnei-der sometimes held his tongue when asleep; but if this was the case, I never noticed, for I was asleep myself at such times.

It was not surprising that we wondered about the dissimi-lar couple; they were the only guests aside from us.

However, something else preoccupied me more at this time: the swallows. There were countless swallows here; they nested in the marvelous old smithy. When I sat at the wooden table in the garden, writing in my notebooks, they darted over-head, very close to me. I kept watching them for hours and hours. I was spellbound. Sometimes, when my brothers wanted to go off, I said: "Go on ahead, I'll catch up, I just have to finish writing something." But I wrote very little. I mostly watched the swallows, and I just couldn't part from them.

For two days, there was a kermess in Sankt Agatha; this was the event that has remained brightest in my memory. The booths stood around the tremendous linden tree in the square in front of the old smithy. However, the booths also reached all the way to the house we were living in. Right under my window, a young man had set up a table with a huge pile of shirts. The hawker tossed the shirts about with a quick, violent motion, picked up one shirt, then another, but usually two or three, raised them aloft, and dropped them with a smack. And he kept shouting:

> "It makes no difference today
> Whether I have cash or hay!"

He shouted it with conviction, and with a nervous gesture, as though he wanted nothing more to do with his shirts, as though he wanted to throw all of them away. So peasant women kept coming over to his stand, to grab some of the shirts that had been chucked away. A few of the women skeptically examined a shirt, as if they knew something about shirts; he would yank the shirt out of their hands and throw it back at them, as if he wanted to give it away. And no woman who grabbed hold of a shirt failed to take it along; it was as if the shirt had stuck to her hands. When she paid, he didn't even appear to see the money. He tossed it away, into a large box, which filled up very quickly. The piles of shirts melted in a very brief time. I watched him from my window, which was right over his head; I had never seen anything so fast; and I kept hearing his shout:

> "It makes no difference today
> Whether I have cash or hay!"

I noticed that the seeming frivolity of his words infected the farmers' wives; they forked over their money as though it were nothing. Suddenly, not one shirt was left. His stand was bare. He raised his right arm, shouted, "Stop! One moment!" and vanished around the corner with the cardboard box of money. I couldn't see where he went; I thought he was done; and I left the window. But I hadn't even reached the door of my small room, when I heard that same call, even louder than before, if possible:

> "It makes no difference today," etc.

Piles of shirts were lying on the table again. He held them up with a bitter grimace and scornfully tossed them back. The farmers' wives approached from all sides and walked into his trap.

It was no huge fair. When I passed among the booths, I kept turning up at his stand again. No one else was as good a huckster. He did notice me; he had already noticed me in the window, and in one of the rare moments when he was alone at his stand, he asked me whether I was a student. I wasn't surprised, he looked like a student, and he was already pulling out his registration booklet from the University of Vienna and holding it under my nose. He was in his fourth semester of law and earned his living at fairs. "You see how easy it is," he said. "I could sell anything. But shirts are best. These dumb broads think you're giving them something." He despised his victims. After a week, he said, the shirts were in tatters, you could wear one four or five times, but then . . . He didn't give a damn. By the time they'd find out, he'd be a thousand miles away.

"What about next year?" I asked.

"Next year! Next year!" He was dumbfounded at my question. "By next year, I'll have kicked the bucket. And if I haven't kicked the bucket by next year, I'll be somewhere else. Do you think I'll come back here? I'll make damn sure I won't. Are you coming back here? You'll make damn sure you won't either. You won't because you're bored, and I won't because of the shirts." I thought of the swallows, I thought of coming again for their sake, but I made damn sure not to say so, and he turned out to be right.

There were all sorts of other things to see at the fair, but the only person I made friends with was a red-haired man with a wooden leg. He was sitting on the steps in front of the old tavern; a crutch lay next to him, and his wooden leg was stretched out before him. I wondered what he was doing here; it would never have occurred to me that he was begging. But then I noticed that passersby occasionally handed him a coin, and he, without compromising himself, said, "Thank you kindly!" I would have liked to ask him where he came from. He looked foreign with his enormous red mustache, which seemed even redder than the hair on his head. However, the words "Thank you kindly" sounded utterly Austrian. I was embarrassed to ask him, a beggar, what he did, as if I hadn't noticed. For the time being, I gave him nothing, planning to make up for it later on. I'm sure my question didn't sound condescending when I asked where he came from. But he named neither a town nor a country. Instead, to my great astonishment, he said: "I am a Mormon."

I hadn't realized there were Mormons in Europe. But perhaps he had been to America and had lived among Mormons there. "How long were you in America?"

"Never been there!" He knew his answer would surprise me, and he waited a bit before enlightening me about Mormons in Europe and even in Austria, and not so few at that. They had their meetings, he said, and kept in touch with one another. He could show me their newspaper. I had the feeling I was disturbing him at work; he had to watch out for the people who went in and out of the tavern. And so I left him, saying I'd come back later on. But by then, he was gone, and I couldn't understand why I hadn't seen him leave. There was no possibility of overlooking him with his wooden leg and crutch and fiery redness.

I stepped into the tavern, which was filled to the rafters. And there, in the huge front room, I suddenly saw him, among many other people at a huge table, with a small glass of wine the color of his hair. He seemed alone; no one talked to him, or perhaps he talked to no one. It was odd to see him mingling with all the other customers, from whom he had only just been begging. He didn't appear to be bothered by this. He sat there quiet and upright; there may have been more room on either side of him than between any two other people. He stood out because of his fiery hair and especially the mustache. He was the only person I would have noticed at his table, even if I hadn't spoken with him earlier. He looked pugnacious, but no one was arguing with him. The instant he noticed me, he gave me a friendly wave and invited me to join him. He didn't have to shift very much to make room for me: there was even a chair nearby since someone got up and left. Finally, we were sitting close together, like old buddies, and he insisted on treating me to a glass of wine.

He had the feeling, he said, starting right in, that I was interested in Mormons. Everyone was against Mormons, he said. No one wanted to have anything to do with him, just because of that. They all thought he had a lot of wives. This was the only thing that people knew about Mormons, if they knew anything at all. It was so silly. He had no wife at all; she had skipped out on him, and that was why he had joined the Mormons. They were good people, all of them worked. They didn't loaf around, they didn't drink any alcohol, absolutely none, not like here, he angrily pointed to my glass—his was already empty, or else he'd forgotten all about it—and with a motion of his arm, he embraced all the glasses in the room. He liked talking about it, he said; he always repeated it; the Mormons were good people. But other people were simply annoyed about it; no sooner did he open his mouth than they said: "Shut up!" or "Go to your Mormons in America!" He had already been kicked out of taverns, just because he had started talking about the Mormons. Everyone had something against him, just because of that. He didn't want anything from these people; he never took anything from anybody when he was inside here, only outside. That was none of their business. Was he hurting them in any way? But they couldn't stand anyone finding something good about the Mormons. For them, the Mormons were heathens or heretics, and he had even been asked whether all redheads were Mormons. His wife had always told him: "Don't come near me with your red hair. You're drunk. You stink." Back then, he had drunk a lot, and sometimes he had gotten furious at his wife and hit her a couple of times with the crutch. That was why she'd left him. It was the fault of the liquor. Then someone had told him: the Mormons could get people off alcohol: none of them drank at all. So he had gone to them, and it was true; they had cured him, and now he didn't touch a drop of liquor. And again, he stared furiously at my glass, which I didn't dare empty.

I sensed the hostility of the others at the same table. He didn't stare at their glasses, but he was all the more audible. His sermon against alcohol grew louder and more violent. He had long since drunk up, but ordered nothing else. I didn't dare offer to treat him. I left for an instant and asked the waitress to bring him a new glass, but not right away, only after I'd be sitting a while. I sensed her question on the tip of her tongue, but forestalled her and payed instantly. Then, suddenly, the full glass was in front of him again; he said, "Thank you kindly" and downed it in one gulp. You had to drink to people's health, he said, even the Mormons did that. You just couldn't imagine what good people they were. Every one of them would give you something; they still had a heart for poor devils; a whole tableful of them would keep ordering a fresh glass for a poor devil, and they'd keep toasting him until they were all drunk, but out of *commiseration*. This was altogether different; you were allowed to drink out of *commiseration*. Why didn't I bump glasses with him? He had ordered a wine for me out of commiseration, and now, someone else had sent him a wine out of commiseration, so we could certainly drink. The Mormons did the same and they were strict, and if those strict people allowed it, then no one could say anything against it.

But it didn't occur to anyone to say anything. As soon as he drank, no one was hostile to him. The looks of the men at the table (there were a couple of strong young guys among them, and they had been raring to beat him up) became friendlier and less baleful. They toasted America with him. He said I came from there; I was visiting him. He told me to say something, so they could see how well I knew the language. Totally embarrassed, I blurted out a few English sentences. They bumped glasses with me, perhaps to check whether I was really drinking. For because of him, they plainly regarded me as an envoy of the Mormons.

The School of Hearing

Returning to Vienna, I continued living in Frau Weinreb's apartment on Haidgasse; and against my will—I couldn't help it—I listened to the evil sounds of the "Executioner" in the kitchen. Since Frau Weinreb's nocturnal visit, I slept more lightly, expecting recurrences of the incident. What particularly unnerved me was her hectic relationship with her husband's pictures, which hung everywhere. There were so many of them, almost indistinguishable from one another except in size and layout; but each single one was important, each had its effect. Frau Weinreb paid her homage in rotation; but since I wasn't at home during the day, I couldn't tell what the routine was. I had the feeling that she was in my room every day; how could she have neglected the pictures hanging in my room?

When she had come at night, she had been in a kind of trance. What was she like during the day, when the Executioner wasn't asleep, and anything that Frau Weinreb did was observed and inspected? Perhaps she was always in the same state; perhaps her state was determined by the sight of the pictures, which she could see on the wall at any time. One pair of eyes replaced another; they were always the same eyes, and always gazing at her. Herr Weinreb was old in every picture; there seemed to be no photographs of his youth. She probably hadn't known him without his full beard; and if any pictures of his youth *had* turned up at his death, they had been discarded, like the pictures of a stranger. It would be wrong to assume that his gaze was strict. He had a kind, mild look, always the same. He didn't appear ominous even in a group of colleagues, but rather assuaging, a peacemaker, a mediator, an arbitrator. Hence Frau Weinreb's disquiet was all the more incomprehensible. What was it that drove her restlessly from picture to picture; what order had he left her, an order that kept her moving, that kept renewing itself as in a "multiple" hypnosis in front of every pair of eyes?

Once, when I ran into her in the vestibule and exchanged a few words with her, I had to force myself not to ask how Herr Weinreb was. Yet every time, she asserted what a dear, good, fine, what an educated gentleman Herr Dr. Weinreb had been. I once said regretfully: "How terrible that he has been deceased for such a long time."

To which she broke in, terrified: "It hasn't been such a long time."

"How long has it been?" I asked, trying to look as friendly as Herr Weinreb; but I didn't succeed without a beard.

"I can't say," she said. "I don't know." And she quickly vanished into her room.

No sooner did I enter the apartment than I became nervous, like her; only I didn't show it, and I tried not to see the pictures, which I felt a distaste for. The frames were always dusted and the glass plates always freshly washed. I looked at them as if they consisted purely of frames and glass plates. I believe I was waiting for a catastrophe, a destruction of the pictures as a dreadful solution.

Once, I dreamt that the Executioner was in my room, the cook, Ružena's aunt, who actually never entered my room. In my dream, she was grinning from ear to ear and holding an enormous burning match, as she moved from one picture of Herr Weinreb to another, very calmly setting fire to all of them. She kept her arm, hand, and the match at the same level and she glided rather than walked. I couldn't see her feet; they were hidden under the long skirt, which reached down to the floor. The pictures instantly burned, but very quietly, like candles. The room was transformed into a church; but I knew that my bed was still there and that I was lying in it; and then I woke up, terrified at blasphemously lying abed in a church.

I told Veza about this dream. She took dreams seriously, never debilitating them with current interpretations. She hadn't failed to notice how eerie I found Frau Weinreb's picture worship. "Perhaps," she said, "it's the Executioner who demands this cult. She knows about it and she keeps her employer dependent on her by means of these pictures. It's the church of Satan, and you live and sleep right in the middle of it, and you'll never have peace again so long as you stay there." I sensed that with a few words she had translated my dream into our more intimate language without confusing the finer dynamics of the dream.

I knew I had to get away from this room, this apartment, this street, this neighborhood. Yet it was no more than ten minutes to Ferdinandstrasse, where Veza lived; and this was the true reason why I had taken this room. I could appear unexpectedly on the street in front of Veza's room and whistle up to her; fidgety as I was, I exercised a kind of supervision over her. Not only did I know whether she was at home or out, whether she was alone or had company, but even whether she was reading or studying by herself; no matter when I felt like showing up, she had to ask me in. She never made me feel I was intruding; perhaps I never did intrude, but it *was* a constraint: for her, because she could never be sure I might not suddenly come by; for me, because my motives were unworthy: I wanted to know exactly what she was doing.

I would have been drawn there in any event, for nothing was lovelier than being with her, admiring her, and, in the midst of this admiration, telling her what I had thought or done. She listened, nothing escaped her, she caught every word; but she reserved the right to voice her opinion. Nothing could hold her back. If she found anything intelligent, she noted it; it came up again in our talk. It wasn't idle or arrogant to deal with intellectual matters, it was perfectly natural. There were thoughts by other people that responded to you like echoes and strengthened you. She knew them; she opened Hebbel's *Journals* and showed you what you had just said, and you weren't ashamed, for you hadn't known he'd said it. Her quotations were never paralyzing: they came only if their effect was animating. She also had her thoughts, inspired by the many she was familiar with. It was she who brought Lichtenberg into my life at that time. I was opposed to other things, so I soon noticed that she felt something like a chauvinism for everything that was female. She gave in unresistingly to glorifiers of women; and Peter Altenberg, whom she had often seen (sometimes running into him in the Town Park when she was a little girl), was a man she worshipped as much as he had worshipped women and little girls. I found this ridiculous and I made no bones about my feelings. It was good that there were things that helped me stake off my territory against her; otherwise, I would have gradually surrendered to her rich literary background. I opposed Altenberg with my Swiss writers: Gotthelf's *The Black Spider* and Keller's "The Three Just Kammachers."

We had a few important pairs of opposites: she loved Flaubert, I Stendhal. When she, annoyed at my distrust or my immense jealousy (which she enjoyed in small doses), was looking for a fight, she would hit me over the head with Tolstoy. Anna Karenina was her favorite female character; and in regard to her, Veza could get so violent that she actually declared war against Gogol, *my* great Russian. She demanded an *amende honorable* for Anna Karenina, whom I found boring, because she had absolutely nothing in common with Veza. And since I wouldn't give in (as steadfast as a martyr in such issues, I would rather have been torn limb from limb than sacrifice to a false goddess), she unhesitatingly reached for her torture instruments and raked Gogol over the coals instead of me. She knew his weaknesses, and she instantly pounced on Taras Bulba, the Cossack, who reminded her so much of Walter Scott.

I wasn't about to defend Taras Bulba. But when I tried to turn the conversation to the grand, the enormous things, "The Overcoat," *Dead Souls,* she hypocritically regretted that so little of the second part of this novel had survived. Perhaps this part would have improved after the first few chapters. And just what did I think of Gogol's Russian years after his return home, when he became terrified at his own impact and tried to prove at any cost how pious and how devoted to the government he was, writing those woeful "Letters to His Friend" and tossing his real works into the fire.

She said she knew of nothing more horrible in world literature than those final years of Gogol's; yet he was only forty-three when he died. Could one still respect this epitome of cowardice—even if it was fear of the fires of hell? And what did I think—in comparison with that—of the later development of Tolstoy, who had grown twice as old, and written *Anna Karenina,* which I absolutely didn't understand at all (said Veza), and had then produced various works that even I, an inveterate misogynist, would have to respect? But until the very last hours of his life, he had demonstrated an unparalleled stubbornness, courage, even magnanimity—what the English call "spirit." She just couldn't take a person seriously if he had a higher regard for Gogol than for Tolstoy.

I was destroyed, but I didn't give in, even if I *was* destroyed. I asked her what had *happened* to Tolstoy, the count, with all his courage? Had he ever landed in prison, had he ever been put on trial? Had he ever left his manor? Had he ever been exiled?

The woman was what happened to him, she said, and he *had* left his "manor" and died in exile.

I also made an effort to save Gogol's honor. He had ventured further, I said. In those works of his that counted, he had been bolder than anyone else. He hadn't realized how bold he was; he had suddenly been confronted with his own boldness and was scared to death of himself. He had seen himself as that which he had attacked, and the zealots surrounding him after his return had threatened him with hell, the punishment of hell, for all his characters together. His terrible end proved the power and also the newness of his characters. She could mock him, but she was mocking his faith. Yet what else was it but his faith that she so greatly venerated in the old Tolstoy?

She couldn't stand my talking about them in the same breath: the terrible zealotry of orthodox bishops, who had such an effect on Gogol, and Tolstoy's self-acquired faith, which he subjected to incessant testing by his conscience. She said that the zealotry and Tolstoy's faith were two utterly incommensurable things. Our bitter, drawn-out feud came to a sort of compromise, which, consistent with the literary topic, was a literary work, but one that we both equally admired: Gorky's jottings about the old Tolstoy, which I had given her to read. It was the best thing Gorky had ever written, loose jottings that he had put aside for a long time before publishing them, without destroying them through a false, external unification. Veza was deeply moved by this picture of old Tolstoy. She called it the most beautiful present I had ever given her. When we approached *these* jottings, we both knew the worst was over. She could then say something that tore my heart: "That's the thing I wish for most in the world: that you may write like this someday."

This was no goal one could set for oneself. It was not just unattainable. (Many things are unattainable, yet one can try to sail in their direction.) However, the greatness of this memoir was due more to its subject than to its author. Was there a Tolstoy in the world today? And if there was, would people know that he was? And even if one could develop so far as to deserve it, would one encounter him? It was a preposterous wish, and perhaps she shouldn't have articulated it. But even though I have never thought of her words without feeling the same sharp pain they caused me at that moment, I believe that it is right to utter the unattainable. After that, one can never get off easily again, and the unattainable remains unattainable.

The astonishing thing about these conversations was that we didn't influence one another. She stuck to the things she had acquired on her own. Some of the things I offered her did impress her; but when she found them in herself, she made them her own. There were battles, but there was never a victor. The battles went on for months and, as it turned out later, for years; but there was never a capitulation. Each of us *awaited* the other's position, but without bringing it up. If what had to be said had been uttered by the wrong side, it would have been nipped in the bud. Veza made an effort to avoid this very danger; she applied her secret caution, a tender concern, but not a motherly one, for we were equals. Despite the vehemence of her words, she never acted superior. Nor would she ever have yielded in submission; and she would never have forgiven herself, had she kept back her opinion for the sake of peace or out of weakness. Perhaps *battle* is the wrong word for our disputes. Complete knowledge of the other was involved, and not just an estimation of his strength and his quickness of mind. It was impossible for her to wound me deliberately. I would never have hurt her for anything in the world. However, we had a compulsion for intellectual truthfulness, a compulsion no smaller than the one I had known in my earlier youth.

I could not discard my legacy of intolerance, even here. However, I learned intimacy with a *thinking* person, which means one must not only hear every word, but try to understand it as well, and demonstrate this understanding by replying exactly and undistortedly. Respect for others begins with not ignoring their words. I would like to call this the *quiet* apprenticeship of this period, although this apprenticeship took place in so very many words; for the other, the utterly contrasting apprenticeship, which I began instantly, was vociferous and glaring.

I learned from Karl Kraus that one can do anything with other people's words. Whatever he read, he operated with it in a breathtaking manner. He was a master of accusing people with their own words. Which didn't mean that he then spared them his accusation in *his* express words. He supplied both accusations and crushed everyone. You enjoyed the spectacle, because you recognized the law dictating these words, but also because you were together with many other people, feeling the tremendous resonance known as a crowd, in which one no longer bruises oneself on one's own limits. You didn't care to miss any of these experiences; you never skipped a single one. You went to these lectures even if you were sick and running a high fever. You thus also gave in to your proclivity for intolerance, which was naturally powerful and which now intensified legitimately, as it were, and in an almost inconceivable way.

Far more important was the fact that you were simultaneously learning how to *hear*. Everything that was spoken, anywhere, at any time, by anyone at all, was offered to your hearing, a dimension of the world that I had never had any inkling of. And since the issue was the combination—in all variants—of language and person, this was perhaps the most important dimension, or at least the richest. This kind of hearing was impossible unless you excluded your own feelings. As soon as you had put into motion what was to be heard, you stepped back and only absorbed and could not be hindered by any judgment on your part, any indignation, any delight. The important thing was the pure, unadulterated shape: none of these acoustic masks (as I subsequently named them) could blend with the others. For a long time, you weren't aware of how great a supply you were gathering. You only felt an eagerness for manners of speech, which you wanted cleanly and clearly delimited, which you could take hold of like an object, which occurred to you suddenly without your discerning their connection to anything else, so that you had to say them aloud to yourself; not without astonishment at their perfect polish and the sure blindness with which they excluded everything else that could be said in the world, almost everything, everything; for they had only one characteristic: they had to keep repeating themselves over and over.

It was, I believe, in Sankt Agatha, during the summer of 1926, that I first felt a need for such masks, their self-sufficiency, as it were, independent of the ones I heard in Karl Kraus's *The Last Days of Mankind*, which I already knew by heart. I felt this need while watching the swallows hour after hour, listening to their swift, light motion and their simultaneous and unchanging sounds. Despite their repetition, these sounds never wore me out, any more than the wonderful movements of the swallows' flight. Perhaps I might have forgotten them eventually; but then came the kermess with the shirt hawker under my window and his unchanging spiel:

"It makes no difference today
Whether I have cash or hay!"

I had heard barkers as a child and had wished they would remain nearby and not go on all that soon. This barker remained in the same place for two days, never budging from under my window. But when the noise drove me to the wooden table in the small garden, where I wrote, I found the swallows again. Undisturbed by the bustle of the fair, they flew in the same way, emitted the same sounds. One repetition seemed like the others; everything was repetition; the sounds—which I couldn't get out of my mind—consisted of repetition. And even though it was a *false* mask that the shirt vendor donned, even though he revealed himself to be a law student in our conversation, a student who knew quite well what he wanted and what he was saying, his consistent use of this mask, together with the unchanging but natural sounds of the swallows, made such an impact on me that my later hunt in Vienna for manners of speaking led to restless nightly rounds through the streets and taverns of Leopoldstadt.

By the end of the year, this district became too confining for me. I began to wish for longer streets, longer walks, different people. Vienna was very large, but the distance from Haidgasse to Ferdinandstrasse was short; Praterstrasse, where I had lived with my brother for several months, seemed exhausted. My routes had become a routine. On Haidgasse, I expected a catastrophe night after night. Perhaps that was why I often had bad thoughts and dashed over to Veza's window on Ferdinandstrasse, so that the light in her room could calm my nerves. If her room was dark and she was out, I was dismayed, even though she had already told me she'd be out. Something in me seemed to expect that she would always be there, no matter what obligations she had.

Gradually, I realized that the possibility of supervision, the short stroll to her home, the temptation to yield to every such emotion, increased my distrust, becoming a danger for us. A distance had to be created between us. I had to leave Haidgasse, and it would have been best if the whole of Vienna lay between us, so that every walk to her and from her would offer me the chance to get to know all streets, doors, windows, taverns of the city, hear all their voices, not take fright at any voice, surrender to them, incorporate them within me, and yet constantly remain open to new ones. I wanted to find and create a place of my own, at the other end of town, and Veza, at least occasionally, was to visit me there, free of the tyranny of the tamed evil old man, whom she always had to listen for with half an ear, for who could tell when he might not suddenly tear himself away from his fire, leave his hell, and break into the holy precinct.

The Invention of Women

During Easter vacation 1927, I went to Paris to see my mother and my brothers. They had been installed there for almost a year, and weren't doing all that badly. My brothers managed to get along in their new schools. French, which they had learned at a much younger age, during two years in a Lausanne boarding school for boys, caused them no problems. They felt fine here, and particularly Georg, the younger one, now called Georges, who was developing in a way that I had wished for. He was a tall, dark-eyed young man, who had a way with words, and who excelled especially in his philosophy class. His proclivity for logical distinctions surprised me (it certainly wasn't due to my influence), and it gave him, at sixteen, a certain independence that he exhibited felicitously in long letters to me and also in the conversations we had during my visit. He was subtle and resourceful; at his school, they assumed he would devote himself to philosophy. He had as much of an aptitude for French as I for German, and yet neither had been our first language. However, we spoke German with one another. He, too, was a faithful reader of *Die Fackel*, which I had to keep sending him from Vienna. And one of his respectable qualities was that when he had mastered a language (and there were many in the course of time), he spoke it no differently from a native, and usually better.

For all the acuity and clarity of mind, he was a tender person, who couldn't do enough for our mother. He replaced what she had lost in me, and he avoided any conflict with her. He was aware of how deeply I had hurt her. In his emotional maturity, which went far beyond his years, he understood what had happened between us and he always kept it in the front of his mind. He listened patiently to her harsh accusations against me without contradicting her, but also without agreeing with her to such an extent as to block any path to eventual reconciliation. It was as if he had taken over my earlier love for her, enriching and refining it with his tenderness, which I lacked. It was a boon for the family that I was gone, and it was a boon for me. But to make the boon perfect, for her as for myself, I had to pull the deepest thorn out of her heart; and this thorn had a name.

Before they moved to Paris, I had understood that there was one single way of assuaging Mother's torment and—what I wanted even more—of protecting Veza against Mother's hatred: the invention of women. I started my inventing in letters and soon got to enjoy the everchanging stories. There had to be *several* women. Any woman I took too seriously, any woman who prevailed, would have frightened my mother and aroused her hatred. Mother would have feared this woman's influence on me and turned her into a satanic figure causing her sleepless nights. And so variety was of the essence. After some experimenting, I hit upon the happiest solution: there had to be *two* very different women, between whom I wavered, one of them not living in Vienna and the other also not too close, so that my studies didn't suffer under the pressure. But also so that neither woman could carry the day against the other; for this would have given her a dangerous preponderance; I would have been, as my mother wrote, at her mercy. I had no scruples about inventing these stories; I did not take them as lies in the ordinary sense of the word. Odysseus, who had always been my model, helped me over the embarrassing aspects of this situation. Something that was well invented was a story, not a lie; and the fact that the purpose of this enterprise was a good, nay, a charitable one, was soon demonstrated by its effect.

The greatest difficulty was that I had to inform Veza. Without her knowledge, without her agreement, I could neither invent these stories nor keep spinning them. And so, it was unavoidable: bit by bit, in small doses, as gently as possible, I had to tell her the truth about Mother's deep animosity toward her. Fortunately, Veza had read enough good novels to understand what had happened. Since I had already begun my enterprise before she knew about it, she couldn't have prevented it anyway. She feared that Mother could learn the truth from others: this would only make matters worse. I argued that *gaining time* would be wonderful. In later years, when Mother got used to my independent life style, when I'd have actually published a book that she could respect with conviction, then learning the true facts would hurt her less. I succeeded in persuading Veza; she also sensed—but without saying so—how deeply I feared that Mother would commit a physical act of jealousy against her.

However, there was one thing I hadn't considered: the animating effect my not very elaborate tales would have on my mother's imagination. By the time I arrived in Paris at Easter, there was, according to my letters, a "Maria" in Salzburg and an "Erika," a violinist, in Rodaun, whereas I allegedly saw little of Veza and didn't like her anymore. I was still standing in the hall of the Paris apartment—nothing had been shown me as yet, I had been greeted only casually—when Mother asked about Erika. And only when we were alone for an instant, without my brothers, did she say: "I haven't told the boys anything; but what is Maria doing? Have you come directly from Vienna or did you stop off in Salzburg?" She didn't feel it was right that the boys should find out about this double life; it could demoralize them. She had told them about Erika, she said. She hoped I didn't mind; it had exorcised the bugaboo of Veza for everyone in the family, and they could think of me in Vienna without worrying too much.

So that was how things stood, and I had to satisfy my mother's curiosity as she asked countless questions. She wanted to know everything, but her questions varied, depending on whether or not my brothers were present. She was endlessly delighted that Maria, the Salzburg girl, was a secret between the two of us. She also advised me not to tell any of our relatives; it could damage my reputation. It looked a bit licentious, whereas she had to admit she would never have expected me to show so much wisdom in a practical question of life. However, she added, it had probably just happened like that, and she shouldn't praise me for something that was sheer chance.

A few days later, when I took my first long walk with Georg (he wanted to show me things he was sure I'd never seen despite my earlier visits to Paris), we first spoke about other, "real," namely intellectual, matters. But then he told me that Mother was a lot better. The fact that the business with Veza was over had worked wonders for Mother. Then he looked at me earnestly and hesitated, as though not really wanting to come out with something. I plied away at him, though sensing what I was about to hear. "You don't have to ask how I feel about it," he said. "I hope you won't always toy with people the way you toyed with Veza." He hesitated again. "Do you have any idea of how she's getting on? Aren't you scared she could do something to herself?"

I had always liked him, but now I loved him even more. I made up my mind to tell him the truth before anyone else. Now was still too early. It was bad, I felt awful about letting him think he was more worried about a person so close to me than I was, even though he barely knew her. I hadn't considered this facet of the stupid lie; it was good that I was now confronted with it.

Georg always thought about this matter whenever we were alone. He was convinced that a person so vilely abandoned was in danger and required special care. The insight and concern he showed Mother in Paris were feelings he had for Veza, too, in Vienna. He tried to make me feel warm about her, yet he didn't mention her, much less give me advice. In the Louvre, which we sometimes visited together, he stopped in front of Leonardo's *St. Anne, Mary, and Jesus,* took a long look at St. Anne and then at me. Her smile reminded him of Veza's. He remembered her so clearly. He had seen her, but hadn't exchanged two words with her. As though we were talking about painters and nothing else, he asked me whether I liked Leonardo. Some people found the smile on Leonardo's faces saccharine, but Georg didn't. It all depended, I said, on whether you knew people who were capable of such a smile but whose lives weren't determined by saccharine things. He agreed with me. I sensed that he wanted to know my true opinion of Veza, whom, as he thought, I had treated so badly. But I also sensed that he wanted justice for her, since he had heard the most dreadful things about her at home, yet held his tongue, although he felt he knew better.

We came to Géricault's *Raft of the Medusa*, which fascinated both of us. I was surprised that he, sixteen years old, couldn't tear himself away from this painting. "Do you know why these heads are so *true?*" he said, and he then told me that Géricault had painted the heads of executed bodies to train himself for the figures on his *Raft*. "I couldn't have done that," I said; it was new to me.

"That's why you didn't become a doctor. You wouldn't have been able to make it through an autopsy." I saw he hadn't given up the idea of studying medicine, and I was very happy. Philosophy was in the foreground now, but he wouldn't remain with it. His sympathy, his knowledge of pain, his ability to endure the sight of death without falling prey to it, his patience, and also his fairness, which gave every person his share of respect—all these things made him appear to be a born doctor. And he would succeed at something that I had failed in despite my awe of this profession.

We vied with each other in thoroughness, and it was a bit comical of us to halt at paintings we were indifferent to, while others attracted us more, ones we were more familiar with because we liked them so much. Georg was cordial enough to ask whether I felt like visiting the Babylonian antiquities; he was alluding to my passion for Gilgamesh. He hadn't forgotten this either; he hadn't forgotten anything. The chaos on Radetzkystrasse had snuffed out none of his earlier experiences. I forwent the Babylonians, because they bored him. And as a reward, he took me to *The Four Cripples*, a very beautiful small Breughel. "So that you'll visit us again," he said. "Do you think I don't know why you can't get away from Vienna? It's the Breughels and Karl Kraus and . . ." He couldn't bring himself to say the last thing, which he would have said earlier.

We were closer than ever. Georg was worried about the person who had been the most important thing in the world for me, a person whom I had sinned against. And Georg's concern gave me a sense of relief. I knew I was guiltless, for how else could the matter have developed? Nevertheless, I felt guilty. And it was only when I was alone with Mother and watched her blossom during her questions about "Maria" (because I answered them in such detail) that I felt free of guilt. Mother was interested only in Maria. She was not interested in the violinist, who was already giving concerts and receiving critical notice. Mother felt sorry for Maria, because Maria was far away from me. She had to live in Salzburg, and yet this great distance was good for her. Mother was impressed with how beautiful Maria was, and told me I was lucky. She was not too astonished that Maria liked me even though I, compared with our youngest, the handsome one, was really not attractive. "You're a poet," Mother said all at once, as I was spinning out my yarn for her. "You can invent things. You're not boring, like so many young men. In a town like Salzburg, people are receptive to poets. She doesn't think of you as a chemist. You're lucky."

I spent three weeks in Paris, at the apartment on Rue Copernic; and not a day passed without her coaxing something new about Maria out of me. Mother had a way of asking that I couldn't resist. I didn't conceal certain dubious items, for instance, the dreadful avarice of Maria's mother, which made Maria suffer.

"It happens in the best families," Mother replied. "Just think of Veza's stepfather!" This alone demonstrated her change of mood. She must have occasionally thought about what an awful pressure Veza lived under at home. At my departure, however, half an hour before we ordered the taxi to take me to the station, she had a generous stirring, and spoke as she had spoken in the past: "Do not be hard on her, my son." She meant Veza. "She has been struck down and is on the ground. Do not tell her everything. She does not have to know how beautiful your two loves are. Do not forget, she has to keep on living now, alone. It is difficult for a woman to preserve her self-respect after such a defeat. It is most difficult of all for a woman to live alone. She has done nothing wicked to you, for you have escaped from her toils. She won't find another like you to catch in her toils, for no one else would be as callow as you were at that time. I brought you boys up pure, and she realized it instantly. It's to her credit that *you*, my son, were the one at whom she cast her eye. Visit her from time to time, not too often; otherwise you will feed her pain. Tell her you cannot come because your studies are more demanding than in the past—you are preparing for life now, things are becoming serious, and you cannot fritter away your time."

These words were in my head as I left. I was glad that the Burgtheater hadn't died out entirely in her. But I was even gladder that her hatred had reversed into pity. She was so imbued with my tale that she could freely prefer one of the two women over the other. It wasn't even certain which one *I* liked more; but she threw all her weight on Maria's side. It was always better, she said, to think of someone far away. If people are too near one another, there's too much friction; everything becomes insipid. Also, Erika's violin brought something false into the relationship. After all, one loves a person and not his instrument; otherwise, one could be satisfied with his concerts. But I was not to think, said Mother, that she wanted to meet Maria. She considered it possible that I would stay attached to Maria until the end of my studies, another two years, simply because she was in Salzburg and not in Vienna. Mother admitted to being curious about Maria, by all means. She said I tended to exaggerate and perhaps she might not think Maria as beautiful as I did. But getting to know my mother would give Maria an importance in her own eyes that ill befitted her. One should not get attached, I had my whole life ahead of me. Nowadays, only a fool would get attached at twenty-two.

The View of Steinhof

In Kolmar, I spent an entire day in front of the Grünewald altar. I didn't know when I had come, and I didn't know when I would leave. When the museum closed, I wished for invisibility, so that I might spend the night there. I saw Christ's corpse without plaintiveness; the dreadful state of his body struck me as true. Faced with this truth, I realized what had bewildered me about crucifixions: their beauty, their transfiguration. Transfiguration belonged to an angelic concert, not on the cross. The thing that people had turned away from, horrified, in real life, could still be grasped in the painting: a memory of the dreadful things that people do to one another. Back then, in February 1927, war and gassings were still close enough to make the painting more credible. Perhaps the most indispensable task of art has been forgotten too often: not catharsis, not solace, not disposing of everything as if it would end well, for it does not end well. Plague and boils and torment and horror—and for the plague that is overcome, we invent even worse horror. What can the comforting deceptions signify in the face of this truth, which is always the same and should remain visible to our eyes? All horror to come is anticipated here. St. John's finger, enormous, points it out: this is it, this is what will be again. And what does the lamb mean in this landscape? Was this putrefying man on the cross the lamb? Did he grow up and become a human being in order to be nailed to the cross and called a lamb?

When I was there, a painter stood in front of the Grüne-wald, copying it. He did not seem fascinated or self-conscious, nor did he think very long about any stroke of the brush. I wished he were gone; no one else was there, and I figured he would start a conversation with me. But he didn't start a conversation; he wanted peace and quiet himself. The only striking thing about him was that he ignored others. I tried to imagine that his copy wasn't there. I stood in such a way as not to see it. But it was impossible not to think of it. Also, I was embarrassed at staying so long. Without doing anything, I kept standing there, a little like him: he never left either, but he held a brush in his hand and was making an effort at something. He was a solidly built man, middle-aged, his face was blank and not marked by pain, it was incredible that this face should be near the one in the painting, that it should be there at the same time, in the same room, occupied as with a craft with the immensity that it never lost sight of.

I was so ashamed in front of the copyist that I vanished in the back from time to time as though to see other parts of the altar. I had to escape the copy of the crucifixion, as well as the painting itself, and the painter must have thought I was being considerate of him. Perhaps he changed when alone, perhaps he made grimaces in order to endure this confrontation. He looked relieved when I reemerged from behind; he seemed to be smiling. I observed him observing me. Is it any surprise that one should notice a real human being in this presence? One needs that person because he is not hanging on the cross. As long as he is busy copying, nothing can happen to him. This was the thought that struck me most. You were shielded against what you saw only by never looking away. You were rescued by *not* turning your head away. It is no cowardly rescue. It is no falsification. But would the copyist be perfection in this salvation? No, for by seeing, he *breaks down* what he sees. He takes refuge in parts, whose connection to the totality is delayed. So long as he paints those parts, they are not part of the totality. They will be part of it once more. But there are times when he absolutely cannot see the totality, since he is absorbed in the detail, which must be accurate. The copyist is a semblance. He is not like St. John's finger. The copyist's finger doesn't show, it moves and executes. The most unselfconscious thing about him is the way he *sees,* namely in such a way that it doesn't change him. Were it to change him, he could not finish the copy.

I forgot the copyist only after several years, when I managed to find the large phototypes, which I hung up in my room. Upon returning from Kolmar, I had to find the room in which to hang the phototypes. I soon found the room, right off the bat and without being able to tell what good it would do me.

I wanted to have trees, many trees, and the oldest trees that I knew around Vienna were in the Lainz Park. The first advertisement I came across was for a room near the park. I went to Hacking, the last stop on the urban railroad, crossed the woeful rivulet known as the Vienna River (about whose dangerous past the most incredible stories were told), and climbed up the slope, crossed Erzbischofgasse (which began here, running along a wall until Ober Sankt Veit; I had always liked this street), and turned into Hagenberggasse. The advertised room was in the second house on the right, up the slope.

The landlady took me up to the third floor, which consisted purely of this room, and she opened the window. The instant I looked out, my mind was made up: I had to live here; I would live here a long time. The window showed an open playing field, and, beyond the field and Erzbischofstrasse, you could see trees, many trees, big ones. I assumed they belonged to the Archbishop's garden. Beyond them, however, on the other side of the Vienna River valley, on a hill, I could see the town of madmen, Steinhof. It was surrounded by a long wall, inside of which there would have been enough room for a town in earlier days. Steinhof had its own cathedral. The dome of Otto Wagner's church shone all the way over to me. The town consisted of many pavilions, which looked like villas from afar. Ever since first coming to Vienna, I had heard about Steinhof; six thousand people lived in this town. It wasn't really nearby, but it seemed very distinct. I tried imagining that I could peer through the windows and into the rooms.

The landlady, most likely misinterpreting my gaze through her window (she must have been sixty, her skirt reached down to the floor), gave a compact speech on the youth of today and potatoes, which had already doubled in price. I heard her out, never interrupting; perhaps I sensed I would be hearing this speech frequently. But to forestall any misunderstandings, I immediately declared, when she was finished, that I would have to have the right to receive visits from my girlfriend. She instantly called her "the Fräulein Fiancée" and insisted it could be only one Fräulein Fiancée. I told her I would also have to bring my books, I had a lot of books. This seemed to put her mind at ease; she said books were proper for a Herr Student. I had a harder time with the pictures I wanted to hang on the walls; I didn't care to part with the reproductions of the Sistine Chapel, which I had had about me since the Villa Yalta in Zurich. "Does it have to be tacks?" she said, but gave in. I had promptly agreed to the rent, which wasn't high, and my books filled her with confidence. She didn't like changing roomers, and anyone bringing a lot of books intended to remain.

So I came with the Sistine pictures, but I never forgot my real goal: to seek phototypes of the Isenheim altar and to nail them to the walls in all the details I could lay hold of. It took me a very long time to find what I was looking for. I spent six years in this room; and it was here, as soon as the reproductions of Grünewald hung around me, that I wrote *Auto-Da-Fé*.

I didn't see much of the landlady, who lived on the ground floor with her husband and grown children: only once a month, when I handed her the rent, and right after that, when she brought the receipt up to my room. Occasionally, however, someone dropped by while I was out. The landlady would then catch me at the front door when I returned, and I was given a detailed account of the visitor's appearance, manner, and wishes. She distrusted everyone who came by; and if it was some neighbor whom I had gotten to know by chance and who wanted to borrow something to read, she emphatically warned me against people with nasty intentions who came purely to check out what could be stolen. Anything the landlady had to tell me ended with her speech on the youth of today.

At the bottom of the house, in the basement, lived a sort of janitress, a forester's widow, who had spent most of her life with her husband in the middle of the park. She was supposed to make my bed and clean up the room. On days when I didn't go to the laboratory, remaining at home for the morning, I would see her, and she talked about her days in the Lainz Park. Frau Schicho was a friendly old woman, white-haired, very fat, with a red face. She broke into a sweat at the least strain, at every movement; and if I was present during her cleaning (which I wasn't very often), the room was soon filled with a powerful smell, even though the window and the door stayed open, creating a draft that was supposed to ventilate. It was not a repulsively pungent smell; more like butter that was neither quite fresh nor quite rancid. I would have gone out, if only to avoid this smell. But Frau Schicho had a way of telling stories that I couldn't resist. She didn't talk about the forest and her forester house, unless I asked her about boars and owls, which she told me about willingly, but unemotionally. Instead, her thoughts went back to the high-ranking guests who had visited the park in the kaiser's retinue. Proud, but not solemn, she talked about the Three Emperors' Day, when the Russian tsar and the German kaiser, on horseback, had halted next to Kaiser Franz Joseph in front of the forester's house, and she had served them a welcoming drink. She could see all three of them, as though they were still standing there; she described their panaches, their uniforms, their faces; she still knew what types of horses they had been riding and what words they had used when thanking her for the beverage. She didn't sound servile, more as if everything were still present; and while her arms reached up to show me how she had offered the welcoming beverage to each of the emperors, she appeared a bit surprised that no one was taking the cup from her hands. Everything was gone. Where were the emperors? How was it possible that nothing was left? And while she never put these thoughts into words and also never betrayed any regret, I sensed it was no less enigmatic for her than for me, and that it was because of this enigma that she told me about the past so powerfully and graphically.

I never breakfasted in this room; I didn't even keep fruit or bread here. I had always wished for a place free of food, undisturbed by anything that I found trivial or bothersome. I jokingly called this my "domestic purity." And whenever Veza came by, she understood, and never tried to establish a household here, as women are apt to do. In her original and flattering way, she interpreted as follows my desire to keep my room free of such things: she said it was my respect for the prophets and sibyls, who were still on the walls, and perhaps also my respect for Michelangelo, who could work endlessly without thinking of food.

But this didn't mean that I deprived myself of anything, much less starved. On Auhofstrasse, five minutes down the hill, there was a dairy shop, where you could buy yogurt, bread, and butter, and consume them in peace and quiet at the one table, while sitting on the one chair. Here, I ate my breakfast before going to the laboratory. If I stayed home, I would climb down during the day. Throughout those years, I gladly lived on yogurt and bread and butter, for anything I managed to save went for books.

Frau Fontana, who ran this branch of the dairy, had nothing in common with Frau Schicho. Her voice was as sharp as her nose, which she stuck into everything. During my repast, I learned details about every customer who left the shop and about every customer who would presumably appear. When this subject was exhausted, which didn't happen all that swiftly, her marriage was next on the list. From the very start, her marriage hadn't been quite right. Frau Fontana's first husband had been a prisoner of war in Siberia, where he spent several years, eventually dying of some illness. A friend of his had come back from there very late, bearing final greetings, the husband's wedding ring, and a photo—a group picture of the deceased, his friend, and other prisoners. It was a precious photo, with which its owner never parted, though he liked showing it. All the men had grown beards, and no one was recognizable. The owner used to point to one beard, the second from the right on the bottom, and say: "That was me! Don'tcha recognize me? Damn it, those were the days!" Then he assumed a solemn mien and pointed to another beard, the second from the left on the bottom, and declared: "And this was my friend and predecessor. Go ahead, you can say the first Herr Fontana, but naturally his name was different. You'd better ask my wife. She can sing his praises for you."

For Frau Fontana could not sing the praises of her second husband. She got up very early, the store opened early. He slept all morning. He would come home in the middle of the night on the last train, sometimes even later, on foot, returning from his pub in town. By then, the wife was fast asleep, and he never saw her. During the afternoon, while she was in the dairy, he would get up and go back to his cronies in town.

She readily began nagging; he avoided her as much as he could. But in the early afternoon, before going to town, he occasionally spelled her in the shop. This was how I met him, and he told me about Siberia. After some two years, the tension between the two of them got so bad that she kicked him out of their home. She said it was no marriage; they had nothing to do with one another. He used their home only to sleep in. Otherwise, he never talked to her anymore. Whenever she was awake, he was asleep, and no sooner did she fall asleep than he woke up again.

He finally left, and she told me so the next morning, both content and embittered. He had scarcely brought anything; he had had nothing, after all. But whatever he had brought, he took along, even a couple of rusty nails. "Just imagine, he took along the rusty nails; he didn't leave me a single nail." She sounded as if she would have liked to keep one of his rusty nails—as a memento? to annoy him?—and he had begrudged her even a nail. Had they been new . . . But they weren't, they were old, rusty nails.

Herr Fontana was very short and also buckled and hunched, as though he had a serious hernia. He was totally bald, looked haggard and somewhat the worse for wear. His eyes seemed about to drip, yet they never did. When he was in the store, he sometimes had a special customer: the splendid, opulent countess, who lived nearby with her family, a tall, strong woman, apparently a horsewoman, trained to hunt—although I had never seen her mounted or hunting. She had a loud voice and always did her shopping as if the dairy existed purely for her sake. Yet she never bought all that much, for she never had enough money on her. Sometimes, she brought along her three little children, whereby one instantly had to think of her tremendous bosom. Herr Fontana's eyes fell out of his tired sockets. He waited on the countess readily and not hatefully; otherwise, he was annoyed at everyone who came in during his shift. She was scarcely out the door when he turned to me and said enthusiastically, with eyes that now really dripped: "What a goddamn mare! What a goddamn mare!"

I believe he came into the dairy at these hours purely to see her—perhaps he might otherwise have slept longer. And she, virtually on schedule, always came at the same time and would have no one but him wait on her. Sometimes, everything she had ordered was gathered before her on the counter. Then—she was very bad at figures—she began to add up. Herr Fontana, who liked to keep her there in order to gaze at her for a longer time, helped her count. She always had too little cash; but even though he liked her, she never got credit. And so one requested item after another had to disappear under the counter again. She was never ashamed of this operation; it was no disgrace that she couldn't do arithmetic. To make up for it, she knew about horses. So, never showing chagrin, she handed back one item after another. Herr Fontana took the liberty of opening her hand with a gentle pressure; he quickly saw how much money she had. It was he who then suddenly stopped her in the midst of her giving back the items, and he said: "Now it's right. You've got just enough for what's left!"

She missed him after he left; for now she was waited on by Frau Fontana, who was less sympathetic with the countess's poor arithmetic and secretly inferred dishonest intentions behind her inability. The proprietress, too, had something to say when the lady with the children had left the shop: "She's never been to school. She can't add, and she can't write either. Now just imagine someone like her running my shop!" The countess, not insensitive to this hostility, said to *me*, outside the shop: "Too bad that fine man is gone! He *was* a fine man!" It was clear that she had heard nothing about the rusty nails.

I, too, missed Herr Fontana, especially the conversations about Siberia. In reality, he was still living there. His buddies in his pub liked to hear him tell about Siberia. He *had* to go to the pub every day, he told me: they were waiting for him, they wanted to hear more. There was a lot left to tell; he was a long way from being finished. He could write a book about Siberia, he said. But he found it easier to tell about it orally. His wife had fallen asleep the first time he said something about Siberia to her. For her, everything was: the wedding band. His friend, her first husband, had told him so: For

God's sake, bring her back the wedding ring, otherwise she won't have a minute of peace! For her, it's a valuable object. After all, he said, he could have held on to it. But if he made a promise to a dead friend, he kept it. And even if it had been a million, he would have given it back for a reward. And what had he gotten for all his honesty? Now he had a milk woman on his back instead of a countess.

One year after he left, Siberia surfaced again in the area.

Among Death Masks

What attracted me about Ibby Gordon was her wit and her merriment; she came out with one flash of inspiration after another. I never heard an expected sentence from her; it was always something else. She was Hungarian, but she managed to surprise you even with her nationality, so that every mistake of hers turned into a bright flash. There were some words that she first made you conscious of; if she particularly liked a German word, she would suppress it, letting it out only in new formations, which reminded you that it had vanished, and which now kept referring to the lost word in one new way after another. She never spoke fast; nothing she said went under; every syllable had its weight. No word was hurried or pushed out by the next. But since she *thought* quickly, many things in her waited for their turn to come and were mirrored in their own joy before becoming visible. Many joys, all new, lined up, and their never ending merriment left no room for grief, terror, chagrin, or anxiety. When you were with her, you never believed that there was grief anywhere in the world; for any grief that she laid eyes on or that was brought to her was transformed into something that lost its heaviness and grew wings. And since she never complained about anything that happened to her, you were not so resentful that she made fun of the terrors of other people.

She looked like a Maillol figure, a rustically classical shape, and her face was like a fruit that would soon shimmer in its ripeness. All the incongruence and grotesqueness she saw was her nourishment. You might have considered her ruthless; but she was ruthless toward herself, too. You were amazed that her witty and entertaining mockery had such a good effect on her. Ibby, an epitome of utterly blissful health, often had nothing to eat, but she did not waste a word on her hunger, unless she had a story to tell about it: how well nourished she seemed to male gazes, which could not get their fill of the splendor of her shoulders.

All things of tradition, order, a regulated daily life had slid off her without a trace. Anything she told about her background was as indifferent as if it had never existed. She came from a place called Marmaros Sziget in Eastern Hungary, at the foot of the Carpathians; and I noted the name of her birthplace because it reminded me of the German word *Marmor*, marble, the marble from which Maillol had carved her. Her first name, Ibolya, Hungarian for *violet*, sounded ridiculous; luckily, you never thought of it because she was nicknamed Ibby. I preferred her maiden name, Feldmesser; she was embarrassed by it, perhaps because of her family, whom I knew nothing about. She had taken the pen name of Gordon, and she loved it; it seemed to be the only thing she cared about.

In Budapest, she had met Fredric Karinthy, a Hungarian satirist, famous in his country. I had read nothing by him; her descriptions of his writings made him sound like Swift. She became his mistress. She wrote poems that he liked; supposedly, he had fallen for both her poems and her beauty. Aranka, his wife, a violent woman, with a dark Gypsy beauty, as Ibby said, was so jealous that she jumped out of a fourth-floor window. Although seriously injured, she survived by a miracle. Her desperate act made such an impression on Karinthy that he decided to break off with Ibby on the spot. And in order to save Aranka's life, he *exiled* Ibby from Budapest and from Hungary.

A friend of his took her across the border to Vienna; she arrived with no baggage except for a toothbrush, which she liked to flaunt. It was a harsh fate, but she talked about it uncomplainingly. She had as little pity for Aranka as for herself; all she felt was the ridiculous quality of her situation. The famous writer had asked his most reliable friend to escort her. The friend was to make sure that she didn't sneak back across the border into Hungary. He rented a room for her on Strozzigasse; she had to report to him in a coffeehouse every day. He would then promptly go to the phone and call Karinthy in Budapest: "Ibby's in Vienna. Ibby hasn't disappeared." She would then get something to eat. The rent was paid for her, she got nothing else. They were afraid she might buy a train ticket for Budapest. If she didn't report, Karinthy's friend would go to Strozzigasse to check up on her; but in that case, she got nothing to eat. Thus she stood before me the first time I saw her: the goddess Pomona, with a toothbrush in her hand instead of an apple.

It took a few weeks, and then Ibby found herself in a circle of Vienna's *jeunesse dorée*, the object of a conflict between two brothers. Every man in this circle was after her; and since there were many, all courting her at the same time, she deployed utmost cunning to play the men off against one another, fending off all attacks. She had an especially hard time with the two brothers; they were both very serious about her.

She remained in Vienna for almost a year. I saw a lot of her; we would meet in a coffeehouse, where she told me stories about everything that happened around her. She talked in her calm, impartial way, cold and radiant and hysterically funny. I *had* to listen, but she also had to tell about it. She was grateful that I didn't try to take advantage of the situation. She was resting with me, as she put it, resting from her innocent beauty. She sensed that I felt the same way about her beauty as she did: it was a burden the effects of which you were helplessly exposed to.

One of the two brothers ran a large bookstore, which he

had taken over after their father's death. The second brother, regarded as more intelligent and more knowledgeable, had studied all sorts of things, constantly switching majors; at this point, it was philosophy. Rudolf, the bookseller, was a little nothing of a person, tiny and homely; he tried to make an impact by dressing carefully and styling what little hair he had left. He was as much under Ibby's spell as his brother; but because of his rather dry, unimaginative ways, he had a much harder time arousing her interest than his brother, a good listener, who gave lightly stuttering but persistent advice. Rudolf, who needed advice and never gave any, had to rely on new books, particularly art books, to which he had access through his bookstore; he would surprise Ibby with them, giving her something to busy her mind. Once, he brought her *The Eternal Countenance,* a collection of death masks, which had just come out. I came by just as Ibby was about to open the book, and after only a few pages, both she and I were captivated. Something happened that would have been unthinkable between us: we lapsed into silence. We sat down side by side. Rudolf, who couldn't endure the rapport of our silence, left us the book and vanished.

I had never seen death masks: they were something completely new for me. I sensed that I was close to the moment that I knew least about.

I accepted the title of the book, *The Eternal Countenance,* without giving it a second thought. I had always been fascinated by the variety among human beings; but I had never expected this variety to intensify into the moment of death. I was also astonished that so many things can be preserved. Since childhood, I had suffered from the disappearance of the dead. Preserving a name or one's works did not suffice for me. I cared about their physicality, too, every feature, every twitching of their faces. When I heard a voice that lodged in my mind, I futilely looked for the face; it appeared in dreams, when I did not wish for it; but I could not evoke it by will. If ever I did see the face (seldom enough), it had become different, subject to its own laws of decomposition. And now I saw the people with whose thoughts and works I lived, whom I loved for their deeds, hated for their misdeeds; they were before me, unchangeable, their eyes closed— as if these eyes could still open, as if nothing irreparable had happened. Were these people still in control of themselves? Could they still hear what was said to them alone? I reeled from one face to another, as though I had to catch and hold each single one. It did not hit me that they were together in this book. I was scared they would decamp in all directions, each in a different one. There were few faces that I recognized without looking at the name. Without a name, they were expelled into helplessness. But the instant you tied a face to a name, the face felt safe from decay. I leafed on and then unexpectedly leafed back; and there they were still, each single one of them; none had decamped, none resented the structure of the sequence in which he had been taken in; the random way this book was put together was not unworthy of them.

The final instant before decay: as though a man had taken up, once and for all, anything that he could be, consenting to this final presentation. *This consent,* however, is not given to all masks: there are some that wound you—masks that expose. Their purpose is the dreadful truth that they churn up, the dominating principle in which this specific life had to end: the burden on Walter Scott, the sharp madness of old Swift, the terrible, consuming disease of Géricault. One could seek only horror in all masks, the horror of death. They would then be murder masks. But that would be a falsification: there is something in them that goes beyond murder.

It is the bating of breath, but as if the breath were preserved. Breath is man's most precious possession, most precious of all at the end; and this ultimate breath is preserved in the mask, as an image.

But how can breath become an image? The mask that I opened up to, sought, and always found again was that of Pascal.

Here, pain achieved its perfection; here, it found its long-sought meaning. Pain that means to remain thought is not capable of anything more. If there is a dying beyond lament, then this is where we are confronted with it. A gradually acquired nearness to death, in ineffably tiny, minute steps, borne by the wish to cross the threshold of death, in order to gain unknown things beyond it. One can read a great deal about believers and martyrs who, for the sake of the afterlife, wish to be saved from this life. But here, we have the picture of one of them in the moment of achieving his wish—a man who did know how to castigate himself, but who thought infinitely more than he castigated himself. Thus, everything he did against his life was reflected in his thought. *His* countenance can be called an eternal one, for it expresses the eternity that he was after. He *rests* in his pain, which he does not wish to abandon. He wants as much pain as eternity is willing to absorb; and when he has reached the full measure permitted by eternity, he will present that full measure to eternity and enter eternity.

The Fifteenth of July

A few months after I had moved into my new room, something occurred that had the deepest influence on my subsequent life. It was one of those not too frequent public events that seize an entire city so profoundly that it is no longer the same afterwards.

On the morning of July 15, 1927, I was not at the Chemical Institute on Währingerstrasse as usual; I happened to be at home. I was reading the morning newspaper at the coffee-house in Ober Sankt Veit. Today, I can still feel my indignation when I took hold of *Die Reichspost:* the giant headline said: "A JUST VERDICT." There had been shootings in Burgenland; workers had been killed. The court had declared the murderers not guilty. This acquittal had been termed, nay, trumpeted, as a "just verdict" in the organ of the government party. It was this mockery of any sense of justice rather than the verdict itself that triggered an enormous agitation among the workers of Vienna. From all districts of the city, the workers marched in tight formations to the Palace of Justice, whose sheer name embodied the unjust verdict for them. It was a totally spontaneous reaction: I could tell how spontaneous it was just by my own conduct. I quickly biked into the center of town and joined one of these processions.

The workers, usually well disciplined, trusting their Social Democratic leaders and satisfied that Vienna was administered by these leaders in an exemplary manner, were acting *without* their leaders on this day. When they set fire to the Palace of Justice, Mayor Seitz mounted a fire engine and raised his right hand high, trying to block their way. His gesture had no effect: the Palace of Justice was *burning*. The police were ordered to shoot; there were ninety deaths.

Fifty-three years have passed, and the agitation of that day is still in my bones. It was the closest thing to a revolution that I have physically experienced. Since then, I have known quite precisely that I would not have to read a single word about the storming of the Bastille. I became a part of the crowd, I fully dissolved in it, I did not feel the slightest resistance to what the crowd was doing. I am amazed that despite my frame of mind, I was able to grasp all the concrete individual scenes taking place before my eyes. I would like to mention one such scene.

In a side street, not far from the burning Palace of Justice, yet out of the way, stood a man, sharply distinguished from the crowd, flailing his hands in the air and moaning over and over again: "The files are burning! All the files!"

"Better files than people!" I told him, but that did not interest him; all he could think of was the files. It occurred to me that he might have some personal involvement in the files, be an archivist. He was inconsolable. I found him comical, even in this situation. But I was also annoyed. "They've been shooting down people!" I said angrily, "and you're carrying on about files!" He looked at me as if I weren't there and wailed repeatedly: "The files are burning! All the files!" He was standing off to the side, but it was not undangerous for him; his lament was not to be missed—after all, I too had heard him.

In the following days and weeks of utter dejection, when you could not think of anything else, when the events you had witnessed kept recurring over and over again in your mind, haunting you night after night even in your sleep, there was still *one* legitimate connection to literature. And this connection was Karl Kraus. My idolization of him was at its highest level then. This time it was gratitude for a specific public deed; I don't know whom I could ever be more thankful to for such an action. Under the impact of the massacre on that day, he put up posters everywhere in Vienna, demanding the voluntary resignation of Police Commissioner Johann Schober, who was responsible for the order to shoot and for the ninety deaths. Kraus was alone in this demand; he was the only public figure who acted in this way. And while the other celebrities, of whom Vienna has never had a lack, did not wish to lay themselves open to criticism or perhaps ridicule, Kraus alone had the courage of his indignation. His posters were the only thing that kept us going in those days. I went from one poster to another, paused in front of each one, and I felt as if all the justice on earth had entered the letters of Kraus's name.

Some time ago, I set down this account of July 15 and its aftermath. I have quoted it here verbatim. Perhaps, although brief, it can offer a notion of the gravity of what happened.

Ever since, I have often tried to approach that day, which may have been the most crucial day of my life after my father's death. I have to say "approach," for it is very hard to get at this day; it is an outspread day, stretching across an entire city, a day of movement for me too, for I biked all over Vienna. My feelings on that day were all focused in *one direction*. It was the most *unambiguous* day that I can remember, unambiguous only because one's feelings could not be diverted from the day as it went by.

I don't know *who* made the Palace of Justice the goal of the tremendous processions from all parts of the city. One could think that the choice was spontaneous, even though this cannot be true. Someone must have blurted out the words "to the Palace of Justice." But it is not important to know who it was, for these words were taken in by everybody who heard them; they were accepted without qualms, waverings, or deliberation, without delay or demur, and they pulled everybody in one and the same direction.

Perhaps the substance of July 15 fully entered *Crowds and Power*. If this is so, then it would be impossible to trace anything back completely to the original experience, to the sensory elements of that day.

There was the long bike ride into town. I cannot remember the route. I do not know where I first bumped into people. I cannot *see* myself clearly on that day, but I still feel the excitement, the advancing, and the fluency of the movement. Everything is dominated by the word *fire*, then by actual fire.

A *throbbing* in my head. It may have been sheer chance that I did not personally see any attacks upon policemen. But I did see the throng being shot at and people falling. The shots were like whips. I saw people run into the side streets and I saw them reemerge and form into crowds again. I saw people fall and I saw corpses on the ground, but I wasn't right next to them. I was dreadfully frightened, especially of these corpses. I went over to them, but *avoided* them as soon as I got closer. In my excitement, they seemed to be *growing bigger*. Until the Republican Defense Corps arrived to carry them away, the corpses were surrounded by empty space, as if people expected bullets to strike here again.

The mounted Defense Corps made an extremely horrible impression, perhaps because they were frightened themselves.

A man in front of me spat and pointed his right thumb halfway back: "Someone's hanging there! They've pulled his pants off!" What was he spitting at? The victim? Or the murder? I couldn't see what he was pointing at. A woman in front of me shrieked: "Peppi! Peppi!" Her eyes were closed and she was reeling. Everyone began to run. The woman fell down. However, she hadn't been shot. I heard galloping horses. I didn't go over to the woman, who was lying on the ground. I ran with the others. I sensed that I had to run with them. I wanted to flee into a doorway, but I couldn't get away from the running throng. A very big, strong man running next to me banged his fist on his chest and bellowed as he ran: "Let them shoot me! Me! Me! Me!" Suddenly, he was gone. He hadn't fallen down. Where was he?

This was perhaps the eeriest thing of all: you saw and heard people in a powerful gesture that ousted everything else, and then those very people had vanished from the face of the earth. Everything yielded and invisible holes opened everywhere. However, the overall structure did not disappear; even if you suddenly found yourself alone somewhere, you could feel things tugging and tearing at you. The reason was that you *heard* something everywhere: there was something rhythmic in the air, an evil music. You could call it music; you felt elevated by it. I did not feel as if I were moving on my own legs. I felt as if I were in a resonant wind. A crimson head popped up in front of me, at various points, up and down, up and down, rising and dropping, as if floating on water. I looked for it as though I were to follow its directives; I thought it had red hair, then I recognized a red kerchief and no longer looked for it.

I neither met nor recognized anyone; any people I spoke to were unknown to me. However, there were few people I spoke to. I heard a great deal; there was always something to hear; most cutting of all were the boohs when the police fired into the throng and people fell. At such moments, the boohs were relentless, especially the female boohs, which could be made out distinctly. It seemed to me as if the volleys of gunfire were elicited by boohs. But I also noticed that this impression was wrong, for the volleys continued even when no more boohs could be heard. You could hear the gunfire everywhere, even farther away, whiplashes over and over.

The persistence of the crowd, which, driven away, instantly erupted from the side streets. The fire would not let the people go; the Palace of Justice burned for hours, and the time of the burning was also the time of utmost agitation. It was a very hot day; even if you did not see the fire, the sky was red for a great distance, and the air smelled of burned paper, thousands and thousands of files.

The Defense Corps, which you saw everywhere, recognizable by their windbreakers and armbands, contrasted with the police force: the Corps was unarmed. Its weapons were stretchers on which the wounded and the dead were carried off. Its eagerness to help was obvious; its members stood out against the fury of the boohs as though they were not part of the crowd. Also, they turned up everywhere; their emergence often signaled victims before these victims were seen by anyone else.

I did not personally see the Palace of Justice being set on fire, but I learned about it before I saw flames: I could tell by a change of tone in the crowd. People shouted at one another about what had happened; at first, I did not understand; it sounded joyous, not shrill, not greedy; it sounded liberated.

The fire was what held the situation together. You felt the fire, its presence was overwhelming; even if you did not see it, you nevertheless had it in your mind, its attraction and the attraction exerted by the crowd were one and the same. The salvoes of gunfire by the police aroused boohs, the boohs new salvoes. But no matter where you happened to be under the impact of the gunfire, no matter where you seemingly fled, your connection with others (an open or secret connection, depending on the place) remained in effect. And you were drawn back into the province of the fire—circuitously, since there was no other possible way.

This day, which was borne by a uniform feeling (a single, tremendous wave surging over the city, absorbing it: when the wave ebbed, you could scarcely believe that the city was still there)—this day was made up of countless details, each one etched in your mind, none slipping away. Each detail exists in itself, memorable and discernible, and yet each one also forms a part of the tremendous wave, without which everything seems hollow and absurd. The thing to be grasped is the wave, not these details. During the following year and then again and again later on, I tried to grasp the wave, but I have never succeeded. I could not succeed, for nothing is more mysterious and more incomprehensible than a crowd. Had I fully understood it, I would not have wrestled with the problem of a crowd for thirty years, trying to puzzle it out and trying to depict it and reconstruct it as thoroughly as possible, like other human phenomena.

Even were I to assemble all the concrete details of which this day consisted for me, bring them together hard and un-adorned, neither reducing nor exaggerating—I could not do justice to this day, for it consisted of more. The roaring of the wave was audible all the time, washing these details to the surface; and only if this wave could be rendered in words and depicted, could one say: really, nothing has been reduced.

Instead of approaching individual details, however, I could speak about the effects that this day had on my later think-ing. This day was responsible for some of my most important insights in my book on crowds. Anything I looked for in widely separate source works, repeating, testing, taking notes, reading, and then subsequently rereading in slow motion, as it were, I was able to compare with the memory of that cen-tral event, which remained fresh—notwithstanding subse-quent events, which occurred on a greater scale, involving more people, with greater consequences for the world. For later years, when agitation and indignation no longer had the same weight, the isolation of the Fifteenth of July, its restriction to Vienna, gave it something like the character of a model: an event limited in both space and time, with an indisputable cause and taking a clear and unmistakable course.

Here, once and for all, I had experienced something that I later called an *open* crowd, I had witnessed its formation: the confluence of people from all parts of the city, in long, steadfast, undeflectable processions, their direction set by the position of the building that bore the name *Justice*, yet embodied injustice because of a miscarriage of justice. I had come to see that a crowd has to fall apart, and I had seen it fearing its disintegration; I had watched it do everything it could to prevent it; I had watched it actually see itself in the fire it lit, hindering its disintegration so long as this fire burned. It warded off any attempt at putting out the fire; its own longevity depended on that of the fire. It was scattered, driven away, and sent fleeing by attacks; yet even though wounded, injured, and dead people lay before it on the streets, even though the crowd had no weapons of its own, it gathered again, for the fire was still burning, and the glow of the flames illuminated the sky over the squares and streets. I saw that a crowd can flee without panicking; that mass flight and panic are distinguishable. So long as the fleeing crowd does not disintegrate into individuals worried only about themselves, about their own persons, then the crowd still exists, although fleeing; and when the crowd stops fleeing, it can turn and attack.

I realized that the crowd needs no *leader* to form, notwithstanding all previous theories in this respect. For one whole day, I watched a crowd that had formed *without a leader*. Now and then, very seldom, there were people, orators, giving speeches that supported the crowd. Their importance was minimal, they were anonymous, they contributed nothing to the formation of the crowd. Any account giving them a central position falsifies the events. If anything did loom out, sparking the formation of the crowd, it was the sight of the burning Palace of Justice. The salvoes of the police did not whip the crowd apart: they whipped it together. The sight of people escaping through the streets was a mirage: for even when running, they fully understood that certain people were falling and would not get up again. These victims unleashed the wrath of the crowd no less than the fire did.

During that brightly illuminated, dreadful day, I gained the true picture of what, as a crowd, fills our century. I gained it so profoundly that I kept going back to contemplate it anew, both compulsively and willingly. I returned over and over and watched; and even today, I sense how hard it is for me to tear myself away, since I have managed to achieve only the tiniest portion of my goal: to understand what a crowd is.

The Letters in the Tree

The year following this event was totally dominated by it. My mind revolved around nothing else until summer 1928. I was resolved more than ever to find out just what the crowd was—the crowd that had overwhelmed me both mentally and physically. I pretended to go on studying chemistry, and I began to work on my dissertation; but the assigned topic was so uninteresting that it barely grazed the skin of my mind. I devoted every free moment to studying the things that were really important to me. In the most diverse, seemingly far-fetched ways, I tried to approach what I had experienced as a crowd. I sought crowds in history, in the histories of *all* civilizations. I was more and more fascinated by the history and early philosophy of China. I had already started in with the Greeks much earlier, while attending school in Frankfurt. I now delved further and further into ancient historians, especially Thucydides. It was natural that I study revolutions, the English, French, and Russian ones. Furthermore,

I began to get insights into the meaning of crowds in religions; it was at this time that I developed my eagerness to know about all religions, a desire that has never left me. I read Darwin, hoping to learn something about the formation of crowds among animals, and I thoroughly perused books on insect societies. I must have gotten little sleep, for I read through many nights. I wrote down a number of things and tried to pen a few essays. These activities were all tentative and preliminary work for a book on crowds, but they were fairly meaningless, since they were based on too little knowledge.

In reality, this was the beginning of a new expansion in many directions at once; and the good thing about it was that I set myself no limits. True, I was after something specific, I wanted to find testimony to the existence and effect of crowds in all realms of life. But since little attention had been paid to this phenomenon, such documents were sparse; and as a result, I found out about all sorts of things that had nothing whatsoever to do with crowds. I became familiar with Chinese names and soon Japanese names as well; I began to move freely among them, as I had done among the Greeks during my school days. Among the translations of Chinese classics, I came upon Chuang Tzu, the philosopher I am now most familiar with; under the impact of his works, I began to write a paper on Taoism. To rationalize straying so far from my actual theme, I tried to convince myself that I would never understand crowds without first learning what extreme *isolation* is. However, the true reason for my fascination with this original trend in Chinese philosophy was (without my realizing it) the importance of *metamorphoses* here. It was, as I see today, a good instinct that drew me to metamorphoses; my probing kept me from giving in to the world of concepts, and thus I have always remained at the edge of this world.

It is strange with what skill—I cannot call it anything else— I avoided abstract philosophy. In it, I found no trace of what I was hunting as a crowd, a both concrete and potent phenomenon. It was not until much later that I understood the disguise of crowds and the form in which they appear in certain philosophers.

I do not believe that any of the numerous things I experienced in this pushing, tempestuous way remained on the surface. Everything struck roots and spread into adjacent areas. The connections between things that were remote from one another were created under the ground. They remained concealed from me for a long time, which was a good thing, for they then emerged years later, all the more strongly and surely. I do not feel that it is dangerous to make plans that are too all-encompassing. A narrowing comes with the process of life; and while you cannot prevent such narrowing altogether, you can at least hold it up and work against it by spreading out as far as possible.

The despair right after July 15, a kind of paralysis caused by horror, sometimes coming over me as I worked and making it impossible for me to continue, endured for six or seven weeks, until early September. Karl Kraus's poster, put up at this time, had a cathartic effect, releasing me from my paralysis. However, I retained a sensitive ear for the voice of a crowd. That day had been ruled by raging boohs. Those were lethal boohs, they had been answered with gunfire, and they had intensified when people, hit by bullets, had fallen to the ground. In some streets, the boohs faded out; in others, they swelled up; they were most indelible in the vicinity of the conflagration.

A short time later, the boohs moved to the area around Hagenberggasse. A mere fifteen minutes from my room, on the other side of the valley, over in Hüttelsdorf, lay the Rapid Stadium, where soccer matches were held on Sundays and holidays. Huge throngs poured into the stadium, unwilling to miss the famous Rapid soccer match. I had paid little heed since soccer did not interest me. But on a Sunday after July 15, a hot day again, I was expecting company; and through my open windows, I suddenly heard the shouts of the crowd.

I mistook them for boohs; I was still so filled with my experience of the terrible day that I was confused for a moment and looked out for the fire that had illuminated that day. However, there was no fire; the golden dome of the church of Steinhof was glowing in the sun. I came to my senses and realized that the noise was pouring over from the playing field. By way of confirming this, the noise was soon repeated; I listened very strenuously; these were no boohs: the crowd was shouting.

I had been living here for three months and never paid attention to these shouts. They must have wafted over to me earlier, just as powerful and bizarre as they were now; but I had been deaf to this noise. It was only the Fifteenth of July that had opened my ears. I did not budge from the spot; I listened to the entire game. The triumphal shouts were triggered by goals and came from the winning side. One could also hear a different noise, a cry of disappointment. I could see none of this from my window: there were trees and houses in the way; the distance was too great. But I could hear the crowd, and it alone, as though everything were taking place right near me. I could not tell from which of the two sides the shouts were coming. I did not know who the teams were. I paid no attention to their names and made no effort to find them out. I avoided reading any newspaper items about them, and I never conversed about them during the week.

But throughout the six years that I lived in this room, I missed no opportunity to listen to these sounds. I saw the torrent of people down by the urban rail station. If the throng was denser than normal at this time, I knew that a match was scheduled and I went over to my window. I find it hard to describe my excitement when following the game from a distance. I did not root for either side, since I did not know which side was which. There were two crowds, that was all I knew; both equally excitable and speaking the same language. At this time, detached from the place that had given rise to them, not diverted by a hundred circumstances and particulars, I developed a feeling for what I later understood and attempted to describe as a double crowd. Sometimes, when deeply absorbed by something, I sat writing at my desk in the middle of the room, while the game went on. But whatever I was writing, no sound from the Rapid Stadium eluded me. I never got *habituated* to the noise. Every single sound made by the crowd had its effect on me. Reading through manuscripts of those days, I believe even today that I can discern every point at which such a sound was heard, as though it were marked by a secret notation.

It is certain that this locality kept alive my interest in my project, even when I concentrated on other things. It was a loud nourishment that I received in this way, at intervals that were not too large. In my isolation at the edge of the city, an isolation that I had had good reasons for seeking and to which I owe what little my years in Vienna produced, I remained in contact—even unwillingly—with that most urgent, most unsettled, most enigmatic phenomenon. At times that I did not choose myself, it talked away at me, forcing me back to my project, which I might have escaped by seeking refuge in more comfortable problems.

Starting in autumn, I went to the Chemical Laboratory again every day, to work on my dissertation, which did not interest me at all. I thought of it as a secondary occupation, something I did because I had already begun it. To finish anything I had begun was an inexplicable principle of my character: even chemistry, which I admitted I despised, was something I could not break off, since I had gone so far with it. My attitude involved a secret respect that I had never owned up to: the knowledge of poisons. Since Backenroth's death, they were constantly on my mind; I never entered the laboratory without thinking how easily each of us could get hold of cyanide.

In the laboratory, there were students who, if not quite openly, then at least unmistakably, were of the opinion that wars are inevitable. This opinion was by no means restricted to people already sympathizing with the National Socialists. There were many such sympathizers, but none of those we knew in close proximity in the laboratory were aggressive or hostile to anyone. In this daily work environment, they almost never voiced their opinions. I personally caught, at best, a certain restraint, which, however, sometimes turned into cordiality when they noticed my disgust at any pecuniary mentality. There were rustic figures among our students, utterly thrifty people, who could not otherwise have attended the university; they were beside themselves with happiness whenever you gave them some object or other without expecting payment. I enjoyed the stunned face of a country boy who scarcely knew me and who expected me—notwithstanding all outer appearances—to have the well-camouflaged character of a livestock dealer.

However, I also met students whose openness and innocence I still recall with amazement today. At one lecture, I met a boy whom I instantly noticed in the crowd because of his radiant gaze and his powerful and yet cautious way of moving. We got into a conversation and then occasionally met again. He was the son of a judge, and, unlike his father, as he told me, he trusted in Hitler. He had his own reasons for this faith, which he advocated with complete openness—I might almost say, with grace: He said there should never be war again; war was the worst thing that could happen to mankind, and the only man who could save the world from war was Hitler. When I advocated the opposite conviction, he insisted that he had heard Hitler speak, and Hitler *had said so himself*. That was the reason he supported him, he said, and no one would ever talk him out of it. I was so flabbergasted that I saw him again for that very reason, continuing the same conversation several times. He would then come out with the same or even lovelier statements about peace. I can see him before me, his glowing face of peace, the countenance of an apostle, and I hope that he did not have to pay for his faith with his life.

I lived so intensely *next* to chemistry that I cannot think back to those days without recalling faces and conversations that have nothing to do with chemistry. Perhaps I showed up punctually at the laboratory, attended the lectures regularly, because I came together with so many young people whom I did not have to seek out deliberately: they were simply there. I thus got to know all the attitudes of the period, naturally and on the side, without making much ado about it. Generally, no one really thought about war back then; or if someone did think about it, then only about the past war. It is horrifying to recall how remote people felt back then, in 1928, from any new war. The fact that war could suddenly exist again, and as a *faith,* was connected with the nature of a crowd; and it was no false instinct that led me to find out the tricks of this nature. I did not realize how much I learned in the laboratory from seemingly absurd or insignificant conversations. I encountered advocates of all opinions that were affecting the world. And had I been open to all concrete things (as I mistakenly imagined myself to be), I might have gained a good number of important insights from these supposedly trivial conversations. But my respect for books was still too great, and I had barely set out on the road to the true book: each individual human being, bound in himself.

The road to Veza was long, now that I lived on Hagenberggasse; all Vienna, in its greatest extension, lay between us. On Sundays, she came out to my place in the early afternoon, and we went to the Lainz Park. The tone of our conversations never changed; I still handed her every new poem of mine; she preserved all of them carefully in a small straw handbag. During the week, she wrote me lovely letters about them, letters which I preserved no less carefully. There was a great deal of air between us, and we actually developed a tree cult in the park. The park had splendid examples of trees. We sought them out with the faces of connoisseurs and settled at their feet.

One of these trees played an unusual role. I had gotten to know death masks through Ibby Gordon, the cheeriest of people. I was so preoccupied with these masks that I gave Veza a copy of the book. I failed to realize how tactless this was, for everything connected to death was part of Veza's province. When I brought her the book, which I had told her about, she made a nasty face and angrily threw the book on the ground. I picked it up, she threw it down again, refusing to open it. She said it didn't belong to her, it belonged to that other woman, who claimed to be a poet and was always grinning; she was the one who had introduced me to these masks. She really did say "grinning." Veza did not know Ibby personally, but I had told her about Ibby's merriment; and since merriment was the thing that Veza lacked most, she thought that Ibby's merriment was my only reason for regarding her as a poet. Now Veza could not get over the fact that Ibby had interloped with these death masks.

I took the book along again; she threatened to hurl it out the window, and she would have done so. I liked her jealousy, which I had never experienced. I told her everything: I was completely open with her; she knew and believed that all I had with Ibby was conversations. But during these conversations, Ibby would recite her poems to me in Hungarian. One day, I had come to Veza full of enthusiasm, carrying on about the beauties of the Hungarian language, even though I had not liked the sound of it earlier. I said that it was beyond any doubt one of the most beautiful languages, and then I told Veza about Ibby's attempts to translate her poems into her comical German. I had put some order into this impossible German, which was bristling with mistakes, and Ibby had then written down the corrected versions. They were very funny poems, I said, by no means wild and frenzied like my own, always cool and witty, each one composed in terms of a specific, always different voice. Veza listened attentively. And though I made it clear that—in terms of my truth back then—I could not regard these pieces as poetry, anyone could tell how much I enjoyed listening to them and correcting them.

This had gone on for a while, until the outburst over the death masks; it is not easy for me to report on what happened next. I would have to tell how Veza once came to Hagenberggasse and went up to my room (I was out). She took all her letters (she knew where I kept them) and then went to the Lainz Park. She had to walk quite a while until she found a defective spot in the wall, which she could climb across with no great effort. She then looked for a tree that forked approximately at the level of her eyes and had a hollow space; she stuck the large package of letters inside. She then returned to Hagenberggasse. I was home by now. I saw that she was terribly upset and I soon wormed it out of her: her letters were gone, and she admitted carrying them off. She said she had thrown them away in the forest. Panicking, I begged her to show me the spot. I was sure no one had been there. The park was closed on that day; we could surely find her letters and save them. My panic was beneficial for her, it was obvious how important the letters were to me; so she relented and, at my urging, she took me back along the rather lengthy path to the park. We climbed over the wall, she found the tree, which she had noted carefully, she told me to reach into the fork. I did so, and my finger struck paper. I instantly knew that these were her letters. I pulled them out; I hugged and kissed them. I danced with them over the wall and back to Hagenberggasse. Veza came along, but was unheeded, all my attention focused on the retrieved letters. I held the package in my arms like a child, I leaped up the steps to my room, and I placed the package in its drawer. Veza was very moved by my actions, her jealousy was gone. She believed how much I loved her.

It is possible that I saw less of Ibby after that, but I did see her; and when we met in the coffeehouse, I asked about her new poems. She enjoyed reciting them. I always wanted to hear them in Hungarian first, and then, when I was enchanted by their sound, we attempted to translate them. "Suicide on the Bridge" was one title, or "The Sick Cannibal Chief," "Bamboo Cradle," "Pamela," "Refugee on Ringstrasse," "City Official," *"Déjà Vu,"* "Girl with Mirror." In time, Ibby had a small supply of German versions; but so long as she remained in Vienna, nothing happened with them; we were the only ones to enjoy them. If I had not first heard them in a language I had no inkling of, they might have meant nothing to me. But I liked their lack of gravity, the want of any higher or deeper demand, the parlando with light, always unexpected phrasing—things I had never associated with poetry. I was afraid to show her any of my own verse. Because of our imaginative and varied conversations, she assumed that my poems were tremendous things of which she was not quite worthy. She thought I was simply being considerate, trying to spare her, unwilling to embarrass her with them; she was grateful and entertained me with all the stories about the stupid men who courted her and uselessly pestered her.

This went on until spring of the following year. Then the situation became too much for Ibby. The two brothers especially had gotten into a conflict that was taking on serious proportions. It annoyed her because it bored her. One day, she vanished from Vienna. I didn't hear from her for over two months. Then, when I had almost given up on her, a letter came from Berlin. She was well, the translations of her poems had brought her luck. I don't know who had given her recommendations to people in Berlin; she never breathed a word about this even later. But all at once, she found herself among so many interesting people; she knew Brecht and Döblin, Benn and George Grosz; her poems had been accepted by *Querschnitt* and *Die Literarische Welt* and would soon be printed. She wrote me again, urging me to come to Berlin, at least for summer vacation: I would have time from July to October, she pointed out, three whole months. A friend of hers, a publisher, would like to hire me. He needed someone to help him compile material for a book. I would have an easy time getting in with the people there, and she had so much to tell me that three months wouldn't be enough.

Her letters became more frequent and more pressing as the summer approached. Did I always have to go to the mountains? I must know them well enough by now, and what was more boring than mountains? The terrible thing about mountains was that they never changed, so they wouldn't run away from me. But it was highly questionable whether Berlin would remain this interesting for long. And what should she do when she had no more poems? No one could translate them as well as I; it was no work whatsoever, we were simply together and talking, and all at once the poems were there. Could I really have the heart to let her starve there when she finally had the chance to live on her poems?

She probably *was* thinking about the translations of her poems, but I believe she cared more about our conversations. She could tell me everything she felt like, without spoiling things with her friends there. How could she possibly keep silent about such an endless number of things? Once, she wrote me that I would be reading a story in the newspapers about a silent poetess being blown up in Berlin, if I didn't come soon.

Her letters were structured in such a way that they always conspicuously held something back: something she couldn't write about, she would tell it to me personally in Berlin. There were exciting and peculiar things in Berlin, she said; you just couldn't believe things you saw with your own two eyes.

My curiosity grew with each of her letters. She never mentioned anyone who wasn't famous for something. I had read little by the writers she named, but, like anyone else, I knew who they were. However, the man who meant more to me than any writer was George Grosz. The thought of seeing him made up my mind.

On July 15, 1928, right at the end of the semester, I went to Berlin for the summer.

Part Four

The Throng
of Names

Berlin 1928

The Brothers

Wieland Herzfelde had a garret apartment at 76 Kurfürst-endamm. The building stood right in the middle of the hubbub, but things seemed quiet way up there; you scarcely thought about the noise. During the summer, he lived with his family by Nikolassee. Renting out part of his city garret, he left the other part for me to work in. I had a small bed-room and, right next to it, a study with a lovely round table. Here, everything I needed for work was piled up. I was thus left undisturbed, which greatly pleased me. I did not have to go to the publishing house, which was cramped and noisy. Herzfelde would come up to the garret for a few hours to discuss the project. He was planning a biography of Upton Sinclair, who was celebrating his fiftieth birthday.

The Malik house was well known for publishing the draw-ings of George Grosz. But it was also interested in new Rus-sian writers—and not just the new ones. Along with a com-plete edition of Gorky, Malik also brought out one of Tolstoy; Malik also focused on authors who had become known since the Revolution. For me, the most important of these authors was Isaac Babel, whom I admired no less than I did George Grosz.

Now the Malik publishing house not only had a good name, it was also lucky enough to be commercially successful, something it owed to its star author, Upton Sinclair. Since his exposé of the Chicago stockyards, he had become one of the most widely read American authors. He was a prolific writer, always striving to find new abuses to pillory. There was no lack of them. He was hardworking and courageous: he brought out a new book each year. His books grew thicker and thicker. Sinclair was greatly respected, particularly in Europe. By now, around his fiftieth birthday, he had written enough books to fill someone else's life's work in addition to his own. It has also been proved that his Chicago book led to abolishing certain abuses in the stockyards. No less important for his reputation was the fact that modern American literature, which was to conquer the world, was only just emerging. Upton Sinclair's fame was a "material" fame, bound to America as its material. And, not insignificantly, Sinclair, who, as America's true muckraker, attacked pretty much everything, aroused the widest interest in his country and even contributed most to the "America" fad, which was rampant in Berlin and to which Brecht, George Grosz, and others had succumbed. Dos Passos, Hemingway, Faulkner, writers of an incomparably higher rank, did not have their impact until later.

Back then, in the summer of 1928, Wieland Herzfelde could not be blamed for taking Upton Sinclair seriously and even wanting to write his biography. Kept busy by his publishing house, Herzfelde needed help for this project and had invited me, at Ibby's recommendation, to spend the summer months in Berlin.

So here I was in Berlin, never taking more than ten steps without running into a celebrity. Wieland knew everyone and introduced me to everyone right away. I was a nobody here and quite aware of this; I had done nothing; at twenty-three, I was nothing more than hopeful. Yet it was astonishing how people treated me: not with scorn, but with curiosity, and, above all, never with condemnation. I myself, after four years under Karl Kraus's influence, was filled with all his contempt and condemnation and acknowledged nothing that was determined by greed, selfishness, or frivolity. All objects to condemn were prescribed by Kraus. You were not even allowed to look at them; he had already taken care of that for you and made the decision. It was a *sterilized* intellectual life that we led in Vienna, a special kind of hygiene prohibiting any intermingling whatsoever. No sooner was something universal, no sooner had it gotten into the newspapers, than it was taboo and untouchable.

And suddenly, the very opposite came in Berlin, where contacts of any sort, incessant, were part of the very substance of living. This brand of curiosity must have agreed with me, though I did not realize it; I yielded naïvely and innocently, and just as I had strolled into the maws of tyranny right after my arrival in Vienna, where I had been kept nicely aloof from all temptations, so too, in Berlin, I was at the mercy of the hotbed of vice for several weeks. Nevertheless, I was not alone: I had two guides, and they were so different from each other that they helped me doubly: Ibby and Wieland.

Wieland knew everyone, because he had been here for such a long time. He had arrived in Berlin before the war, at the age of seventeen, and had become friends with Else Lasker-Schüler. Through her, he had met most of the writers and painters, especially the *Sturm* people. Wieland owed her even more: the name of his publishing house, which he had founded at the age of twenty-one with his brother and Grosz; and it is not just my opinion that the exotic name Malik helped to make the house known. To everyone's amazement, Wieland turned out to be a good businessman. His ability contrasted so sharply with his boyish freshness that it seemed almost incredible. He was not really an adventurer, but he won over a good many people with the adventurous quality that they ascribed to him. He got close to people quickly, like a child, but never became overattached, and he detached himself easily. You never had the feeling that he fully belonged to anyone. It was as if he could get up and leave at any time. He was considered footloose, and people wondered where he got his energy from. For he was always on the go, agile and active, never burdened by superfluous knowledge, averse to traditional education, informed by "snooping," not by zealous abstract reading. However, when he had to produce something, he was amazingly precise, suddenly as obstinate as an old man. Both attitudes, the boyish one and the old, experienced one, existed simultaneously, coming into play alternately, whenever he found either attitude suitable.

There was one person who was more than near and dear to him. They were bound by a navel cord, which may not have been so secret, but which you did not notice for a long time, because the two men were as different as if they had come from separate planets: John Heartfield, his brother, who was five years older than he. Wieland was soft and easily moved. You might have regarded him as sentimental, but he was sentimental only intermittently. He had various tempi at his disposition, all of them natural to him; and only one tempo, the emotional one, was gradual. Heartfield was always swift. His reactions were so spontaneous that they got the better of him. He was skinny and very short, and if an idea struck him, he would leap into the air. He uttered his sentences vehemently as if attacking you with his leap. He would angrily hum around you like a wasp. I first experienced this on Kurfürstendamm. Walking along unsuspectingly between him and Wieland, I was asked about termites by the latter and I tried to explain: "They're completely blind and they move only in underground corridors." John Heartfield leaped up at my side and hissed at me, as though I were responsible for the blindness of termites, perhaps also as though I were putting them down for their blindness: "You termite, you! You're a termite yourself!" And from then on, he never called me anything but "termite." At the time, I was frightened: I thought I had insulted him, I did not know how. After all, I had not called him a termite. It took me a while to realize that this was how he reacted to everything that was new to him. It was his way of learning: he could only learn aggressively; and I believe one could show that this is the secret of his montages. He brought things together, he confronted things after first leaping up at them, and the tension of these leaps is preserved in his montages.

John, I feel, was the most thoughtless of men. He consisted of spontaneous and vehement moments. He thought only when he was busy doing a montage. Since he was not always calculating away at something like other people, he remained fresh and choleric. His reaction was a kind of anger, but it was no selfish anger. He learned only from things that he regarded as attacks; and in order to experience something new, he had to see it as an attack. Other people let new things glide off them or swallowed them like syrup. John had to shake new things furiously in order to hold them without enfeebling them.

Only gradually did it dawn on me how indispensable these two brothers were to one another. Wieland never criticized John for anything. He did not excuse his brother's unusual behavior, nor did he seek to explain it. He took it for granted; and it was only when he spoke of his childhood that I understood the bond between them. They were four orphans—two brothers and two sisters—and had been taken in by foster parents in Aigen, near Salzburg. Wieland was lucky with his foster parents. The elder brother, Helmut (this was John's name before he changed it to his English name), had a harder time. The two brothers were always aware that they did not have their real parents, and they became very close to one another. Wieland's true strength was his bond with John. Together, they gained a foothold in Berlin. Helmut had officially changed his name to John Heartfield in protest against the war. This took courage, since he did so before the war ended.

George Grosz, whom they met during that period, became equally good friends with both of them. When the Malik publishing house was started, John quite naturally designed the dust jackets. Each brother had his own family, his own home. They never pressed or pestered one another; but they were both there at the same time; they were both together in the turbulent and incredibly active life of Berlin.

Brecht

The first thing that struck me about Brecht was his disguise. I was taken to lunch at Schlichter, the restaurant in which the intellectual Berlin hung out. In particular, many actors came there. They were pointed out; you recognized them on the spot: the illustrated magazines made them part of your image of public things. However, one must admit that there was not very much theater in their outer appearance, in their greetings and order, in the way they bolted down their food, swallowed, paid. It was a colorful picture, but without the colorfulness of the stage. The only one I noticed among them all—and because of his proletarian disguise—was Brecht. He was very emaciated. He had a hungry face, which looked askew because of his cap. His words came out wooden and choppy. When he gazed at you, you felt like an object of value that he, the pawnbroker, with his piercing black eyes, was appraising as something that had no value. He was a man of few words; you learned nothing about the results of his appraisal. It seemed incredible that he was only thirty. He did not look as if he had aged prematurely, but as if he had always been old.

The notion of an old pawnbroker haunted me during those weeks. I could not shake it off, if only because it seemed so absurd. It was nourished by the fact that Brecht prized nothing so much as usefulness, and he let on, in every way he could, how greatly he despised "lofty" convictions. What he meant was a practical, a solid usefulness, and in this respect there was something Anglo-Saxon about him, in its American variety. The cult of America had already taken root in Berlin, especially among left-wing artists. Berlin emulated New York with neon lights and cars. There was nothing Brecht felt so tender about as his car. Upton Sinclair's books, those exposés of abuses, had a two-edged effect. People shared his attitude about scourging these abuses; but at the same time, they absorbed the American substratum from which those abuses had sprung; they assimilated it like food and pinned their hopes on its expansion and extension. Chaplin happened to be in Hollywood, and, even in this atmosphere, one could applaud his success with a clear conscience.

One of the contradictions about Brecht was that his outer appearance had something ascetic to it. Hunger could also seem like fasting, as though he were deliberately forgoing the object of his greed. He was no pleasure-seeker: he did not find satisfaction in the moment and did not spread out in the moment. Anything he took (and he took anything that might be useful to him from right and left, from behind him and before him) had to be utilized instantly: it was his raw material, and he produced things with it incessantly. Thus, he was a man who manufactured something all the time, and that was his true goal.

The words I annoyed Brecht with, especially the demand that one could write only out of conviction and never for money, must have sounded downright laughable in the Berlin of those days. He knew precisely what he wanted, and was so driven by his goal that it made no difference whatsoever whether he got money for it or not. On the contrary: after a period of straitened circumstances, it was a sign of success if he did receive money. He had great respect for money; the only important thing was *who* received it and not where it came from. He was certain that nothing could make him swerve from his path. Anyone who helped him was on his side (or else cutting into his own flesh). Berlin was teeming with patrons: they were part of the scenery. He used them without falling prey to them.

The things that I said to him, and that annoyed him,

weighed less than a thread against all that. I rarely saw him alone. Ibby was always present; typically he regarded her wit as cynicism. He noticed that she treated me respectfully; she never took sides with him. He loved terrifying me or showering me with scorn when she asked me for information in his presence. Sometimes, he made a mistake in some trivial matter; she would not be put off. She accepted my information, included it definitively in the conversation without batting an eyelash, but also without mocking Brecht. The fact that she did not make fun of him to his face should have indicated that she was not indifferent to being with him. In her own way, she had surrendered to the pervasive avantgarde atmosphere around him.

He did not care much for people, but he put up with them; he respected those who were persistently useful to him; he noticed others only to the extent that they corroborated his somewhat monotonous view of the world. It was this view that increasingly determined the character of his plays, while, in his poems, he started out far more vividly than anyone else in his day; later on, with the help of the Chinese (but this does not belong here), he found his way to something like wisdom.

It must sound surprising when I say how much I owe him, despite all my hostility toward him. During the period of our (almost daily) brief collisions, I was reading his *Manual of Piety.* I was enchanted by these poems, I took them up in one swoop without thinking of him. There were some that cut me to the quick, for instance "The Legend of the Dead Soldier" or "Against Seduction," and others: "Memory of Marie A.," "Poor B.B." Many things, most of the volume, struck me deeply. My own writings crumbled into dust. It would be too much to say that I was ashamed of them; they simply no longer existed; nothing was left of them, not even shame.

For three years, my ego had been feeding on the poems I wrote. I had shown them to no one outside of Veza, but I

showed her almost everything. I had taken her encouragement seriously, trusted her opinion. Some of my poems had
filled me so intensely that I felt as vast as the universe. I had
written all sorts of other things, not just poems; but the poems
were what counted for me—along with the plan to write a
book on crowds. This was still a plan, however; it could take
years. And for the moment, at least, almost nothing existed
of it: a few notes and preliminary jottings, things I had
learned for the book. For the time being, however, the things
I learned were not yet my own; this was still to come. My
own things, I had thought, were the many completed pieces,
short and long poems. And now, everything had been shattered at one blow. I had no pity for all my stuff, I swept it
away with no regret: garbage and rubbish. Nor did I praise
the man who had written the real poems; everything about
him repelled me, from his compulsive disguise to his wooden
speech. But I admired, I loved, his poems.

I was so repulsed by him personally that I said nothing
about the poems when I saw him. Every time I saw him, and
especially every time I heard him speak, I felt furious. I did
not let on about my fury any more than about my enthusiasm for the *Manual of Piety*. No sooner had he uttered a cyn-
ical sentence than I replied with a severe and highly moral
sentence. Once—it must have sounded funny in Berlin—I said
that a true writer has to *isolate* himself in order to accomplish
anything. I said he needed periods in the world and periods
outside the world, contrasting strongly with one another.
Brecht said his telephone was always on his desk, and he could
write only if it rang often. A huge map of the world hung in
front of him on the wall, he said, and he looked at the map
so as never to be outside the world. I would not give in and,
shattered as I was by realizing the futile wretchedness of my
verse, I insisted on my advice, facing the man who wrote the
best poems. Morality was one thing and matter was another,
and when I dealt with this man, who cared only about matter, then nothing but morality counted for me. I railed against

the advertisements contaminating Berlin. They did not bother him; on the contrary, he said, advertisements had their good points: he had written a poem about Steyr Automobiles and been given a car for it. For me, these were words from the devil's own mouth. His boastful confession floored me. I was dumbstruck. No sooner had we left him than Ibby said: "He likes riding in his car," as though it were nothing. But I—crazy as I was—saw him as a murderer. I had "The Legend of the Dead Soldier" on my mind, and he had entered a contest for Steyr Automobiles! "He flatters his car even now," said Ibby. "He talks about it as if it were his girlfriend. Why shouldn't he flatter it *beforehand* in order to get it?"

Brecht liked Ibby; he put up with her witty, unsentimental ways, which contrasted so greatly with her radiant country looks. Nor did she disturb him with any demands. She never competed with anyone. She had surfaced in Berlin as Pomona and could vanish any moment. But it was different with me: I came from Vienna with lofty tones, devoted to the purity and rigor of Karl Kraus, more in thrall to him than ever before because of his Fifteenth of July poster. Nor did I keep his fortifying pomp to myself: I *had* to blurt it out. It was only two or three years since I had escaped the domestic money talk; it still had an effect on me: I never once saw Brecht without expressing my disdain for money. I *had* to hoist my flag and reveal my colors: one did not write for newspapers, one did not write for money; one was committed heart and soul to every word one wrote. This irritated Brecht for more than one reason: I had published nothing; he had never heard of me; my words had no substance for this man, who so greatly valued concrete realities. Since no one had offered me anything, I had refused nothing. No newspaper had asked me to write for it, so I had not resisted any newspaper. "I write only for money," he said drily and hatefully. "I wrote a poem about Steyr Automobiles and I got a car for it." There it was again; it popped up frequently. He was proud of this Steyr car, which he drove into the ground.

After an accident, he managed to wangle a new one by means of an advertising trick.

However, my situation was a lot more complicated than one might assume from what has been said so far. For the man who was faith and conviction for me, whom I venerated more than anyone else in the world, without whose wrath and zeal I wouldn't have cared to live, whom I had never dared to approach (only one single time: after July 15, I had addressed a prayer to him, not a plea, a prayer of gratitude, and I did not even assume that he paid it any heed)—Karl Kraus—was in Berlin at this time and friendly with Brecht. He saw Brecht frequently, and it was through Brecht that I met him, several weeks before the premiere of *The Three-penny Opera*. I did not see Kraus alone, only together with Brecht and other people who were interested in this production. I did not say a word to Kraus. I was afraid to show him how much he meant to me. I had attended every one of his readings since spring 1924, when I arrived in Vienna. But he didn't know this. And even if Brecht (who certainly guessed my state of mind) had made some joking remark about it to him (which wasn't very likely), Kraus let nothing on. He had ignored my exuberant letter of thanks for his poster after July 15; my name meant nothing to him: he must have received countless such letters and thrown them all away.

I much preferred his knowing nothing about me. I sat next to Ibby in the round and kept quiet. I was oppressed by the thought of sitting at the table of a god. I felt unsure of myself, as though I had sneaked in. He was altogether different from the way I knew him at lectures. He hurled no lightning bolts, he damned no one. Of all the people sitting there— some ten or twelve—he was the most polite. He treated each person as if he or she were an unusual creature, and he sounded solicitous, as if assuring that person of his special protection. One felt that nobody escaped his notice; thus he lost nothing of the omniscience attributed to him. However, he deliberately stepped back behind the others, an equal among equals, peaceful, concerned with their sensitivities. His smile was so relaxed, I felt as if he were concealing himself. Given the countless parts I had heard him play, I knew how easily he could conceal himself. However, the role I saw him in now was the one I would never have expected; and he carried it off: he remained the same for an hour or more. I expected something tremendous from him, and what came were cordialities. He treated everyone at the table with tenderness; however, he treated Brecht with love, as though Brecht were his son, the young genius—his *chosen* son.

The people at the table were talking about *The Threepenny Opera,* which did not have this title as yet; they were trying to hit on a name. Many suggestions were made. Brecht listened quietly, in no way as if it were his play. You could not tell that the ultimate decision was his. There were so many suggestions that I can no longer remember who said what. Karl Kraus had a suggestion, which he advocated without getting domineering; he tossed it into the debate, skeptically, as though doubting it. His suggestion was instantly superseded by another, a better one. I do not know from whom the title finally came. It was Brecht who presented it, but perhaps he had gotten it from someone not present and wanted to hear what these people thought about it. In his work he was astonishingly free with demarcations and property lines.

Ecce Homo

"We're visiting Grosz," said Wieland. I did not quite believe that one could go there just like that. Wieland wanted to get something he needed for his publishing house, but he also wanted to impress me, for he had instantly noticed that there was *one* figure in Berlin whom I was dying to meet. Wieland enjoyed showing me everything that Berlin had to offer. He sort of liked my inexperience. It reminded him of his own when he had first come here. He was not domineering like

Brecht, who was always surrounded by adepts. Brecht wanted people to think him hard-boiled, and he must have started at an early age. Be older than you are, just don't appear young. Innocence was despicable to him: he hated innocence, equating it with stupidity. He wanted to be nobody's fool; and long after there was nothing more to prove, he flaunted his precocity, a schoolboy smoking his first cigar and gathering others whom he is trying to cheer-lead. Wieland, however, was in love with the innocence of his own childhood, seeing it as an idyll. He managed to hold his own in the cynicism of Berlin. By no means was he defenseless: he knew all the tricks of the trade, and he demonstrated his capabilities in the so-called struggle of life, which requires hardness, but above all, indifference. However, he managed to hold his own purely by sticking to the image of the innocent orphan boy that he had been. He could speak about it as if he still were that orphan boy. While working, we sometimes got into these conversations; and, as hurried as life in Berlin may have been, when we sat at the round table in that room in his garret, we often wandered away from Upton Sinclair, the object of our work, and turned to the younger Wieland. This present Wieland was no more than thirty-two, but it seemed like a huge leap to the Wieland of fifteen years earlier.

He showed me everything to be seen in Berlin, namely the people, as though I were he himself, coming to Berlin for the first time. And he enjoyed my astonishment without observing it too carefully, for he was concerned not so much with me but with himself, as he had been at my age. It was good for me that he never put me down; he always introduced me as his "friend and colleague." Yet I had only known him for a few days, and I had not yet begun working. He did not ask me for any proof of my abilities; he did not want to read any of my writings. Perhaps it would have been a bother to read something of mine (it is amazing to think that he, the publisher whom I eventually knew best and most intimately, never, not even later, brought out any of my own writings). It was enough for him that we talked. He had heard some things from Ibby; I told him some things myself. Most important for him was that he could tell me, in *his* Berlin, about his innocent ways, his love for his youth, and that I listened. I thus gained his friendship by listening, and I cannot even say that this was cunning on my part; I enjoyed listening. I have always enjoyed listening when people speak about themselves. This seemingly quiet, passive tendency is so violent as to constitute my innermost concept of life. I will be dead when I no longer hear what a person is telling me about himself.

Why did I expect so much from Grosz? What did he mean to me? Ever since Frankfurt, when I had seen books of his displayed at the Bookstore for Young People—that is, for the past six years—I had been admiring these drawings and carrying them around in my head. Six young years are a long time. His drawings had struck me to the core at first sight. They expressed precisely what I felt after the things I saw around me during the inflation, after Herr Hungerbach's visit, after the deaf ears of my mother, who refused to notice anything happening around us. I liked the strength and recklessness you saw in these drawings, the ruthlessness and dreadfulness. Since they were extreme, I regarded them as Truth. A truth that mediated, that weakened, that explained, that excused was no Truth for me. I knew that Grosz's characters really existed. I had known it since my childhood in Manchester, when I had installed the ogre as my foe, which he then always remained for me. A short time after seeing Grosz's drawings, I heard Karl Kraus in Vienna, and the effect was the same. Except that being a verbal person, I began to imitate Kraus. From him, I could learn, above all, how to hear, but also, to a certain degree (and not without some reluctance) the rhetoric of accusal. I never imitated George Grosz: drawing has always been beyond me. I did seek and find his characters in real life, but the distance to a different medium always persisted. His talent was unattainable for me:

he spoke in a different language, which I understood, but which I would never be able to master for my own use. This meant that he never became a model for me—he was the object of my utmost admiration, but never a model.

The first time I entered his home, Wieland, as usual, introduced me as a "friend and colleague." The result was that I never felt *too* small. It did not cross my mind that Grosz was well acquainted with all of Wieland's friends and must have known that I was not one of them. Ibby was suddenly there; I had never been discussed; Ibby had announced that I would shortly be coming from Vienna, that was all. However, I soon managed to get over such insecurities, for Grosz began to show Wieland and me some of his works. I was close to things that had just been created. Grosz was accustomed to showing Wieland his drawings; Wieland had published them and made them renowned. They had picked them out together, and Wieland had found titles for these drawings. Now too, titles were dropped, out of habit. Wieland loved spouting them quickly. There was no discussion of them. Grosz would accept Wieland's titles: they had brought him luck.

Grosz was dressed in tweed, he was strong and tan in contrast to Wieland, and he sucked at his pipe. He looked like a young skipper, not an English one, he talked a great deal, he seemed more American. Since he was extremely open and cordial, I did not regard his costume as a disguise. I felt free with him and I let myself go. I was enthusiastic about everything he showed us. He was delighted by my enthusiasm, as if it were very important to him. He sometimes nodded at Wieland when I said something about a graphic. I sensed that I was on target; and while I couldn't open my mouth in front of Brecht without triggering his sarcasm, I aroused Grosz's interest and delight. He asked me whether I knew the *Ecce Homo* folder. I said no; the set had been banned by law. He went over to a chest, raised the lid, and removed a folder, which he then handed me as if it were nothing special. I thought he wanted me to have a look, and I opened it up; however, I was quickly enlightened: he said I could take it home, the folder was a present. "Not just anybody can get one," said Wieland, who knew how impulsive his friend was. But he did not need to say it. No act of magnanimity has ever eluded me, and I was overwhelmed by this one.

I put down the folder so as not to get into comical movements of happiness, and I had not quite finished thanking him when a visitor appeared: it was the last person I would have wished for or expected: Brecht. He came with all signs of respect, slightly bent; he was bringing a present for Grosz, a pencil, a completely ordinary pencil, which he placed on the drawing table, emphatically and significantly. Grosz accepted this modest homage and transformed it into something greater. He said: "This pencil was just what I needed. I can use it." I felt intruded on by the visit, but I enjoyed seeing Brecht from a different side. This was how he acted when he wanted to show approval; the fact that it occurred in such a restrained and economical way made it all the more impressive. I wondered how Grosz felt about him, whether he liked him. Brecht did not stay long. When he had left, Grosz said to Wieland—casually, as though it were not meant for my ears: "He's got no time, the European stew." It did not sound hateful or hostile, perhaps skeptical, as though he had various opinions about Brecht, conflicting ones.

Wieland and I went our separate ways after leaving Grosz: Wieland to the publishing house, I to my round table in the garret, where the work on Upton Sinclair's documents was waiting for me. In contrast with the things he had exposed as a muckraker, Sinclair's own life seemed boring. This was due not to the *circumstances* of his life (which had been hard), but to his straight and narrow views. He was Puritanical through and through. And even though I was just as Puritanical and ought to have felt a kinship with him, even though I wholeheartedly approved of his attacks against terrible conditions, against humiliation and injustice, I felt that his assaults lacked all satirical brilliance. Thus it was not surprising that I did not get right down to work that day; instead, I opened the *Ecce Homo* folder: it contained everything that one missed in Upton Sinclair.

The folder had been banned as obscene. There is no denying that certain things in it could appear obscene. I took it all in with an odd mixture of horror and approval. These were dreadful creatures of Berlin's night life that you saw here, but they were here because they were viewed as dreadful. I regarded my disgust at them as the artist's disgust. I knew very little about all this, I had been in Berlin for only about a week. Grosz was one of the first people I visited. Ibby had introduced me to Brecht at Schlichter; she regarded him, if only because he was a writer, as the most interesting thing that she could offer me in Berlin. We had gone to this restaurant every day. Brecht liked seeing Ibby, but she always dragged me along, and perhaps that was one reason why he made me the butt of his scorn. Wieland, however, was a generous man; Grosz was far more important to me than Brecht, and that was how it had come to this visit (I believe on the sixth day of my sojourn).

Now, however, I had brought home the *Ecce Homo* folder. It inserted itself between me and Berlin, and from then on, it colored most things for me, especially all the things I saw at night. Perhaps it would otherwise have taken these things a lot longer to penetrate me. My interest in the freedom of sexual matters was still not great. Now these unbelievably hard and ruthless depictions threw me into the sexual world, and I regarded this world as true. I would never have dreamt of doubting its truth. And just as one sees certain landscapes only through the eyes of certain painters, so too I saw Berlin through the eyes of George Grosz.

I was swept off my feet by this first viewing and also terrified, so deeply that I could not part with the folder when Ibby came by and saw the watercolors, which I had found as loose pages in the folder and spread across the table. She had never seen me with anything like this, and she found it funny:

"You've become a Berliner very quickly," she said. "In Vienna, you were crazy about death masks, and now . . ." She spread her arm over the paintings, as though I had gathered them on the table cautiously and with some deliberate plan. "You know," she said, "Grosz likes this. When he's drunk, he talks about 'ass.' He means women, and he looks at you in such a strange way. I pretend I don't understand. But he sings a hymn to 'ass.'"

I was beside myself: "That's not true! He hates this! That's why his things are so good. Do you believe I would look at them if what you said were true!"

"*You* don't like that," she said. "I know, I know. That's why I can tell you everything. But he *does* like it! Wait till you see him drunk and he starts carrying on about 'ass.'"

It was characteristic of Ibby that she could say this. She used the word *ass*, and there was no mistaking what she meant: Grosz, being drunk, had tried to make a pass at her and sung the praises of her physicality, an action that might have offended or at least annoyed other women like her. The word *ass* referred to her; she repeated it, and it sounded as if it had nothing to do with her. She remained unmoved, as if he had never gotten too close for comfort, as if all that interested her was the unvarnished report that she gave me.

That was why she had wanted me to come to Berlin—so she could tell me everything. She was pursued by men; wherever she appeared, they would get personal. Three or four men tried it at the same time; one had to succeed. When none of them did succeed, people found her enigmatic. They set up the most abstruse hypotheses; for instance: she was not really a woman, she only looked like one; there was something different about her—her vagina was probably closed up. One particularly distrustful man named Borchardt, who was in Brecht's circle, declared that she was a spy: "Where does she come from? She popped up out of nowhere. Who is she? She's everywhere and listens to everything." Ibby laughed at his remarks and remained in high spirits. She found him ridiculous, but, so long as she was alone in Berlin, she could not say so to anyone, for these people, who saw everything as permissible, were deadly serious about sexual activity, and they would have greatly resented Ibby's mockery (that was all she felt). She could not live without mockery. She had to, was driven to, express her mockery with wit and verbal surprises. And that was why she hadn't rested until she finally managed to lure me to Berlin.

Common to both of us was an insatiable interest in *every* kind of human being. Her interest was colored by humor, and I enjoyed it when she regaled me with her accounts. But I myself did not really find human variety comical. I found it unsettling. People wriggled in every possible way to communicate. But they failed to understand one another. It was every man for himself. And even though every man did remain alone, notwithstanding all delusions, he kept on wriggling indefatigably. I listened to all the flagrant misunderstandings that Ibby told me about. I was confronted with many of them myself, but she brought special testimony into my world, things that I as a man could not experience. Beautiful and sought after as she was, she received nothing but the most absurd propositions, as though she herself did not exist, as though there were only a seemingly live statue of her to receive suggestions. Her answers, however, were not heard: they never reached the ears of those men, who cared only about having their say and, if possible, getting what they lusted after. They did not realize why they never succeeded, for they would have been utterly incapable of grasping an answer. Nor would it have interested them to find out anything about their rivals; such information, even though they all seemed to have the same goal, would have been strange and unintelligible to them. For no matter how precisely and inalterably Ibby retained their words and deeds, each man, in order to *understand* them, would have had to disregard himself, and this was something none of them wished to do.

Isaac Babel

A large portion of my memories of Berlin is filled with Isaac Babel. He could not have been there very long, but I feel as if I had seen him every day for weeks on end, for hours and hours, yet we never spoke very much. I was so fond of him—more than any of the countless other people I met—that he has spread out in my memory, which would like to grant him every one of the ninety days of Berlin.

He came from Paris, where his wife, a painter, was studying with André Lhote. He had stayed in various places in France. French literature was his promised land; he regarded Maupassant as his true master. Gorky had discovered Babel and watched over him; he had counseled Babel in a manner that could not have been wiser and more promising. He had perceived Babel's possibilities and had been intent on helping *him*, not himself, with unselfish criticism, serious and unmocking, knowing quite well how easy it is to destroy someone younger, weaker, unknown, before the tyro can know what is in him.

Babel, after traveling abroad for a long time, had stopped off in Berlin on the way back to Russia. I think he was here in late September, actually remaining no more than two weeks. The two books that had made him famous, *Red Cavalry* and *The Odessa Tales*, had both been published in German by the Malik publishing house. I had read the latter book more than once. I could admire him without feeling all too remote from him.

I had heard about Odessa as a child. The name went back to the earliest phase of my life. I laid claim to the Black Sea, even though I had known it for only a few short weeks in Varna. The colorfulness, wildness, and energy of Babel's Odessa stories were virtually nourished by my own childhood memories. Without realizing it, I had found the natural capital for that smaller town on the lower Danube; and I would have found it suitable if this Odessa had developed at the mouth of the Danube. Then, the famous voyage that had determined the dreams of my childhood, up the Danube and down again, would have stretched from Vienna to Odessa and from Odessa back to Vienna. And Ruschuk, which lay very far downstream, would have had a proper place on this route.

I was curious about Babel, as though he came from this region, which I only halfheartedly acknowledged as my own. I could feel at ease about a place only if it was open to the world. Odessa was such a place. That was how Babel felt about Odessa and its stories. In my childhood home, all windows faced Vienna. Now, on a previously averted side, a window was opened toward Odessa.

Babel was a small, squat man with a very round head. The first thing you noticed about him was his thick glasses. Perhaps it was these glasses that made his wide-open eyes seem particularly round and gaping. No sooner had he appeared than you felt viewed, and, virtually as recompense for so much attention, you told yourself that he looked broad and powerful and by no means feeble—an impression that would have been more consistent with the effect of the glasses.

I first saw him at Schwanecke, a restaurant that struck me as luxurious, perhaps because people went there at night and after the theater. It would then teem with famous theatrical figures. No sooner had you noticed one than another went by, an even greater celebrity. There were so many celebrities during this efflorescence of the theater that you soon gave up noticing each and every one of them. There were also writers, painters, patrons, critics and fancy journalists. And Wieland, with whom I had come, was always attentive enough to explain to me who these people were. He had known them all so long already that they made no impact on him. He didn't sound as if he were name-dropping, more as if he were questioning their right to fame, as though they were overrated and would soon vanish from the scene. He had his own horses in the running, the people he had discovered himself, whose books he published and whom he was trying to bring to the attention of the public. Hence he naturally preferred talking about them, and certainly in greater detail. At Schwanecke in the evening, he never sat at a separate table with his loyal followers, dissociating himself from the outside world. Instead, he mingled in larger groups, where friend and foe sat together; here, Wieland looked for someone to attack. He advocated his cause aggressively, not defensively, but he generally didn't stay long, for he had already noticed another group where there was someone who inspired his urge to attack. I soon realized that he was not the only one employing this aggressive method. Then too, there were people who asserted themselves by complaining, and even those who came right into the midst of this noisy turbulence in order to keep quiet—a minority, but a highly conspicuous one: mute, pinched face-islands in the seething landscape, turtles who knew how to drink, and whom you had to ask about because they never reacted to any questions.

The first evening that Babel appeared at Schwanecke, a large group was sitting at a long table in the front room. I had come late and had sat down shyly at the far end of the group, right near the door. I hovered on the edge of my chair as though sliding off and about to vanish. The "handsomest" man in the circle was Leonhard Frank. He had a deeply furrowed face with chiseled features; it looked as if it had gone through all the ups and downs of life, gladly marked by experience and for all to see. Frank's slender, muscular body was clothed in an elegant custom-made suit and seemed about to leap; one jump, and he would have swung as a panther across the entire length of the table, and the suit would not have been crumpled or twisted in any way. Despite his deep furrows, he didn't look the least bit old, more like a man in the prime of life. In his youth, people said in awesome tones, he had been a blacksmith (others said, less poetically, that he had been a locksmith). Not surprising, given his strength and agility. I imagined him at the anvil, not in this suit, which bothered me. However, there was no denying that he felt absolutely wonderful here, at Schwanecke.

The same was true in a different way for the Russian writers at the table. In those days, they traveled frequently and they liked coming to Berlin; the devil-may-care turbulence suited their temperaments. They were very friendly with Herzfelde, their publisher; he was not their only publisher, but he was certainly the most effective. Any author he brought out was not overlooked; this was impossible, if only because of the jackets designed by his brother John Heartfield. Anya Arkus sat there; people said she was a new poet. She was the most beautiful woman I had ever seen: it sounds incredible, for she had the head of a lynx. I never heard her name again; perhaps she wrote under a different name, perhaps she died early.

I ought to speak about others who sat there, especially those who are forgotten today and whose faces I may be the only one to recall, though without their names. This is not the place to bring them up, however, because that evening was significant for a very special reason; everything else pales next to it. It was the evening when Babel appeared for the first time, a man not distinguished by anything that was typical of Schwanecke. He did not come as an actor of himself; although lured by Berlin, he was not a "Berliner" in the same sense as the others—he was a "Parisian." The lives of celebrities did not interest him more than other lives, perhaps even less. He felt uncomfortable in the circle of the illustrious and he tried to get away from it. That was why he turned to the only person here who was unknown and did not belong. This person was I, and the sureness with which Babel recognized this at first sight speaks for his sharp eyes and the staunch clarity of his experience.

I can't remember the first few sentences. I made room for him, he remained standing. He didn't appear determined to stay. Yet he seemed immobile, standing there as if in front of an abysmal fissure, which he knew and was trying to block.

Berlin 1928 / 289

My impression may have been caused partly by his broad shoulders, which were blocking my view of the entrance. I saw no one else who came, I saw only him. He made a dissatisfied face and tossed a few sentences to the Russians at the table. I couldn't tell what his words meant, but they inspired confidence in me. I was certain that he had said something about Schwanecke, which he disliked no less than I; *he*, however, could say so. It is possible that I first became aware of my dislike of the place through him. For the poetess with the lynx face sat not too far from me, and her beauty made up for everything else. I wanted him to stay; I pinned my hopes on her. Who would not have stayed for her sake? She waved to him and signaled that she wanted to make room for him next to her. He shook his head and pointed his finger at me. This could only mean that I had already offered him a seat; his cordial gesture delighted and confused me. *I* would have sat next to her unhesitatingly, although greatly embarrassed. But he didn't wish to offend me, so he turned her down. I now forced him to sit on my chair and went off in search of another. There was none to be found. I went past every table; I wandered around futilely for a while. By the time I returned empty-handed, Babel was gone. The poetess told me that he hadn't wanted to rob me of my chair, so he had left.

This first act of his, occasioned by myself, may seem unimportant; but it was bound to have a great impact on me. Standing there in his solid, sturdy way, he had reminded me of his *Red Cavalry*, the wonderful and dreadful stories that he had experienced among Cossacks in the Russian-Polish War. Even his dislike of the restaurant, which I thought I had read in his face, fitted in with his stance; and the same man who had gone through those rough, harsh times had now shown such tenderness and consideration toward a very young man, whom he didn't know and whom he now distinguished with his interest.

He was very curious: he wanted to see everything in Berlin; but for him, "everything" meant the *people*, and indeed all kinds of people, not those who hung out in the artists' restaurants and the fancy pubs. His favorite place was Aschinger's restaurant. There we stood side by side, very slowly eating a pea soup. With his globular eyes behind his very thick eyeglasses, he looked at the people around us, every single one, all of them, and he could never get his fill of them. He was annoyed when he finished the soup. He wished for an inexhaustible bowl, for all he wanted to do was keep on looking; and since the people changed rapidly, there was a great deal to see. I have never met anyone who looked with such intensity. He remained utterly calm; the expression of his eyes changed incessantly because of the play of muscles around them. He rejected nothing when seeing, for he felt equally serious about everything; the most usual as well as the most unusual things were important to him. He felt bored only among the spendthrifts at Schwanecke or Schlichter. When I was sitting there and he came in, he would look for me and then sit down nearby. But he wouldn't stay seated for long; very soon, he said: "Let's go to Aschinger!" And no matter what people I may have been with, I regarded it as the greatest possible honor in Berlin that he liked taking me there. So I stood up and left.

However, it was not the extravagance of these fancy restaurants that he carped at when uttering the name "Aschinger." It was the peacock ways of the artists that repelled him. Everyone wanted attention, everyone played himself, the air was simply rigid with heartless vanities. Babel himself was generous; to reach Aschinger faster, he would take a cab, even for short distances. And when it was time to pay, he would zoom over to the driver and explain to me with exquisite politeness why he *had* to pay. He had just received some money, he said; he was not allowed to take it along, he *had* to spend it in Berlin. And though my instinct told me that none of this could be true, I forced myself to believe him, because I was enchanted with his magnanimity. He never put into words what he thought about my situation: that I was a student and probably not earning anything. I had admitted to him that I hadn't published yet. "That doesn't matter," he had said. "It'll come soon enough." As if it were shameful to have published already. I believe he took me into his care because he empathized with my embarrassment at being among so many trumpets of glory. I said little to him, a lot less than to other people. Nor did he talk very much; he preferred looking at people. He became loquacious in my presence only when the conversation turned to French literature; he admired Stendhal and Maupassant above anything else.

I thought I would hear a great deal from him about the great Russians, but he must have taken them for granted, or maybe he found it boastful to expatiate on the literature of his own countrymen. But perhaps there was more to it; perhaps he recoiled from the inevitable shallowness of such a conversation: he himself moved in the language in which the great works of that literature were written, and I had read them at best in translations. We would not have been speaking about the same thing. He took literature so seriously that he must have hated anything vague and approximate. However, my timidity was no weaker than his; I couldn't get myself to say anything to him about *Red Cavalry* or *The Odessa Tales.*

Yet in our conversations about the French, about Stendhal, Flaubert, and Maupassant, he must have sensed how important *his* stories were to me. For whenever I asked him about anything, my question secretly referred to something of his that I was focusing on. He instantly recognized the tacit reference, and his answer was simple and precise. He saw how satisfied I was; perhaps he even liked the fact that I didn't keep on asking. He spoke about Paris, where his wife, a painter, had been living for a year. I believe he had just called for her there and was already missing Paris. He preferred Maupassant to Chekhov, but when I mentioned Gogol (whom I loved more than anything), he said, to my joyful amazement: "That's one thing the French lack—they don't have Gogol." Then he reflected a bit and, to make up for what might have sounded like boasting, he added: "Do the Russians have Stendhal?"

I realize how few concrete things I have to say about Babel, and yet he meant more to me than anyone else I met in Berlin. I saw him together with everything of his that I had read—not much, but it was so concentrated that it colored every moment. And I was also present when he absorbed things in a city that was alien to him, and they were not in his language. He didn't throw around big words and he avoided drawing attention. He could *see* best if he was hidden. He accepted everything from others; he didn't reject things he didn't care for. The things that tormented him most were the things that he allowed to exert the longest effect on him. I knew all this from his Cossack stories; everyone was enthralled by their blood-filled brilliance without being intoxicated by the blood. Here, where he was confronted with the brilliance of Berlin, I could see how indifferent he was to things in which other people bathed in blabbering vanity. He disapproved of any empty reflex; instead, his thirsty eyes lapped up countless people eating their pea soup. One sensed that nothing was easy for him, even though he never said so himself. Literature was sacrosanct to him; he never spared himself and would never have *embellished* anything. Cynicism was alien to him because of his strenuous conception of literature. If he found that something was good, he could never have *used* it like other people, who, in sniffing around, implied that they regarded themselves as the culmination of the entire past. Knowing what literature was, he never felt superior to others. He was obsessed with literature, not with its honors or with what it brought in. I do not believe that I saw Babel any differently from what he was because he spoke to me. I know that Berlin would have devoured me like lye if I hadn't met him.

The Transformations of Ludwig Hardt

One Sunday, I happened to be at a morning performance by Ludwig Hardt: a reciter after the poets' own hearts, recognized by all of them, especially the avant-garde. No one made a face when his name came up; not even Brecht pronounced a wooden verdict (just imagine all the things he did reject). Ludwig Hardt was said to be the only speaker of both classical and modern literature who could handle both with equal mastery. People praised his faculty for metamorphoses; they said he was really an actor, but an unusually intelligent one. His programs, they said, were cunningly arranged. Never had anyone been bored by him, which meant a great deal in Berlin, where everyone was trying his luck. In terms of my thralldom back then, there was one more thing that occupied my thoughts: Hardt had been friends with Karl Kraus, and, in earlier years, he had recited portions of *The Last Days of Mankind*. But they had had a fight about this and had broken with one another. Now his program lacked nothing of any importance in modern literature, except this one thing that had been forbidden him: Karl Kraus.

Hardt's reading, which I attended with Wieland, was devoted to Tolstoy. Hardt was planning to read from the Malik edition of Tolstoy, otherwise Wieland wouldn't have gone. Wieland never enthused about actors, and he watched them perform only if he absolutely had to. This was his way of defending himself against the glut of Berlin. He explained to me how quickly Berlin used up people. Anyone who didn't know how to arrange things for himself was doomed. You had to husband your curiosity, saving it for things that were important to your own work. After all, you were no tourist who'd be leaving again after a couple of weeks. You had to face the fact that you'd be living here, year in, year out, and you had to grow a thick skin. He went to hear the universally admired reciter Ludwig Hardt only in honor of the Tolstoy edition, but he talked me into coming along.

I went and I did not regret it. I have never been able to forget his recital, and our subsequent meeting in the home of a maecenas led to one of those embarrassing incidents from which you learn more than from any insult. Eight years later, in Vienna, he became my friend.

He was a very short man, so short that he struck even me as unusually so. He had a narrow, dark, Southern-like head, which could change in a twinkling, so rapidly and so profoundly that you wouldn't have recognized him. He appeared shaken by bolts of lightning, which he *spoke*, however—characters and poems that he knew by heart and that belonged to him as if native to him. He couldn't stay calm for even a moment, unless he turned into a slow, easygoing character; and that was how I first saw him, as Uncle Yeroshka in Tolstoy's *Cossacks*. His head became very round, his body broad and rough. He knew how to twirl a mustache until you could actually see it; I could have sworn that he had stuck one on (and when he later claimed that he hadn't had one and certainly didn't carry a mustache around in his pocket, I simply didn't believe him). Of all the Tolstoy characters, this Cossack has remained the most vivid for me because *Hardt* portrayed him. It was miraculous to see how small, delicate Ludwig Hardt turned into a huge, heavy, massive Cossack—without leaving his chair and table, without jumping up even once or helping his transformation with suitable movements. The piece he read was rather long, but it seemed to be growing shorter and shorter; people feared he might stop. Then came a few of Tolstoy's folktales, especially "How Much Land Does a Man Need?" And they struck me so deeply that I was convinced these folktales were the essence of Tolstoy, his best, his most intrinsic. Any work by Tolstoy that I subsequently took hold of seemed more lifeless, because I didn't hear it in Ludwig Hardt's voice. He spoiled Tolstoy for me in part. His Yeroshka from the *Cossacks* has remained an intimate of mine. Ever since that time, 1928, I have felt that I know him well, better than other people who were close friends of mine.

However, Ludwig Hardt's interference with my relationship to Tolstoy went even further. Soon after the war, I read Tolstoy's "The Death of Ivan Ilyitch," and it moved me as profoundly as the folktales in 1928. I felt as if I'd been transplanted somewhere else, and at first I thought it might be Ilyitch's sickroom. But then, to my astonishment, it dawned on me that I heard the words in Ludwig Hardt's voice. I found myself in the half-darkened auditorium where Hardt had spoken. He was no longer alive, but his repertoire had expanded, and the much longer novella, "The Death of Ivan Ilyitch," had entered the group of folk stories that he had recited back then.

This is the strongest comment I can make about that performance: the way it reached into a later time. To make this account less incredible, I would like to add that I heard many more readings of Ludwig Hardt's in subsequent years. In Vienna, when we had become friends, he often visited our home and recited to us for hours on end, as long as we cared to listen. He had put out a book containing his programs, and little was kept back from us of the wonders he had included. I got to know his voice in all its rich possibilities, and we often spoke about metamorphosis, which preoccupied me more and more. He had given me my first conscious prompting for this interest with his transformation into old Yeroshka during the performance in Berlin. After the war, when I learned of his death, I picked up "The Death of Ivan Ilyitch," and I think it was a kind of obsequy for him when I attributed to his voice something that I had never heard from it during his lifetime.

But let me return to that first incident, which I have not yet fully reported. Ahead of me lay the satyr play, whose patient victim I ultimately became. After that morning performance, Hardt was invited to a rather large party in the home of a Berlin attorney, where the guests were lavishly regaled. They felt so good that they spent most of the afternoon there. Everything was *comme il faut,* not just the hospitality. The walls sported canvases by painters who were talked about, the latest books (at least those that had gotten friendly or unfriendly attention) were spread out on small tables. Nothing was lacking; no sooner was something mentioned than the host eagerly brought it over, held it under your nose, opened it—all you could do was put it in your mouth. You were spared any trouble, well-known people sat around, chewing or burping. However, notwithstanding the host's officious efforts, intelligent or provocative conversations were going on. The most comfortable person was Ludwig Hardt himself. He was the only one more active than the host. He was even more a-bustle, leaping on low tables and reciting famous speeches, by Mirabeau or by Jean Paul Richter. He wasn't the least bit exhausted, he could keep it up forever; strangest of all, he was interested in people he didn't know, and during the recesses between his leaps, he got involved in conversations. He wouldn't rest until he found out what sort of person he was dealing with. He thus found his way to me, and, infected by his expansiveness, I wasn't ashamed to show him my enthusiasm.

He thanked me in his way by telling me interesting things about his background. He was the son of a horsebreeder in Frisia and had done a lot of riding when he was young. Small and light as he was, he looked like a jockey. I understood why he always had to jump around and I respectfully presented this insight. Any sentence that could be agreeable to him was countered with exquisite *politesse*. With his rich imagination and his eccentricity, he reminded you of E. T. A. Hoffmann. He was quite aware of this association, but it did not exclude other associations. It was impossible for him to recite anything without *resembling* the author of the words.

My embarrassment (for this is what I am reporting) began with one of these leaps. He switched from Hoffmann to Heine, and his agility then increased so greatly that you instantly knew that Heine was one of his most important figures. I must have faltered upon realizing this; the process of free exchange slowed down. But he instantly grasped what had happened, and suddenly he began to come out with everything that had ever been said *against* Heine, and in the words of Karl Kraus, which I was all too familiar with. He spoke these words like a role, with conviction. I fell for it. I added some things with textual fidelity. I didn't notice that he was poking fun at me. But it went on for a long time; I felt as if I were being tested on my knowledge of *Die Fackel*. And it was only when he suddenly broke off and went on to other things in *Die Fackel*, to encomiums on Claudius, on Nestroy, on Wedekind, that I suddenly saw the light. I knew that I had made a complete and utter fool of myself. I said, as though somehow apologizing: "You have a different opinion of Heine."

"Indeed I do!" he said. And now came a splendid slap in my face, a thrilling recitation of several Heine poems, which belonged to Hardt's most intimate repertoire.

I believe that this was the first jolting of my faith in Karl Kraus. For Hardt was measuring himself with Kraus on his most personal terrain, as a reciter, and he emerged victorious. He recited "The Wandering Rats" and "The Silesian Weavers," and his power and fury were in no way second to Karl Kraus's. It was an irruption of a taboo; and, despite threats, curses, and prohibitions, my mind was too sound not to make room for the intrusion. The impact was even stronger because Hardt had just listed all the objections to Heine: they crumbled and scattered. I felt the collapse inside me and I had to bear the consequences. For the dams that Karl Kraus had erected in me had been my defense against Berlin. I felt weaker than before, and my confusion mounted. I had been assaulted by the enemy in two places at once. My God had sat with Brecht, who had written an advertising poem for cars, and He had exchanged words of praise with Brecht. And Ludwig Hardt, with whom He had once been on good terms, who had been His friend, had struck an irreparable breach in me for Heine.

An Invitation to Emptiness

Everything was equally *close* in Berlin, every kind of effect was permitted: no one was prohibited from making himself noticeable if he didn't mind the strain. For it was no easy matter: the noise was great, and you were always aware, in the midst of noise and tumult, that there were things worth hearing and seeing. Anything went. The taboos, of which there was no lack anywhere, especially in Germany, dried out here. You could come from an old capital like Vienna and feel like a provincial here, and you gaped until your eyes grew accustomed to remaining open. There was something pungent, corrosive in the atmosphere; it stimulated and animated. You charged into everything and were afraid of nothing. The terrible adjacency and chaos, such as poured out at you from Grosz's drawings, were by no means exaggerated; they were natural here, a new nature, which became indispensable to you, which you grew accustomed to. Any attempt at shutting yourself off had something perverse about it, and it was the only thing that could still be regarded as perverse. And if you did manage to isolate yourself for a brief while, then you soon felt the itch again, and you plunged into the turbulence. Everything was *permeable,* there was no intimacy. Any intimacy was feigned, and its goal was to surpass some other intimacy. It was not an end in itself.

The animal quality and the intellectual quality, bared and intensified to the utmost, were mutually entangled, in a kind of alternating current. If you had awakened to your own animality before coming here, you had to increase it in order to hold out against the animality of other people; and if you weren't very strong, you were soon used up. But if you were directed by your intellect and had scarcely given in to your animality, you were bound to surrender to the richness of what was offered your mind. These things smashed away at you, versatile, contradictory, and relentless; you had no time to understand anything, you received nothing but strokes, and you hadn't even gotten over yesterday's strokes before the new ones showered upon you. You walked around Berlin as a tender piece of meat, and you felt as if you still weren't tender enough and were waiting for new strokes.

But the thing that impressed me most, the thing that determined the rest of my life, even today, was the *incompatibility* of all the things that broke in on me. Every individual who was something—and many people *were* something—struck away at the others with himself. It was questionable whether they understood him; he made them listen. It didn't seem to bother him that others made people listen in a different way. He had validity as soon as he was heard. And now he had to continue striking away with himself to keep from being supplanted in the ears of the public. Perhaps no one had the leisure to wonder where all this was leading to. In any event, no transparent life came about in this way; but then, this was not the goal. The results were books, paintings, plays, one against the other, crisscross, zigzag.

I was always with someone else, Wieland, Ibby; I never wandered through Berlin alone. This was not the right way to get to know a city, but it may have been suitable in the Berlin of that era. You lived in groups, in cliques; perhaps, you couldn't otherwise have endured that harsh existence. You always heard names, usually well-known names: someone was expected, someone came. What *is* a time of brilliance? A time of many great names, all close together, but in such a way that no name suffocates another, even though they are fighting one another. The important thing is daily life, steady contact, the blows that brilliance endures without dimming. A lack of sensitivity in regard to these blows, a sort of yearning for them, the joy of exposing oneself to them.

The names *rubbed* together, that was their goal. In a mysterious osmosis, one name tried to filch as much radiance as possible from another name, after which it hurried off to find yet another one very quickly, in order to repeat the same process. The mutual touching and sloughing of names had something hasty to it, but also something arbitrary; the fun of it was that you never knew which name would come next. This hinged on chance; and since names that were out to make their fortune arrived from everywhere, anything seemed possible.

The curiosity about surprises, about the unexpected or the terrifying, left you in a state of mild intoxication. To endure all these things, to keep from entering a state of total confusion and remaining in it, the people who lived here all the time grew accustomed to taking nothing seriously, especially names. The first person in whom I could observe this process of cynicism about names was someone I saw frequently. His cynicism showed itself, first of all, in his aggressive statements about anyone who had excelled in anything. These statements could appear as expressions of a political standpoint. But in reality, they were something else, namely a kind of struggle for existence. By acknowledging as little as possible, by hitting out in all directions, you yourself became somebody. Anyone who didn't know how to hit out in all directions was doomed and could simply hit the road: Berlin was nothing for him.

One very important thing was to keep being seen, for days, weeks, and months. The visits to the Romanisches Café (and, on a lofty level, to Schlichter and Schwanecke), which were certainly pleasurable, were not meant for pleasure alone. They were also impelled by the need for self-manifestations, a need that no one eluded. If you didn't want to be forgotten, you had to be seen. This obtained for every rank and every stratum, even for any moocher who went from table to table in the Romanisches Café, always getting something, so long as he maintained the character he performed and did not tolerate any distortion of it.

An essential phenomenon of Berlin life in those days was the patrons. There were many. They sat around everywhere, lying in wait for customers. A few patrons were always there; others were just visiting. There were some who commuted frequently from Paris. I met my first maecenas—a man with a mustache, a globular face, and lips revealing a good cuisine—at the Romanisches Café. I was with Ibby. There was little room; a chair was free at our table. The man with the mustache and lips joined us and kept totally quiet. We were talking about Ibby's poems again. She had just been asked for a few. She was reciting them to me. We were trying to decide which ones she ought to show. The man was listening and chuckling as if he understood us. Yet he looked like a menu with nothing but French names. He clicked his tongue several times as if about to speak, but then remained silent. Perhaps he was looking for suitable words. Finally, he found them, with the aid of a calling card that he flashed. He was a cigarette manufacturer and lived in Paris, near the Bois de Boulogne. You could look into every worker's pot, he said; you knew what was in it. The pot and its content sounded ominous and explosive. We were both frightened. Whereupon he invited us to dinner, well-bred and courteous. We begged off, pleading something important that we had to discuss. He insisted. He said he had something to discuss with us, too. He was so emphatic that curiosity got the better of us and we agreed to dine with him.

He took us to an expensive restaurant that we didn't know. He indulged in a few rhetorical flourishes about the French cuisine, mentioned Baden-Baden, where he came from, and then asked me quite discreetly whether he could offer the young poetess a monthly pension of two hundred marks for one year. A tiny amount, almost nothing, he said, but it was a heartfelt need. He said not a word about the poems he had heard. It sufficed for him that he didn't understand them. He had seen Ibby for the first time in his life just one hour ago. She was beautiful, certainly, and when she recited her poems, her Hungarian German also sounded seductive. But I doubt that he had an organ for it. When Ibby, in response to my rather chilly question, agreed to accept his offer, he gratefully kissed her hand—and that was the only liberty he took. Yet this was a man in the best years of his life, and he knew what he wanted (not just in regard to menus). His goal here, however, was to be a patron of the arts; that was what he had wanted to discuss with us. He kept his word; and since he was never in Berlin, he never attempted to force himself on Ibby.

I distinguished between the loud and the silent patrons; this one was a silent patron. Their loudness depended on whether they could have a say; for this, they had to be familiar with the jargon of the circle that they bankrolled. In the group around George Grosz and the Malik people, one often saw a young man, whose name I have forgotten. He was rich and noisy and wanted to be taken seriously. He participated in conversations and liked to argue. Perhaps he knew something about a few subjects, but the first thing I got to hear from him was the Glass-of-Water Theory. This theory was making the rounds; there was nothing more hackneyed in all Berlin. But when he spoke about it, he really picked up an empty glass, brought it to his lips, pretended to drain it, and scornfully put it down on the table: "Love? A glass of water, drained, done with!" He had a blond mustache, which puffed up slightly in pride: every time he came out with the Glass-of-Water Theory, the mustache bristled. This young man was a high-style backer; perhaps he helped to support the Malik publishing house. At any rate, he was a patron of George Grosz.

A truly silent maecenas, who never had his say, because he understood so much about his own field that he didn't want to say stupid things about other fields, was a youngish man named Stark, who had something to do with Osram light-bulbs. He was often around, listening carefully to everything, saying nothing, and sometimes making himself useful when it seemed imperative—but he was always restrained, never making a splash. In a building owned by him or his firm at the center of Berlin, there was a vacant apartment, three lovely rooms in a row. He offered this apartment to Ibby for a few months (it wouldn't be vacant after that). The rooms, with wall-to-wall carpeting, were totally empty. He put in a couch for her to sleep on; that was all. Everything else was up to her.

She had the graceful idea of leaving the apartment empty, not get a single piece of furniture, and invite people into her emptiness. "You have to *say* the furniture," she said. "I want inventive guests." To support their inventiveness, a small porcelain donkey grazed on the green carpet in the middle room. It was a very pretty donkey. She had seen it in the window of an antique store, had gone in and offered to write a poem about the donkey in exchange for getting it. "Brecht a car, me a donkey. Which do you prefer?" she asked me, knowing quite well what my answer would be. The proprie-tress of the store had agreed to the barter (there were such people in Berlin), and Ibby was so astonished that she wrote her "best poem" for the woman—it was lost.

Ibby threw a huge housewarming. Each guest was first led to the donkey, introduced to it, and then asked to have a seat wherever he liked. There was no chair anywhere in the apartment; the guests stood or sat down on the floor. Drinks were taken care of: there were patrons for such things, too. Everyone showed up, no one who had heard about the empty apartment wanted to miss it. But the odd thing was that everyone remained, no one left. Ibby asked me to watch George Grosz. She was afraid he'd get drunk and attack her, saying all the things that I refused to believe he said. When he came, he was enchanting, in his most dandyish elegance. He brought along someone who was loaded up with bottles for Ibby. "Too bad," said Ibby, "that I don't fall in love. To-day it's all starting charmingly. But just wait!"

We didn't have to wait too long. Grosz was already drunk when he came, playing the *élégant*. He sat on the day couch, Ibby sat on the floor not too far from him. He stretched out his arms to her, she recoiled so that he couldn't reach her. Then he blew up and there was no stopping him: "You don't let anyone get to you! No one gets anything from you! What's going on?" He went on in this way, and he grew even worse. Then he switched over to singing the praises of "Ass!" "Ass, ass, you're my delight!" She had predicted this after my very first visit to him, when I had returned with the *Ecce Homo* folder that he had given to me; I had been full of enthusiasm about him, full of veneration for the sharpness of his eye, his relentless scourging of this Berlin society. There he sat now, crimson, drunken, uncontrollably excited because Ibby had turned him down in front of all these people, who weren't even offended by his behavior, his shameless cursing— and all at once, he seemed to me like one of the characters in his drawings.

I couldn't stand it. I was in despair. I was furious at Ibby for putting him in this state, knowing what would happen. I wanted to get away. I was the only guest who didn't feel comfortable here. I sneaked out, but I didn't escape, for Ibby, who had kept her eye on me all the while, was already at the door, blocking my way. She was afraid. She had provoked the entire scene to show me that he really did act toward her as she had told me. However, his outburst was so powerful and so long-lasting that she now feared him. She, who was never afraid, who had managed to get out of countless bad situations (she had told me about all of them, I knew about all of them)—Ibby now didn't dare remain in the apartment, which was full of people, if I didn't stay to protect her. Now I hated her because I couldn't leave her alone. Now I had to remain and watch one of the few people I admired in Berlin, a man who had been magnanimous to me and had acted the way I still expected people to act—I had to watch him demean himself and I had to make sure that Ibby was concealed from him and didn't come within his reach. It was so horrible listening to him rage that I would rather she left with him. No one seemed surprised at his conduct, nor did anyone laugh; people were used to these scenes, they were part of daily life here. I just wanted to get away from there, far away, and since I couldn't get out of the apartment, I wanted to get away from Berlin.

Escape

That was late in September. At the end of August, Ibby and I had attended the premiere of *The Threepenny Opera*. It was a cunning performance, coldly calculated. It was the most accurate expression of this Berlin. The people cheered for *themselves:* this was they and they liked themselves. First they fed their faces, then they spoke of right and wrong. No one could have put it better about them. They took these words literally. Now it had been spoken, they felt as snug as a bug in a rug. Penalty had been abolished: the royal messenger rode in on a real horse. The shrill and naked self-complacence that this performance emanated can be believed only by the people who witnessed it.

If it is the task of satire to lash people for the injustice that they devise and commit, for their evils, which turn into predators and multiply, then, on the contrary, this play glorified all the things that people usually conceal in shame: however, the thing that was most cogently and most effectively scorned was pity. To be sure, everything was merely taken over and spiced up with several new crassnesses; but these crassnesses were what made it so authentic. It was no opera, nor was it what it had originally been: a parody of opera. The only unadulterated thing about it was that it was an operetta. In opposition to the saccharine form of Viennese operetta, in which people found, undisturbed, everything they wished for, this was a different form, a Berlin form, with harshness, knavery, and their banal justifications—things that they wished for no less ardently, that they probably wished for even more than the saccharine things.

Ibby had no feeling for the piece and was no less astonished than I by the raging spectators, who stormed up to the apron of the stage and were so enthusiastic that they were ready to smash everything to smithereens. "Gangster romanticism," she said. "It's all false." And even though I was thankful to her and felt the same word *false*, and used it, we each meant something very different by it. Her idea, which was more original than the play, was that everyone would like to be one of these false beggar characters but was too cowardly to do it. She saw successful forms of hypocrisy, employable whininess, which you held in your hand and manipulated, and the whole thing was placed under a supervision that allowed you to have your fun, but exempted you from the responsibility. I saw it in far simpler terms: everyone knew himself to be Mack the Knife and now he was at last openly declared as such and approved and admired for it. Our opinions went past one another, but since they didn't touch, they didn't disturb one another, and they strengthened our defenses.

That evening, I felt closest to Ibby. Nothing could faze her. The raging crowd of the audience didn't exist for her. She never felt drawn into a crowd. She never even considered public opinions: it was as if she had never heard them. She walked untouched through Berlin's sea of posters. No name of any item stuck in her mind. If she needed anything for daily life, she didn't know its name or where to find it; and at the department store, she had to ask about both in the most haphazard way. Watching a demonstration of one hundred thousand people passing before her very eyes, she felt neither attracted nor repelled; anything she said right afterwards was in no way different from her words beforehand. She had watched carefully and grasped more details than anyone else; yet nothing added up to a direction, an intention, a compulsion. In this Berlin, which was filled with violent political struggles, she never said a single word about politics. Perhaps this was because she could never repeat what other people said. She read no newspapers, she read no magazines either. If I saw a periodical in her hand, I knew that it had printed a poem of hers, which she wanted to show me. I was always right; and when I asked her what else was in the same issue, she shook her head in total ignorance. I often found this unpleasant and accused her of having a big ego. I said she acted as if she were alone in the world. But this was unfair of me, for she noticed more about people—all sorts of people—than anyone else did. It puzzled me that she never let herself be swept up by a crowd; at the premiere of *The Threepenny Opera,* I liked the very thing about her that I had often criticized.

I had seen many things in Berlin that stunned and confused me. These experiences have been transformed, transported to other locales, and, recognizable only by me, have passed into my later writings. It goes against my grain to reduce something that now exists in its own right and to trace it back to its origin. This is why I prefer to cull out only a few things from those three months in Berlin—especially things that have kept their recognizable shape and have not vanished altogether into the secret labyrinth from which I would have to extricate them and clothe them anew. Contrary to many people, particularly those who have surrendered to a loquacious psychology, I am not convinced that one should plague, pester, and pressure memory or expose it to the effects of well-calculated lures; I bow to memory, every person's memory. I want to leave memory intact, for it belongs to the man who exists for his freedom. And I do not veil my dislike for those who perform a beauty operation on a memory until it resembles anyone else's memory. Let them operate on noses, lips, ears, skin, hair as much as they like; let them—if they must—implant eyes of different colors, even transplant hearts that manage to beat along for another year; let them touch, trim, smooth, plane everything—but just let memory be.

Having made this profession of faith, I would like to tell about things that I still see clearly, nor do I wish to seek any further twilight.

When the era found itself in its common denominator, *The Threepenny Opera,* when the joy of feeding your face before talking of right and wrong became a household slogan on which all the conflicting forces could agree—at this point, my resistance began to organize itself. Until then, I had felt more and more tempted to stay in Berlin. You moved in a chaos, but it seemed immeasurable. Something new happened every day, smashing at the old, which had itself been new just three days earlier. Things floated like corpses in the chaos, and human beings became things. This was known as *Neue Sachlichkeit* ("New Thingness"). Little else could be possible after the long and drawn-out shrieks of Expressionism. Nevertheless, whether a man was still shrieking or had already become a thing, he knew how to live well. If you arrived fresh and still didn't let on your confusion even after several weeks, but instead flaunted a clear mind, then you were considered useful and you received good offers, which lured you to remain. You latched on to any newcomer, if only because he wouldn't be new for long. You welcomed newcomers with open arms while looking around for other newcomers; the existence and efflorescence of this era, which was great in its way, hinged on the incessant arrival of the new. You were still nothing, and yet already you were needed, you moved chiefly among people who had likewise been new.

You were considered old-and-established if you had an "honest" profession; the most honest profession (not only in my eyes) was always that of a physician. Neither Döblin nor Benn* was part of the scene. Their work kept them from the routine of incessant self-flaunting. I saw them so rarely and so fleetingly that I have nothing substantial to say about them. But I was struck all the more by the way people talked about them. Brecht, who acknowledged no one, spoke Döblin's name with the greatest respect. A few rare times, I saw him unsure of himself; he would then say: "I've got to talk to Döblin about that." He made Döblin sound like a wise man from whom he sought counsel.

Benn, who liked Ibby, was the only man who didn't pester her. She gave me a New Year's card that he had sent her: he wished her everything that a beautiful young woman would like to have, and he listed these things individually. His list contained nothing that Ibby would ever have thought of. He had judged her by her appearance and he adhered to this impression. Thus, the card, which had absolutely nothing to do with her, seemed to come from some unconsumed writer who was sure of his senses.

I could have remained as a "newcomer," and, regarding my external progress, I would surely have been well off. A certain generosity was part of this bustle. Nor was it so easy to say no when people cordially pressed you to stay. I was in an unusual situation: not only did I have clear sailing to reach anyone, but Ibby's stories had informed me about people in a way that would have been beyond anyone else's reach. She knew people from their most laughable sides; her observations were ruthless, but also accurate. Never did she report anything false or approximate; whatever she hadn't seen or heard herself did not exist for her. She was the *desirable* eyewitness, who had more to say than others, because it is this witness's chief experience to stand back.

During the weeks after the premiere, when the urge to escape this world began to articulate itself, I stuck to Ibby. I

---

*Both physicians.—TRANSLATOR

told her I had to return to Vienna for my examinations; I would then get my doctorate in the spring. That was how it had been planned. Then, in summer of the next year, I could come back to Berlin and make up my mind, depending on what I felt like doing. She was unsentimental. She said: "You'll never commit yourself. You can't commit yourself. With you it's the way it is with me in regard to love." She meant that she wouldn't let anyone talk her into anything, inveigle her, or seduce her. She also felt that it was clever to have the examinations ahead of me. "They'll understand, these artists! Four years of drudging in a lab and then not getting a doctorate—they'd think you were crazy. Forget it!"

She had a good supply of poems. I had turned a whole stock of them into German, more than she would need for a year. The cigarette man, who had listened to our discussion of her poems, had set up her monthly pension for a year; two checks had arrived so far, accompanied by a cordial and respectful card.

She made things easy for me, as I had assumed she would do. While we weren't lovers (we had never even kissed), all the people we had spoken about stood physically between us, a forest that kept growing, that could not die for her or for me. Both of us were poor letter-writers. She must have written me, and I sometimes wrote her, too; but how meager this was when we couldn't see one another and listen to one another.

Then, three weeks after the premiere, came the *soirée* in her empty apartment; the shock destroyed the magic of her stories.

I began to be ashamed of the things I had heard from her about other people. I realized that she led men on merely in order to tell me about it. When I finally understood that the freshness, originality, and accuracy of her accounts were connected to the fact that she provoked men to make fools of themselves for her stories—the conductor of a chorus of voices, of which I couldn't hear my fill—when I finally admitted to myself that I had never, literally not once, heard anything *in favor of* any man, and only because any favorable remark would have sounded boring, I suddenly felt a dislike for her and exchanged her mockery for Babel's silence.

During my last two weeks in Berlin, I saw Babel every day. I saw him alone; I felt freer with him alone; I believe he preferred seeing me alone, too. I learned from him that one can gaze for a very long time without knowing something, that one can tell only much later whether one knows something about a person: only after losing sight of him. I learned that nevertheless, without knowing something as yet, you can carefully note everything you see or hear, and things lie dormant in you, so long as you don't misuse them to entertain other people. I learned something else, which may have seemed even more important after my lengthy apprenticeship with *Die Fackel:* I learned how wretched judging and condemning are as ends in themselves. Babel taught me a way of looking at people: gazing at them for a long time, as long as they were to be seen, without breathing a single word about what you saw. I saw the slowness of this process, the restraint, the muteness, right next to the importance Babel placed on what could be seen; for he sought tirelessly and greedily—his only greed, but also mine, except that mine was untrained and not yet certain of its justification.

Perhaps we met in a word that was never spoken between us, but which keeps crossing my mind when I think about him. It is the word *learn.* Both of us were filled with the dignity of learning. His mind and my mind had been aroused by early learning, by an immense respect for learning. However, his learning was already completely devoted to human beings; he needed no pretext—neither the expansion of a field of knowledge, nor alleged usefulness, purpose, planning, in order to "learn" people. At this time, I, too, seriously turned to people; and since then, I have spent the greater part of my life trying to understand human beings. Back then, I had to tell myself that I was doing so for the sake of some bit of knowledge or other. But when all other pretexts crumbled, I was left with the excuse of *expectation:* I wanted people, including myself, to become *better,* and so I had to know absolutely everything about every single human being. Babel, with his enormous experience—although he was only eleven years my senior—had long since gotten beyond this point. His desire for an improvement of mankind did not serve as an excuse for knowing human beings. I sensed that his desire was as insatiable as mine, but that it never caused him to deceive himself. Anything he found out about human beings was independent of whether it delighted or tormented him, whether it struck him to the ground: he had to "learn" human beings.

Part Five

The Fruit
of the Fire

Vienna 1929-1931

The Pavilion of Madmen

In September 1929, upon returning home to Vienna after a second visit to Berlin, something that I called the "necessary" life began at last. This was a life determined by its own internal necessities. Chemistry was done with: I had gotten my doctorate in June, ending a course of studies that had served as a delay but meant nothing else to me.

The problem of earning a living was solved: I had been commissioned to translate two American books into German. I could make the deadline by working four or five hours a day. Further translations were in the offing. Since the work was well paid (I was living very modestly on Hagenbergstrasse), I had two or three free years ahead of me. Translating, which I took seriously as a livelihood, was easy. However, the substance of these books touched me only superficially; sometimes, while working, I caught myself thinking of entirely different things, my own.

For, by resolutely detaching myself from Berlin, I had obtained external peace and quiet; but this was no idyll to which I returned. I was full of questions and chimaeras, doubts, forebodings, catastrophic anxieties, but also an incredibly powerful determination to find my bearings, take things apart, set their direction, and thus gain understanding of them. None of the things that I had witnessed during two visits to Berlin could be shoved aside. Day and night, everything surfaced, with no rhyme or reason, it seemed, plaguing me in many shapes, like the devils painted by Grünewald, whose altar hung in details on the walls of my room. It turned out that I had absorbed more than I myself was willing to admit. The fashionable term *suppress* was apparently not coined for me. *Nothing* was suppressed, everything was there, always, simultaneously, and as clearly as if one could grab it with one's hands. Tides over which I had no control determined the things that surfaced in front of me on waves and were swept aside by other waves. One always felt the vastness and fullness of this ocean, seething with monsters all of whom one *recognized*. The frightening thing was that everything had its *face*, it looked at you, it opened its mouth, it said something or was about to say something. The distortions it pestered you with were calculated, they were intentional, they tormented you with yourself, they *needed* you, you felt compelled to surrender. But no sooner had you found the strength to do so than they were swept aside by others whose demands on you were no less intense. Thus it went on, and everything came again, and nothing remained long enough to be grabbed and detached. It was no use stretching out your arms and hands, there was too much, and it was everywhere; it couldn't be overcome: you were lost in it.

Now it might not have been so unfortunate that nothing of the weeks in Berlin had oozed away, that I had preserved everything. I could have written it all down; and it would have been a colorful and perhaps not uninteresting account. I could still set it down today; it has been preserved all this time. However, no account would have captured the essence: the ominousness with which that period was charged and the contradictory directions it moved in. For the one, uniform person who had seized it and now seemingly contained it all was a mirage. The things he preserved had been altered because he had stored them in himself together with other people. The true pull of things was a centrifugal pull; they strove apart, leaving one another at top speed. Reality was not at the center, holding everything together as if with reins; there were many realities, and they were all outside. They were wide apart from one another, they were unconnected; anyone attempting to harmonize them was a falsifier. Way, way out, in a circle, almost at the edge of the world, the new realities I was heading toward stood like crystals. As spotlights, these realities were to be turned inward, toward our world, in order to illuminate it.

These spotlights were the true means of knowledge: with them, one could penetrate the chaos one was filled with. If there were enough such spotlights, if they were properly conceived, then the chaos could be *taken apart*. Nothing must be left out. One must drop nothing. All the usual tricks of harmonizing caused nausea. Any man who believed he was still in the best of all possible worlds ought to keep his eyes shut and take pleasure in blind delights; he didn't have to know what lay ahead of us.

Since all the things I had seen were possible *together*, I had to find a form to hold them without diminishing them. It would diminish them if I showed people and behaviors as they had appeared to me, but without my simultaneously communicating what was bound to become of them. The potentiality of things, which was always present as overtones when you were confronted with anything new, which remained implicitly, even though you felt it powerfully, was utterly lost in the depictions that were considered accurate. In reality, everything had a direction and everything increased; *expansion* was a chief characteristic of people and things; to understand any of this, one had to take things apart. It was a bit as if you had to disentangle a jungle in which everything was ensnarled; you had to detach every plant from another without damaging or destroying it; you had to view it in its own tension and let it keep growing without your losing sight of it.

When I returned to an environment marked chiefly by calm and restraint, the things I brought back, my experiences, became more urgent. No matter how hard I attempted to slow down and limit myself, my experiences left me no peace. I tried long walks, picking routes with nothing special about them. I walked down Auhofstrasse, the long stretch from Hacking to Hietzing, and back, forcing myself not to walk too quickly. I figured this would help me get used to a different rhythm. Nothing leaped at me from any street corner. I strolled along low, two-story houses as if I were going down a suburban street in the nineteenth century.

I started out at a leisurely pace; I had no goal; I thought of no tavern I would drop in at, even to write something. It was to be a walk that wouldn't spin my head around, whether to the right or the left, no St. Vitus's dance of sightseeing, no shrill fracas—a strolling prehistoric creature, that was what I wanted to be, an animal that doesn't run from anything, into anything, that doesn't make way, doesn't stumble, doesn't bump into anything, doesn't push, doesn't have to be anywhere, a creature who has time, who's after nothing, who makes doubly sure not to carry a watch.

But the more total the emptiness that I had prepared for myself, and the more footloose and fancy free I started out, then the more inevitable the assault: something hit my eyes, a rock on my head—inevitable because it came from inside myself. Some figure from the time from which I was trying to escape seized hold of me, a figure that I didn't know. It had only just come into being, and even though I knew where it came from—it was marked by its urgency—even though it ruthlessly grabbed everything I consisted of, it was utterly new to me. I had never encountered it. It disconcerted me to a terrifying degree, pounced on me, squatted on my shoulders, crossed its legs around my chest, steered me as fast as it pleased to wherever it pleased. I found myself out of breath on Auhofstrasse, which I had picked because it was innocuous and unanimated. I was obsessed, virtually fleeing, my shoulders weighed down by the danger that I couldn't escape. I was frightened and yet aware that the only thing that could save me from the chaos I had brought along was now happening.

What saved me was that this was a figure that had an outline, that kept going, that gathered the senselessly scattered things and gave them a body. It was a terrible body, but it was alive. It threatened me, but it had a direction. I saw what it was after. I never completely lost the terror it aroused, but it also aroused my curiosity. What was it capable of? Where was it going? How long would it keep on? Was it bound to end? As soon as the figure is recognized in its sketchy outline, our relationship is reversed, and it's no longer quite so certain who is possessed by whom and who is driven by whom.

I would run back and forth in this state of mind for a while, dashing faster and faster along the same route. In the end, I would sit down in some tavern, wherever I happened to find myself. My notebook and pencil were at hand. I began to record; whatever had happened in my movements was turned into written words.

How is one to describe this state of incessant recording? First, there was no coherence. There were thousands of things. An articulation, something that could be called the beginning of an order, started with a division into figures. The activity, to which I mainly devoted myself, was an angry attempt to ignore myself, namely by metamorphosis. I sketched characters who had their own way of seeing, who could no longer cast about promiscuously, but could only feel and think along certain channels. Some of these figures recurred frequently, while others vanished rather early. I was reluctant to give them names; they weren't like individuals one knew: each was invented in terms of his main preoccupation, the very thing that kept driving and driving him, away from the others. Each was to have a completely personal view of things, the dominant feature of his world, not to be likened to anything else. It was important that everything was kept in terms of that view. The rigor with which everything else was excluded from each figure's world may have been the most important aspect. It was a strand that I pulled out of the tangle. I wanted the strand to be pure and unforgettable. It had to lodge in people's minds like a Don Quixote. The strand should think and say things that no one else could have thought or said. It should express some aspect of the world so thoroughly that the world would be poorer without that strand, poorer, but also more mendacious.

One of these characters was the Man of Truth, who savored to the full the fortune and misfortune of truth. However, each of them was concerned with a specific kind of truth: the truth of self-harmony. A few of these figures, not many, sank away, and eight survived, fascinating me for a year, keeping me in motion. Each character was marked with a capital letter, the initial letter of his preoccupation or dominant feature. *W* was for *Wahrheitsmensch* [Man of Truth], whom I have already mentioned. *Ph* was the *Phantast:* he wanted to get away from the earth, off into outer space; his mind was devoted to finding a way; his intense lust for discovery was permeated with a dislike for everything to be seen around him here. His desire for new and incredible things was nourished by his disgust with earthly things. There was *R*, the *Religious Fanatic*, and *S*, the *Sammler* [Collector]. There was the *Verschwender* [Spendthrift] and the *Tod-Feind* [Enemy of Death]. There was *Sch*, the *Schauspieler* [Actor], who could live only in rapid metamorphoses, and *B*, the *Büchermensch* [Book Man].

As soon as such initial letters were jotted down on one side at the top of the page, I felt narrowed down and I furiously zoomed off in this single direction. The endless mass of things filling me was sorted out, broken down. I was after (I have already used this word) crystals, which I wanted to detach from this wild chaos. I had overcome none, absolutely none, of the things that had been filling me with horror and dreadful forebodings since Berlin. What could the outcome be if not dreadful conflagration? I felt how pitiless life was: everything racing by, nothing really dealing with anything else. It was obvious not only that no one understood anyone else, but also that no one *wanted* to understand anyone else.

I tried to help myself by forming strands, a few individual features, which I tied to human beings; this brought the beginning of perspicuity into the mass of experiences. I wrote now about one character, now about another, with no discernible rule, depending on whatever urge came over me; sometimes, I even worked on two different strands on the same day, but rigidly observed their borders, which were never crossed.

The linearity of the figures, each one's limitation to himself, the impetus driving them in one single direction—live one-man rockets—their incessant reactions to a changing environment, the language they used, each in his unmistakable way—intelligible, but unlike anyone else's language—so that they consisted purely of a border and, within this border, of daring, surprising thoughts expressed in that very language. Nothing general I can say about them can give you a conclusive idea of them. An entire year was filled with sketches of these eight, it was the richest, the most unbridled year of my life. I felt as if I were struggling with a *Comédie Humaine;* and since the characters were intensified to an utmost extreme and closed off against one another, I called it a *Human Comedy of Madmen.*

When I wrote at home (I didn't write only in taverns), I had Steinhof before my eyes, the pavilions of lunatics. I thought of these inmates and linked them to my characters. The wall around Steinhof became the wall of my project. I fixed on the pavilion that I saw most clearly, and I imagined a ward in which my characters would ultimately be together. None of them was meant to die in the end. During the year of this sketching, I developed more and more respect for the people who had moved so far away from others as to be considered insane, and I didn't have the heart to kill a single one of my characters. None had evolved far enough for me to foresee his end. But I did exclude their dying in the end, and I saw them together in the pavilion ward, which I had saved for them. Their experiences, which I viewed as precious and unique, were to be preserved there. The ending I had in mind was that they would talk to one another. In their individual isolation, they would find sentences for one another, and these peculiar sentences would have a tremendous *meaning*. It struck me as demeaning them to think of their recovering. None of them was to find his way back to the triviality of everyday life. Any adjustment to us would be tantamount to diminishing them; they were too precious for this because of their unique experiences. On the other hand, their reactions to one another struck me as sublimely, inexhaustibly valuable. If the speakers of these individual languages had anything to say to one another, anything meaningful for them, then there was still hope for us ordinary people, who lacked the dignity of madness.

That was the utopian aspect of my enterprise, and even though I had the town of Steinhof before me in the flesh, as it were, this utopian aspect stayed utterly remote in time. The figures were only just emerging, and their lives were so manifold that anything was possible, any twist of destiny. However, I excluded an irrevocable end, and it was as if I had given the figure most urgent for me, the Enemy of Death, a power over the lives of the others. Whatever was to become of them, they would remain alive. I would look over into their pavilion from my window; now one figure, now another, would turn up at his barred window and signal to me.

The Taming

I frequented a small coffeehouse below in Hacking, right by the bridge across the Vienna River; the place stayed open very late. Once, deep into the night, I noticed a young man. He was sitting with a group of people who didn't really seem to fit in with him. He was tall and radiant, with very light blue eyes. He enjoyed drinking and talking. Something violent was happening at his table, with sudden vituperative outbursts that didn't affect him. I recognized him from a picture. It was Albert Seel, a writer published by a Berlin house; he had been a prisoner of war in Russia and written a book about it. I hadn't read the book; only the title had stuck in my mind. It contained the word *Siberia*. I was at the adjacent table and I unabashedly asked him from table to table whether he was Albert Seel, which he affirmed, still radiant and yet somewhat embarrassed. He invited me to join him and introduced me to his friends. I recall the names Mandi and Poldi; I've forgotten the rest. I introduced myself as a student, although I no longer was one, and a translator, eliciting howls of laughter from Seel's buddies.

They observed me in a way in which I had never been observed before, as though they had great plans for me and were testing me to see whether I was the right man for their project. They were no intellectuals; their language was primitive, coarse, and vehement, and they justified themselves with every sentence as though I had criticized them. I didn't know them at all; I didn't have the foggiest notion who they were. The fact that they were with an author who was anything but famous inspired my confidence; ever since returning to Vienna several months earlier, I had not encountered any authors. I neither distrusted nor feared them, yet I noticed that they were unsure of themselves with me, and I was amazed at how greatly they valued physical strength. Seel did full justice to the wine in front of him and soon stopped reacting to my attempts at literary conversation.

"There's a time and a place for everything," he said, whisking my questions aside like annoying flies. "When I'm with my friends, I like to talk." But perhaps it was a kind of tact on his part to avoid any literary dialogue, which his friends would have been incapable of following. Soon, I contented myself with listening to the others, who, I realized, were preoccupied with "heroic feats," but I couldn't ferret out exactly what they meant. Particularly Poldi, the biggest and strongest of all, liked to show how he had struck down someone or other with his tremendous hand. No one could hold his own against him. Mandi, the shortest one, had an apelike face, he looked incredibly agile and nimble, and he very graphically told about how he had recently managed to provoke the dogs of a villa. I didn't know why he had to provoke these dogs and I was listening as innocently as a baby, when Poldi suddenly punched me in the chest with his paw and asked whether I knew the villa that they wanted to get into— it was, as it turned out, the home of the countess, the "goddamn mare" from the dairy. I thought I'd have some fun and went along with their conversation as though they were actually planning a burglary. I told them they had picked the wrong house. The "count and his family" had nothing worth stealing. I got a second, even more powerful punch in the chest, and Poldi said with ominous scorn: Just what had gotten into me? They wouldn't break into the home of such people: why, everyone in Hacking knew them. They weren't that stupid! Mandi loved to talk through his hat!

I realized my joke had gone awry, but not understanding the reason for Poldi's annoyance, I kept quiet. The conversation went on, louder and louder, more and more vehement. This table, at which no more than five or six people besides myself were sitting, was the most animated table in the tavern. Normally, the place was quiet and lonesome: a few old pensioners, some couples, but no large group. This time, however, the place seemed unusually quiet, as if no one dared to make noise competing with our table. Herr Bieber, the proprietor, was behind the counter: I had a good view of him from my chair, and he seemed irritated. He usually had something to do and was always bustling around; but today, he held himself erect and kept staring at me. I even had the impression that he was discreetly winking at me, but I wasn't sure.

The racket at our table grew more and more ominous. Poldi

and Mandi began to argue and traded insults, ones that struck me as particularly filthy, even for these surroundings. Seel, as unswervingly radiant as ever, tried to mediate, pointing to me, as if their fight could leave me with a poor opinion of the group. But the result was that the two buried the hatchet and kept glaring hatefully at me. Seel said it was time to go home, the place was closing. But his friends did not get up. I did, however, and this was probably what he was aiming at. He was trying to shield me against his buddies, who were getting rougher and angrier. So I said goodnight. Something of my amazement at this utterly new kind of people must have been translated into my warm goodbye; for Poldi said: "We're always here." Mandi, who seemed a lot more cunning, added: "Come aroun', we kin always use a student!"

I went over to the counter to pay my bill, and Herr Bieber received me with a low, sepulchral voice. I had never heard him speak so somberly, much less whisper. "For God's sake, Herr Doktor, you better be careful with those guys, they're tough customers. Don't sit with them!" Afraid that they might suspect him of warning me, he grinned conspicuously, while whispering.

I went along with his secrecy and whispered: "Why, that man's a writer, I know a book of his."

Herr Bieber was flabbergasted. "He's no writer," he said. "He always comes here with those guys; he helps them." There was something shivery about his words; he was really scared for me, but also for himself. The next day, when I was alone in the tavern and could speak in detail with him, he told me that my new acquaintances were a notorious gang of burglars. Each of them had served many prison terms. Mandi, who could climb like a cat, had just been released from jail; he had served time together with Poldi, but then they had been separated. They were all from the surrounding area. Herr Bieber would have liked to keep them out of his tavern, but that was too risky. When I asked him what they could do to me, since I wasn't a house and they couldn't steal anything from me but books, he gawked at me as if I were crazy: "Don't you understand, Herr Doktor, they want to pick your brain, they want to find out what they can burglarize in other places. You didn't tell them anything, did you?"

"But I don't even know what they can burglarize in other places. I don't know anyone around here."

"Yes, but you live up where the villas are, on Hagenberggasse. Just watch out. Next time, one of them is gonna walk you all the way home and question you about every house. Who lives here? And who lives there? Don't say anything, Herr Doktor, for God's sake. Don't say anything. Otherwise, it'll be your fault if anything happens!"

I still didn't really believe him. And a few evenings later, when I returned to the tavern, I sat down with an acquaintance of mine, an elderly painter, and pretended not to see the "gang," who were sitting pretty far away, in the other corner. This time, they had come without Seel. Mandi wasn't there either; I noticed only Poldi when he raised his hand and pointed to something. But something must have happened. No noise could be heard; things were quiet, and I felt that Herr Bieber had been wrong with his Cassandra cries: no one paid any attention to me, I wasn't greeted or called over to the "gang's" table. When Herr Bieber brought me my coffee, he said: "Today, you're not staying till closing time, Herr Doktor. Today, you're leaving early." He sounded as if he knew that I had some special plans for the night. His supervision was irksome; but to have my peace and quiet, I did leave soon.

I had only taken a few steps when I felt that tremendous hand on my shoulder. "We're going the same way," said Poldi. He had followed me quickly.

"Do you live up there, too?"

"No, but I have to go the same way."

No further explanation was forthcoming, and I didn't care for the prospect of walking with him up the dark and narrow footpath, which was the only road to Hagenberggasse. But I let nothing on; I only asked: "Seel wasn't around today? And Mandi wasn't, either?"

What had I done! A gigantic cannonade burst forth. Poldi railed and ranted against Mandi, and a torrent of stories about this "eageristic" person (he meant "egotistic") poured over me. Poldi never wanted to lay eyes on him again. He had never been able to stand Mandi; he'd prefer Seel any day, even though you never knew what he was all about. Just what kind of a book was it that Seel had written?

It was about being a prisoner of war, I said, about the people he had known when he was a POW in Siberia.

"Siberia?" was the derisive response, and Poldi slammed me on the back. "He's never been to Siberia. He's been locked up, all right. But not in Siberia."

"Yes, he was, a while back, when he was very young."

"When he was a little boy, you mean?"

In short, he refused to accept that Seel had been locked up as a POW and not as a criminal. Poldi explained that Seel always lied. None of them ever believed a word he said; he always kept making up things. However, he had never told them that he had written a book himself. He had made sure not to tell them, said Poldi, because they would have found new lies of his. What did I think of a man who always had to lie? He, Poldi, was incapable of lying. He always told the truth.

Mindful of Herr Bieber's prediction, I expected Poldi to question me about the villas as we approached them; but he was so preoccupied with Seel's lies and his own love of truth that he asked me nothing at all. This was lucky for me: I had nothing to say, even had I wanted to, about the villa owners he was interested in. I didn't even know the names of most of them, and if, by hook or crook, something plausible had occurred to me, it would have struck him as absurd or like one of Seel's lies.

We had reached Erzbischofgasse; his protestations of veracity had paused for an instant. I took advantage of the lull and pointed to the right: "Do you know Marek at 70 Erzbi-schofgasse, over there? He lies in a wagon and his mother pushes him around."

Poldi didn't know Marek, which surprised me, for young Marek in his wagon could be seen everywhere; if his mother didn't take him for a stroll, he would lie in the sun outside his house. Whether alone or not, he was always on his back. He couldn't walk, he couldn't move his arms or legs. His head lay up at an angle, and an open book lay on a pillow next to his head. Once, as I passed by, I had seen him stick out his tongue and use it to turn a page of his book. I didn't *believe* it, though I saw it clearly. He had a long, sharp, strikingly red tongue. I passed by a second time, as if by chance, and so slowly that he would have had time to memorize an entire page. And indeed, when I was very close, I saw his tongue shoot out and turn the page.

I had noticed the young man two or three years earlier, after my arrival on Hagenberggasse: his mother was wheel-ing him by. I had politely nodded to both and mumbled "Good morning," but never received an answer from him. I assumed it was as difficult for him to speak as it was for him to move, and so I was reluctant to try conversing with him. He had a long, dark face, a lot of hair, and large, brown eyes, which he always focused on anyone who came toward him, and you felt his eyes on you long after you'd gone on. Some-times, he lay in the sun without reading, his eyes closed. It was very lovely to see them opening at a noise. He seemed particularly sensitive to footsteps; for even if he was fast asleep, you couldn't go by without his eyes opening. You might try to walk softly so as not to wake him up; but he always heard the steps on the gravel, and he always made sure to gaze at the passerby.

I knew that someday I'd get into a conversation with him; since I hoped to be living here for a long time, I was patient. No one in the area was more on my mind than he. I asked everyone whether they knew anything about him, and I had been told certain things that I couldn't really believe. I was told he was studying, his subject was philosophy; hence, the heavy tomes that always lay on the pillow next to him. He was so gifted, they said, that professors at the University of Vienna came all the way to Hacking merely to give him private lectures. This struck me as sheer nonsense until one sunny afternoon when I saw Professor Gomperz—the long-bearded man who looked like my image of the Greek cynics—sitting next to Marek's wagon. I had heard his lecture on the pre-Socratics some time ago. His way of speaking had not been as inspiring as the subject matter, but the latter was abundant. When I actually saw him sitting in front of young Marek, talking to him with vast, slow gestures, I was so startled that I swerved from my route and made a detour to avoid coming near the professor and having to greet him. Yet this would have been the best and most dignified occasion for finally getting to meet the paralyzed man.

Now, it was past midnight and very dark out. At the top end of the narrow footpath, I stretched my arm toward Marek's house and asked my uncouth companion, who was more than one head taller than I, whether he knew the paralyzed man. Poldi was amazed that I was pointing in that direction—to the right of the path. To make sure I meant this direction, he slowly—as was his wont—stretched out his huge paw in the same direction. "There's nothing there," he said, "there's no house there." But there *was* a house, a single one, number 70, albeit a low, humble, one-story house, no villa. The villas, the only houses that Poldi was interested in and knew about, were on the left side of the hill, forming Hagenberggasse, where I lived.

Poldi wanted to know what was wrong with the paralyzed man, and I talked about him. I told Poldi everything I had learned about Marek. Very soon after I started, it occurred to me that the two men had very similar faces: Marek's was a lot narrower and looked like the face of an ascetic; Poldi had a bloated face, and perhaps the resemblance struck me only because I couldn't see him so well in the darkness. However, I had a very clear memory of him from our conversation that earlier night in the tavern; I had noticed him especially, because of his evocative dark eyes, which contrasted so greatly with his clumsy paws.

"You look alike," I now said, "but only in your faces. He's totally paralyzed. He can't move his arms or legs. But don't think he's sad. He's brave, it's unbelievable. He can't move, but he studies. The professors come all the way to Erzbischofgasse and give him lessons. He doesn't have to pay them. He couldn't pay them anyway. He doesn't have any money."

"And he looks like me?" asked Poldi.

"Yes, you've got the same eyes. The very same eyes. If you ever come to see him, you'll think you're looking into a mirror."

"But he's a cripple!" he said, somewhat irritated. I sensed that he was starting to get annoyed at the comparison.

"But not in his mind!" I said. "He's smarter than any of us! He can't go anywhere and he studies! The professors come to him, so he can study. It's unheard of. He must have something on the ball, all right, otherwise they wouldn't come. Do you know what? I've got the greatest respect for him! I really admire him!" This was the first time that I waxed enthusiastic about Thomas Marek. Yet I didn't even know him. Later on, when we had become friends, I couldn't have spoken with more enthusiasm about him.

We had stopped. We hadn't gone any further after I'd pointed toward Marek's house. Thomas Marek's physical state penetrated Poldi very slowly. He asked several times whether the man really couldn't move on his own. "Not at all," I said. "He can't walk a step. He can't even put a piece of bread in his mouth. He can't even bring a glass to his lips."

"But he does drink, doesn't he? And chew? Can he swallow, can he swallow his food?"

"Yes, he can do those things. He can gaze, too! You can't imagine how beautiful he looks when he opens his eyes!"

"And he resembles *me?*"

"Yes, but only your face! He'd be happy if he had your big hands! Imagine how much *he'd* like to walk people home the way you're walking me home now! He couldn't do it even when he was a little boy."

"And you like him! A cripple!"

I was annoyed at this word now; after everything I had said, he shouldn't have used it. "He's not a cripple for me!" I said. "I think he's wonderful! If you don't understand, then I feel sorry for you. I figured you'd understand!" I was so annoyed that I forgot whom I was talking to, and I became vehement. I kept singing Marek's praises. I didn't stop, I couldn't stop. When I no longer had anything concrete to add, I began inventing further details, which, however, I believed in. I believed in them so intensely that Poldi just listened, and only now and then would he throw in the same sentence: "And he resembles me?"

"His face, I told you, his face looks just like yours."

And then it came over me, and I kept on talking. I said women came from far away merely to see Marek. "They stand in front of his wagon and look at him. His mother brings chairs out for them to sit down. I could swear they're in love with him. They wait for him to look at them. He can't caress them, he can't do anything with them. But he *can* look at them, with his eyes." Everything I said was true, even though I made it up that night. A short time later, when I became friends with Marek, I saw the women and girls who came to him; I saw them with my own eyes, and anything I didn't see he told me.

But that night, Poldi and I didn't go a single step further. He had grown quieter and quieter, he didn't use the word *cripple* again. He forgot that he had planned to walk me to the garden gate of my home and look about in his way. He forgot the villas. He was preoccupied with the young man who resembled him but couldn't stand or walk. I shook hands with him but only after my praises were exhausted. He took my hand rather restrainedly, not crushing it as he usually did. He turned and walked down the footpath, which we had climbed together. I had lost all fear of him.

The Provider

My shyness about Marek vanished that night. I had spoken so much about him that I no longer avoided him. My praises had made him seem more familiar. Nor had I failed to notice that my enthusiastic remarks about Marek had tamed the rough customer who had tramped up Erzbischofgasse with me after midnight. I was no longer interested in him and his buddies. I barely noticed them when I went to the tavern. We nodded at one another from a distance, and they were no longer curious about me. I don't know in what form my behavior that night was communicated to them. Whatever they may have thought about the matter now, there was nothing to be gotten from someone who dealt with such poor devils. Nor did their original interest change into scorn or hatred; they left me alone. They left me so utterly in peace that I felt something like a quiet liking in them, albeit a quite undemonstrative, barely perceptible liking—enough, however, to arouse the tavern keeper's hostility.

He hadn't failed to notice that the strongest and most intractable of the men had followed me that night, and he wanted to know what had happened. Nothing, I said, to his disappointment. "But he walked you all the way home?" he said, and it sounded almost like a threat.

"No, only till Erzbischofgasse."

"And then?"

"Then he turned back."

"And he didn' ask you anything?"

"Nothing at all."

"If it weren' you, Herr Doktor, no one'd believe you."

He was convinced I was hiding something, and he was

right; for I didn't say a word about the actual topic of our conversation. I didn't feel the tavern owner was good enough for that. Perhaps I didn't want to hear him—especially him—come out with derogatory comments about people who couldn't stand or walk and were ultimately just a burden on the taxpayer. "He walked along with you and didn' talk. That's not like him."

"I didn't say he didn't talk, but he didn't question me. I wouldn't have known anything anyway."

Perhaps it was this sentence that made him even more distrustful. What did I mean I didn't know anything! I'd been living there for two or three years already. You hear all sorts of things, after all. And in any case, I was shielding the fellow when I stated that he hadn't questioned me, thus hadn't shown any criminal intentions.

I now saw that Herr Bieber carefully noted the time whenever I entered the tavern. When had they come? When did I come? Why didn't they talk to me anymore? Why didn't I ever talk to them? Something must have happened. Since there was no public communication between us, Herr Bieber assumed that there must be a secret communication; and since it was so consistently secret, it had to signify something. He was absolutely convinced that he was on the trail of something, and he waited for the glorious revelation.

I would seldom come to his tavern in the morning. But once, when I did show up that early, he came over and said: "So it didn' work."

"What didn't work?"

"Well, you must have heard about it. They caught all of them! First, they let them into the house, and then the mousetrap closed. All four are in jail already. They'll get years for this! What can you do, they've all got records! It had to end badly. They're hunting for Seel now. He's vanished—the writer!"

He spoke that last word with genuine scorn, which was meant either for me, whom he often saw writing, or for my

claim that I knew of a book that Seel had written. Herr Bieber saw that I was stunned by the news, and he crowned his
report with the precautionary words: "You see how good it
is that I warned you. Otherwise you'd be in trouble now, too."

I pictured my powerful and vigorous escort of that night
in a narrow cell; and now I understood why my account of
the paralyzed man had affected Poldi so deeply that he forgot about his plans and went home empty-handed. He really
hadn't asked me anything, not a single question. He hadn't
had a chance, he had gotten so involved in the story, which
I had cast over his head like a reflecting net. I had talked
about someone who resembled him, but who could move neither his arms nor his legs—a man who was worse off than
Poldi in a cell.

Everything had happened rather swiftly; only a few months
had passed from the nocturnal conversation to the cell in
which the man with the tremendous hand was confined. But
my image of the paralyzed man had been animated and
aroused so vehemently that a real meeting would have to take
place. I no longer made a detour when I saw someone talking to him at his wagon; I would walk by with an audible
greeting and was surprised and delighted the first time I
heard the paralyzed man's voice returning my greeting. His
voice sounded breathy, as if coming from deep inside him, it
gave color and space to his greeting. It stuck in my mind
and I wanted to hear it again. The next day, as luck would
have it, I saw Professor Gomperz sitting there. I recognized
him from far away by his long beard and his physique, which
looked high and straight even when he was seated. I didn't
know whether he would recognize me. In his course, I had
always been among very many students when I had spoken
to him, and only once had I gone to see him about some
matter or other.

However, he now instantly became attentive as I drew near,
and he gave me such an astonished look that I was una-
bashed about stopping and holding out my hand. He only

nodded but did not hold out his hand, and I turned crimson with embarrassment about my want of tact. How could I offer someone my hand in the presence of the paralyzed man! However, Professor Gomperz spoke to me in his slow, affable way, asking me my name, which, he said, had slipped his mind; then, upon learning my name, he introduced me to Thomas Marek. "My young friend often sees you passing here," said the professor. "He could tell that you're a student, too. He has an infallible instinct for people. Why don't you visit him sometime? After all, you live close by."

Marek had told him everything while I approached. He had noticed me, no less than I him, and he had found out where I lived. Professor Gomperz explained that Thomas Marek was majoring in philosophy, and that he, Gomperz, came to see him once a week for two hours. He was so satisfied with Marek that he would like to come more often, but, alas, he didn't have the time. It was quite a long trip, taking him an entire afternoon. However, said the professor, Thomas Marek *merited* his coming twice a week. It didn't sound like flattery, though it was meant to be encouraging; it sounded as direct and clear-cut as one might expect the words of a cynic philosopher to sound. However, the paralyzed man declared with his powerful breath: "I don't know anything now. But I will know more."

From here on, things moved quickly. It was early May. The paralyzed man often basked in the sun outside his house. I visited him. His mother brought me a chair from inside so that I might not leave too soon. I remained for quite a while, one hour the first time. When I was about to say goodbye, Thomas said: "You must think I'm tired already. I'm never tired when I can have a serious conversation. I like talking to you. Do stay!" I was frightened by his hands, which I had never noticed when casually passing by. The fingers were cramped and crooked, he couldn't move them voluntarily; they had reached the twined wire of the garden fence and had twisted around the wire and were clutching it so tightly that they couldn't get loose. When Marek's mother came out again, she carefully loosened his hand from the wire, finger by finger, which was no easy job. Then she moved Thomas's wagon a bit away from the fence, so that his fingers wouldn't get caught again. She gave me a scrutinizing look with her deepset eyes, a prematurely aged woman, and she let me know tacitly, merely with her eyes, that she wanted me to make sure the wagon didn't roll against the fence anymore.

Thomas always kept moving slightly, thus making the wagon move. His mother poured his medicine into his mouth. He took it several times a day, he said after she'd left; he had such powerful convulsions that he couldn't do anything peacefully without this medicament: he couldn't read or talk. But, he said, the medicament was good. He'd been taking it for many years. The effect always lasted for several hours. They had no idea what sort of disease he had. Something totally unknown. He had spent many long periods at the Neurological Hospital. Professor Pappenheim had personally examined him because his was such an interesting case. But the professor couldn't make head or tail of it either. It was a unique disease; it had no name as yet. Marek repeated this several times. It was important for him that no one else had the same disease. Since it had no name, it remained a secret for him, too, and he didn't have to be ashamed of it. "They'll never find out," he said, "not in this century. Maybe later on, but then it won't concern me."

He had had trouble standing as a child, but his limbs weren't twisted. There was nothing special about them. When he was about six, his arms and legs had begun to twist and shrink, and from then on his condition got worse and worse. He never said anything about the time when the convulsions had started. Perhaps he no longer knew about it; and we had a tacit agreement that I would never ask his mother anything. Whatever I learned about him came from his lips and was thereby weightier than if someone else had told me; for the strength of his breath, which came from deep inside him, gave his words their own respiratory shape. They were words *in statu nascendi,* they spread like warm steam when they left his mouth, and they never fell out as finished detritus like other people's words.

The first time we spoke, he told me about a philosophical work he was planning, but he didn't tell me what the subject was. For the moment, he wanted to finish his studies and get his doctorate; this was necessary, he said, if his work was to be taken seriously later on. He didn't want people to read him out of pity when the time came. He wanted to be judged according to merit, like anyone else. On the pillow next to him lay a volume of Kuno Fischer's *History of Philosophy.* Marek had made up his mind to read every sentence of this ten-volume opus, and he was up to the volume on Leibniz, a very thick tome. He was about halfway through. He wanted to show me a typographical error, which he found very comical. His tongue suddenly shot out and leafed back lightning-fast through ten pages. There, there it was. He had the passage, and with a jerk of his head he asked me to see for myself. I didn't know whether to take hold of the book, it didn't seem proper to lift it from the pillow, I was timid about the leaves, all of which—at least the ones he had read—had been touched by his tongue and were soaked by his spit. I hesitated; he said: "You can hold it if you like. It comes from Professor Gomperz's library. He has the greatest philosophical library in Vienna." I had heard about it, and I was deeply impressed that Professor Gomperz's volumes from *this* library had been made available for Thomas Marek's studies.

"He doesn't mind my keeping the books for so long. The Spinoza volume is still inside the house. He says it's an honor for his books to be read so emphatically." Thomas stuck his tongue out and laughed. He sensed how deeply moved I was by everything connected with his way of reading, and he was radiantly happy because he had something so strange to offer me. He wanted to enjoy it before I grew used to it. He had many visitors, as he later told me, but after a visit or two, people felt they had exhausted what was unique about him, and then they didn't come back. This hurt him, for he could have told them so many things that they had no inkling of. But it didn't surprise him; he knew what people were like. He had an infallible method for discerning a person's character: he observed the way a person walked.

When he lay in the sun outside his house and no longer felt like reading and closed his eyes, he never slept. He would be laughing at the people who made an effort to walk softly so as not to wake him. This was one of the methods he used to investigate their characters: the way they changed their gait when approaching and then the way they changed it when they had walked a bit and thought he couldn't hear them anymore. But he heard them a lot sooner than they thought and also a lot later. He always had some sort of footsteps in his mind; there were people he hated because of the way they walked, and people whom he wished to be friends with because he liked the way they walked. However, he envied everyone for walking. The thing he desired most in the world was to be able to walk freely someday, and he had an idea which he confided to me, more timidly than was his wont: he felt that he could *earn* the ability to walk by producing a great philosophical work. "When the work exists, I'm going to stand up and walk. Not earlier. This will take a long time."

He expected a great deal of people who could walk; he listened to steps as though they were miracles. Every new walker was to be worthy of his good fortune and excel with words that he alone and no one else could say. Marek could never get over the triviality of the words spoken by couples when they approached his wagon and thought him asleep. It was always a fresh and extreme disappointment for him when he heard their "nonsense"; he noted it and repeated the stupidest examples with seething scorn. "They ought to prohibit him from walking," he would then say. "Such a person doesn't *deserve* to walk." But perhaps it was lucky for him that couples who approached him didn't come out with lines from

Spinoza. Although he waited for people to address him, he was very selective about whom he condescended to hear. It cost him quite an effort to pretend to be deaf (his particular strength of mind), and he was proud whenever he succeeded at *demonstrating* his rejection in front of a third party. As soon as someone whom he didn't seem to hear had gone away, Marek's face lit up. He could laugh so hard that his wagon began to surge like waves; he would then say: "He thinks I'm deaf. What's he doing standing here! He has no right to stand at all! He feels sorry for me because he thinks I'm deaf. I feel sorry for *him*. What an idiot!"

He was sensitive to everything, but he was most sensitive to people who could stand and walk but didn't realize how well off they were. He was quite aware of the effect of his large, dark eyes, and he used them for some of the movements that were denied his limbs. He would close his eyes in midsentence, breaking off so dramatically that people were a bit frightened even if they were long accustomed to his game. But no one would miss the moment when his eyelids rose very slowly and his eyes opened in majestic calm. At such times, he resembled a Christ on an Eastern icon. During this slow process of opening his eyes, he was very earnest. He was performing his own self; it was a ritual spectacle.

The word *God* never crossed his lips. When he was a little boy, his mother had gotten the other two children, his sister and his brother, to *pray* aloud for his recovery. This had filled him with despair and anger. At first, he had wept when they began to pray. Later, he interrupted them, shrieking, reviling them, reviling God, and raging so wildly that his mother got scared and finally put a stop to the praying. He was resigned to nothing. When he told me about these memories, he justified his early outbursts against God: "What kind of a God is this whom you have to ask for something! He *knows* about it! He should do something of his own accord!" Then he added: "But he doesn't do it." And you could tell by this last sentence that his expectation had not died out.

The second time I came by, I didn't find him in front of the house. I entered. His mother had been expecting me, and she took me into the living room. He lay there in his wagon, right by the family table. A Giorgione painting hung on the back wall over the sofa: *The Three Philosophers*. I had recently seen the original at Vienna's Kunsthistorisches Museum; this seemed like a good copy. He spoke about it right away. I soon realized that he had received me in here in order to talk about his family. It was easier here; he could point everything out. In front of the house, it would have sounded less plausible. His father was a painter, the Giorgione copy was his work. It was his lone masterpiece, the best thing he had ever done. Nothing else of his was worth looking at. I must have seen the father already. He sometimes went on walks, flaunting his artist's mane of hair. He would walk completely upright, a handsome man, boldly fixing his gaze on one thing or another. But there was nothing to him; at home, he merely sat around, never earning anything. Every few years, he might be commissioned to do a copy, but his copies were no longer as good as *The Three Philosophers*, which had been done a long, long time ago.

His mother had left us; she always left him alone with his visitors; thus he could talk about her, too. She came from the countryside. She had been a milkmaid in a small hamlet in Lower Austria. The young painter had been strutting about, a striking man with a flowing mane and a trilby, and the girls ogled him. She fell for him head over heels and became his wife, and felt heaven knows how honored; but there was nothing behind the mane, she had fallen for the strutting; that was his entire art.

The mother had to provide for the family; the father earned next to nothing. Three children came, his sister, his brother, and he, whom she loved most. Starting at the age of six, he became more and more helpless, causing her more work than an entire household. This had been very hard on his mother, he said. She had moved heaven and earth looking for a doctor to cure him. She had pushed his wagon into every hospital, wouldn't take no for an answer, and came back over and over again—this was all she could think of.

But meanwhile, everything had changed; for the past eight years, he, Thomas, had been the provider for the family. His brother had a job, said Thomas; he was a clerk. His sister, in order to get out of the house, had married, much to his displeasure. She was a beautiful woman, he said. Everyone noticed her. She walked like a goddess—she was a dancer and actress and she could have reached the top. As children, they had been very close. His sister had watched him when his mother went to work. They shared all their secrets with one another. She read to him, and he had aroused her ambition, stoking it tirelessly. If only she had remained at home—but she couldn't stand it. The young men who admired her and came by weren't worthy of her, he found, and he put them down in front of her; she sensed that none of them was on his intellectual level. But then came a "painting official," a schoolteacher; Thomas respected him least of all—"a boring fellow, but tenacious." The teacher wouldn't give up, and this was the man she married. Yet by then, Thomas already had his scholarship, and the entire family could live on it. It was true, by studying, he supported his family.

He told me this with scornful pride. He was scornful of his sister, who preferred being kept by her husband rather than by him; she could have lived on Thomas's scholarship, too, if she had stayed at home. I didn't quite understand what he meant by "scholarship." I would have liked to ask him, but I felt it was tactless and I held back. I didn't have to ask, however; he kept talking on his own, explaining in detail what he meant. As soon as the professors who came out to see him were convinced of his gift and forecast a philosophic future for him, they presented his case to a rich old lady who was active as a maecenas. She wasn't interested in charity, however. She looked for very special, unique cases. Any project of hers was to benefit all mankind, not just an individual person. Professor Gomperz, and others, made it clear to her that if Thomas could only complete his education carefully and thoroughly, he would produce an intellectual achievement that no one else was capable of. What seemed like a disadvantage under the given circumstances would prove to be an advantage, and all that was required was patience and a suitable stipend. His mother, they told the patroness, was indispensable for him; if she did it right, she would have to attend to him all day long. And if Thomas were to study with all due concentration, he mustn't think of his father as being impoverished. It was correct, of course, to regard the father as a failure, but if one didn't let him feel all too strongly how helpless he was, then he would not cause any trouble. He wasn't a bad person, after all, merely lamentable, like all people who rely on their legs instead of their minds and strut about instead of reading a serious book.

The lady came just once: the father was waiting for her on the sofa in front of his Giorgione. She looked at the painting for a long time and praised him for it; he had the gall not to mention that it was only a copy. She said the painting was so beautiful that she would love to purchase it—she said "purchase" not "buy," such an elegant woman—whereupon the father rudely declared: "This painting is not for sale. It is my best work, and I will never part with it." She had taken fright and apologized. She hadn't meant to offend him, she said. Naturally he had to keep his best work at hand, if only to inspire him to do further works. Thomas, who was in the room, lying in his wagon, had felt like throwing in: "Wouldn't you like to see the other paintings?" or "Haven't you ever been to the Kunsthistorisches Museum?" When it came to what Thomas called his father's insolence, he felt his oats. However, Thomas kept still. The lady didn't quite have the nerve to look at Thomas, but she could tell that a heavy philosophical book was lying on the pillow next to him, and he would have liked to show her how well he could read. He had planned to read an entire page aloud to her, so she could make certain she wasn't being swindled. But the lady was much too tactful and perhaps she was scared of his tongue—some people were scared of seeing him read with his tongue. She gave him a friendly look and asked his father whether he felt that they could halfway get along on four hundred schillings a month; if that was too little, he should simply say so. The father shook his head and said: No, no, that was quite enough, but, he added, the question was for how long. Such a course of studies could take a long time.

"As long as it takes. Let me worry about that," said the lady. "If it is all right with you, let us establish it for twelve years, for now. That way your son does not have to feel pressured. Perhaps he will also feel like commencing his book already. People expect a great deal from him. I have heard good things about his mind from all sides. If he then wishes to continue working on his book, we can always extend the stipend for another four or five years."

The father, instead of thanking the woman on bended knees for such faith in his son, merely stroked his beard and said: "I believe I can express my acceptance on behalf of my son." The woman thanked him as heartily as if he had saved her life, and she then said to the father, who never did anything: "You must have a great deal to do. I do not want to keep you any longer." She gave Thomas a friendly nod. On the way to the door, almost squeezing past his wagon, she added: "You are giving me great joy. But I am afraid I will not understand your book. I have no head for philosophy." Then she left. Since then, four hundred schillings had come from her punctually on the first of every month. She had begun eight years ago, and she had never once forgotten to send the money.

I felt that I had never heard such a lovely story. The only thing that Thomas had committed himself to was to keep reading. Yet he would have done so in any case: there was nothing he would rather do. It must have been assumed that he might get his doctorate if at all possible. But the lady had not said one word about it. She must have known that there were difficulties involved. Where, for instance, if he ever got that far, would he take his examinations? Would the mother have to bring him to the university in his wagon or did the professors who came to instruct him (there were several) hope to obtain special permission to have him tested at home? After all, his entire education was taking place at home or, on sunny days, outside on Erzbischofgasse.

He mentioned a second teacher who came out specially to see him: this teacher gave him lessons in political economy; he was the secretary of the Chamber of Labor, Benedikt Kautsky, a son of the famous Karl Kautsky (the theoretician of the German Social Democrats). Thomas found it amusing that his two most important teachers, who had accomplishments of their own, were both sons of far more famous fathers. Heinrich Gomperz's father was Theodor Gomperz, the classicist; his multivolumed opus *Greek Thinkers* had even been translated into English. In the Austro-Hungarian Empire, he had been a member of the upper chamber of parliament and was renowned as an important speaker of the Liberal Party. "All parties are represented here," said Thomas. "I reserve the right of independent thinking for myself and so I don't belong to any party."

The scene in front of the father's Giorgione work had sufficed for him, and, consistent with the true conditions in the family, the father stayed entirely in the background. I would see him now and then when I came into the house, but he was out walking a great deal. Something of his love of nature had remained from his youth. But he couldn't always be strolling; I don't know where else he went. He was never to be seen in taverns, and I suspect that, notwithstanding the comments of his son, who had nothing good to say about him, the father did go to work. At home, he always happened to be sitting on the sofa in front of *The Three Philosophers;* one got used to seeing his head as a fourth to the other three. It didn't look so bad next to them. In poor weather, when we had to go indoors and the father was at home, I passed the four heads in the living room and went in back to the parents' bedroom. Thomas's mother had pushed his wagon into this room. I was alone with him here, and we could talk unhindered, as if no one else were at home.

His mother was so deeply focused on him that you never, or at best seldom, noticed her eyes. Her gaze was always fixed on him and on the things she brought him, whether she was dripping medicine into his mouth or feeding him bite by bite. He had a good appetite; she cooked only for him; whatever the others ate was peripheral. But he never praised his food; it was proper for a philosopher to scorn anything as ordinary as food. He had developed an expression for scorn, which was a bit terrifying, because you took it personally, though you learned that it was meant for something else. The interplay of eyebrows, nostrils, and the corners of his mouth made his face look like an Oriental mask, yet he couldn't possibly have seen such a mask. He once admitted to me that he had rehearsed the mimetic expression of scorn. I told him, half jokingly, about the impression made on me by a sentence in one of Leibniz's letters: *"Je méprise presque rien"* [I despise almost nothing]. Whereupon Thomas grew angry and hissed at the Leibniz volume on his pillow: "Leibniz was lying!" He didn't like being watched while "feeding," as he put it. But if someone *were* watching him, he managed to keep the expression of scorn on his face throughout the time of his feeding. He then refused to eat the last two or three bites on his plate and said quite roughly to his mother: "Take it away! I don't want to see it!"

She never contradicted him. She never tried to talk him into anything. Wordlessly, she took each of his directives, which were sometimes so terse and domineering that they sounded like commands. Her deepset eyes didn't seem to be looking as she carried out his directions; she could just as easily have been blind. But in reality, his slightest motion didn't elude her, nor did anything done in regard to him by others. There were people whom she liked, because she felt they were good for him, and others whom she hated because they depressed him. She observed his state of mind when a person left him, and as soon as she noticed that someone had been good for his ego, that person became a desired and preferred visitor. Most of all, she hated people who talked to him about traveling or athletics. There were people who felt impelled by his condition to talk about those things; they were so depressed by the sight of him that they spoke about the things in their lives that were most remote from his condition. If they did seek any rationale for this crudeness, they told themselves that they were "entertaining" him, providing him with the things he lacked most. At such times, he would listen, breathing heavily, and often laughing, which would encourage them even more.

A student, who visited him every week out of "charity," once gave him a dramatic account of how he had won a hurdle race. He spared him no detail, and Thomas, who reported it to me years later, had not forgotten a single detail. He was in such despair when the matador left him that he didn't want to go on living. The thermometer that his temperature had been taken with was still on the pillow; he could grab it with his tongue. He took it into his mouth and chewed it into small pieces, which he swallowed together with the mercury. But nothing happened to him. He was taken to the hospital at once. His intestines, astonishingly strong, played a trick on him; he didn't even have pains, and he survived.

That was his first suicide attempt. Two others followed in the course of time. Since he couldn't do anything with his arms and hands, each suicide attempt required unusual speed and decisiveness. The second time, he chewed up a tumbler and swallowed the splinters. The third time, he ate an entire newspaper. He concluded his descriptions of these attempts with tears of rage. Nothing whatsoever had happened to him either time. "I'm the only person who can't kill himself." He was proud of some of his "unique features," but not this one.

Didn't I feel, he asked, that, given these circumstances, he hadn't tried it so often?

Stumbling

With Marek, I spoke unabashedly about crowds. He listened to me in a different way from other people. He was (after Fredl Waldinger) the second person with whom I had long conversations about crowds. He didn't have the ironic attitude that Fredl had because of his richly developed Buddhist consciousness. When I spoke to Fredl about crowds—especially in earlier years—I felt a bit like a barbarian always repeating the same thing, while he opposed me with complex and carefully defined conceptions, some of which impressed me. In particular, Buddha's starting point, the phenomena of illness, old age, and death, had a meaningful impact on me; anything connected with death was already more important to me than crowds.

But when I said anything about crowds to Thomas, I sensed an altogether different sort of reaction, which initially surprised me. The dissolution of the individual in a crowd was the enigma of enigmas to me, and Thomas saw it in terms of himself, doubting whether he could ever become a crowd. He said he had once asked his mother to take him along to a May Day demonstration. She agreed (reluctantly—he wouldn't give in) and pushed him in his wagon all the long way to the city. But when they tried to join the parade, they were thrust into a group of invalids, who had come rolling up in their wagons. He protested. He shouted as loud as he could that he wanted to march with the others, but they ignored him. They said it wouldn't work; he couldn't even march; he would hold up the procession. No, the invalids would all come together; they would thus have a common tempo. It would look better, too. He wasn't the only one after all: there were many others; all the war invalids were here.

But he wasn't a war invalid, he shouted angrily. He was a student; he was studying philosophy; his place was behind the Academic Legion, which was made of militant socialist students. All the like-minded students were marching behind them. He wanted to be with his fellow students, otherwise the whole thing had no interest for him. However, the demonstration organizers wouldn't yield. They said they had to make sure that everything was orderly, and so they mercilessly placed him among the war invalids in their little wagons. Some of them could move along on their own, others had to be pushed like him.

Throughout the demonstration, he felt raped. He was at the edge, the spectators in their rows had a good view of him; luckily, they didn't understand what he was trying to say in his breathy voice: "I don't belong here! I'm not a war cripple!" That was the last thing he cared to be. *He* had not been in the war. He had not killed anyone. He was serious when he said he wouldn't have gone to war. The others had all gone, out of cowardice, and had been punished with their serious wounds. Many had even gone out of enthusiasm. But their enthusiasm had soon waned. Now, they were all pulling along, behind the giant signs that said "Never Again War!" Of course not. *They* would never go to war again; they couldn't. They weren't lying at least, but all the others walking on their legs, they would dash to war again like sheep and forget all the fine May Day slogans. He spoke with deep hatred about this demonstration. It was just like the army. All the cripples together, a special company. He believed that everyone should march wherever he felt like. He had nothing against dividing the parade according to districts, or according to factories; but division according to cripples was a scandal, and he never went again.

I asked him whether he couldn't imagine some other situation in which he would willingly dissolve into a crowd. After all, he *had* been drawn to the May Day demonstration; otherwise he wouldn't have nagged his mother to take him. She had given in very reluctantly; she may have realized what the upshot would be. However, there were other occasions which might not require locomotion—meetings in a hall, for instance. Didn't he enjoy them? He must have had such experiences. The very way he spoke about war was proof for me that he had heard antiwar speeches, indeed, in the excited state of mind that one has when one is together with many other people.

Thomas made a skeptical face. If he had understood me correctly, he said, such an experience requires a feeling of *equality*, and this was one feeling he didn't have. Did I know the cripple newspaper, he asked, put out by the Association of Cripples? No? He would ask his mother to put aside a copy of this cripple newspaper for the next time I came. These cripples (he used the word so often in order to make clear how utterly he excluded himself from this category), these cripples had their meetings, too. They were announced in the newspaper. He had once had himself taken to such a meeting to see what they were all about. But none of them were in wagons. They sat in their chairs in rows, while some one-armed man sat on the podium in front, trying to keep order. His mother had placed his wagon on the side, toward the front, so that his heckling could be heard, for he was firmly resolved not to spare them anything.

He told me that I just couldn't imagine the level of such a meeting. These people regarded themselves as a sort of union and behaved accordingly. They were always carrying on about some rights or other that had to be fought for—he just couldn't stand the way they wailed on and on about how badly off they were. Yet all they lacked was an arm or an eye. Some had a wooden leg, some had waggling heads, all of them were ugly. He combed the rows of people, looking for an intellectual face. There was none with whom one would have cared to start a philosophical conversation. He would have bet that not a single one of these four or five hundred people in the auditorium had ever heard the name Leibniz. All you heard was demands for higher pensions. A pensioners' meeting, yes, that's what it was. Every time such a demand was brought up, he heckled, shouting they had enough as it was. They were much too well off. Just what did they want anyway? The insolence of these people, who had all come to the meeting on their own legs and actually had the gall to complain! He, in any event, disrupted the meeting as much as he could. He heckled much louder than I realized. He didn't know whether his comments had been understood, but some of them must have been, for the people were annoyed and ultimately they became furious. *This* was freedom of speech, which people made such a to-do about! The one-armed chairman asked him not to disrupt, others wanted to have the floor, too. But Thomas just couldn't stand hearing the nonsense, and he kept heckling, until the one-armed chairman asked him to leave the auditorium!

"How am I supposed to leave?" he had retorted. "Could you tell me how I'm supposed to leave?" The one-armed man had had the gall to tell him: "You found your way into the auditorium. You will find your way out again!" The chairman meant that his mother should push him out, and unfortunately she did so, because she got scared. He wanted to remain in order to see what they would do. Perhaps these people, who could walk, would not have been ashamed to pounce on him and beat him, the defenseless man. What did I think? Would they have beaten him? It would have been worth the trouble to wait and see. He wasn't scared. He would have spat in their faces and yelled "Riffraff!" But his mother wouldn't go along with such things. She was always trembling for him, her precious child. Actually, she treated him like a babe-in-arms, and he was dependent on her and couldn't do anything about it. By and large, she did what he wanted her to do, after all.

But now could I tell him whether this was a "crowd experience"? He hadn't felt at all *equal*. They all thought he was a lot worse off than they, yet these were people who read their cripple newspaper and nothing else. So they were a lot worse off than he; that was why they had very nearly pounced on him. When he thought about it now, in retrospect, he was forced to conclude that they were all *envious* of him. Perhaps they could tell just by looking at him that he was preparing for his doctorate in philosophy.

This was all that Thomas could say about crowds. I began to realize how tactless I had been with my talk about crowds. How could I speak in his presence about the *density* and *equality* inside a crowd? What equality would this have been for him? And how densely could others squeeze against Thomas, who always lay in his wagon? It was a matter of life and death for him to change, being so different—an inalterably painful difference—into something proud. After all, he had learned how to read with his tongue, he stuck to difficult books, which only a few chosen people could know of; and if he so greatly emphasized that he was studying, then it was only something temporary; in reality, he wanted to be known as a *philosopher* and write works so powerful and unique that, someday, thick tomes would be written about him, too—as about Spinoza, Leibniz, and Kant. This was the only rank he recognized; this was where he belonged, even though he hadn't reached that point yet, doubting only in moments of extreme shame and humiliation by others that he would someday really be accepted into this rank.

I had never seen such burning ambition, and I liked his ambition, even though I didn't know what it was based on. For the things that Thomas had already dictated to his mother—scattered thoughts and also sketches for an autobiography—would by no means have struck me had I been unacquainted with the author's life. He had no style of his own as yet, the language of these dictated pieces was colorless and wooden; the things he told me during the long hours of our conversations were a lot more interesting. The most striking thing of all was that in the course of such a conversation he intensified and *became* interesting. He soon noticed that I didn't think much of his pieces, and he said all these things didn't count: first of all, he had dictated them years ago, before he had even learned how to think, and then— referring to his autobiography—it was all whining and sentimental. After all, he couldn't tell his mother his true, hard thoughts. They would make her sick. For such dictation, he needed a friend who was his peer, someone like me, and anyway, it was too early for such things. I liked his notion of fame and immortality so much that I believed him. I *resolved* to believe him, I lulled my doubts, which, however, didn't fully die.

He talked to me about everything. He was more open than any person I had ever known. Many things that were a matter of course for me, things I never gave a second thought, were first brought to my awareness by him. I had paid little heed to physical things: my body meant nothing to me; it existed, it served me, I took it for granted. At school, I had been unspeakably bored by subjects in which the body was on its own, as it were—athletics, for example. Why run when you're in no hurry, why jump into the air when it's not a matter of life and death, why *compete* against others if you don't all have the same prerequisites—no matter whether you're all equally strong or equally weak. You never learned anything new in gym: you kept on repeating the same thing; you were always in the same area, which smelled of sawdust and sweat. Hiking was different. You got to know new places, new landscapes; nothing was repeated.

Yet now it turned out that the things I found most boring were things that Thomas was most interested in. He always kept asking what a person felt like during a high jump; nor was broad jumping to be scorned, or vaulting, or the hundred-meter race. I tried to describe these actions in such a way as to satisfy his curiosity without making him feel too regretful that he couldn't do them himself. But he was never satisfied with my descriptions. He always lapsed into silence, said nothing for a long while, and then next time he usually came out with questions that made it obvious he wanted far more accurate descriptions. Sometimes, he criticized me for the rather summary fashion in which I reported on these things. Such arrogance didn't suit me, he said. I was like a man who has overeaten and is talking to a hungry man about food and trying to prove to the hungry man that eating is not what it's cracked up to be. He thus forced me to pay more attention to physical things. I caught myself suddenly thinking about walking while I was walking, and especially about falling while I was falling. I never lost the feeling that it was important and useful to tell him about *failure*. And even though he never admitted it, I did sense how happy he was when I again spoke shamefacedly about how ridiculous I had once again been.

In high school, I had really been poor in athletics, and I didn't have to invent anything against myself in the past: all I had to do was recall situations that I didn't normally like to remember. As for the present, however, I got used to stumbling more often during walks, falling, and bruising my knees and hands, which I could then show during my visits. I didn't talk about these things right away, but I kept the bruised hand concealed as if I were ashamed of it. He enjoyed this game, observed me closely, and eventually said: "What's wrong with your hand?"

"Nothing. Nothing."

"Show me!"

I held back a bit, but then pulled out my hand, and watched him delight in my clumsiness.

"You've fallen again! You've fallen again!" He remembered the Ionian philosopher Thales, who looked at the stars instead of at the ground and tumbled into a well. "Starting today, I'm going to call you Thales! Why don't you go inside and wash off the blood! Mother's in the house!" The blood wasn't so bad, but it did him good to have his mother find out about my clumsiness. So I went in, and she insisted on washing off the blood.

If, en route to his home, I actually stumbled and fell just a few paces from his wagon, then his jubilation knew no end. This didn't happen frequently; he might have become suspicious. Nevertheless, I learned how to fall credibly, and Thomas made fun of me, even advising me to write an essay on "The Art of Falling"—there was no such essay, he said. He didn't realize how close he had come to the truth; in order to feed his ego, I had become a true artist in falling. Luckily, I had been working toward this turn of events before we ever met. We had observed one another for three years before speaking. I had been so fascinated by him that I really hadn't paid attention to where I was walking, and once, very close to him, I had tripped and fallen. This had made a deep impact on him. He had noticed my fall, and now, when I deliberately resumed and continued this tradition of falling, he could remind me of that previous fall in all its details.

I believe that he got to like me because of these stumbles, which I staged for his sake. Certainly, our conversations were important to him too, for here too I made sure I "stumbled." This wasn't at all easy; I wouldn't have cared to miss our conversations for anything in the world, and in order to win the right to these conversations and his trust, I had to let on that I had read a bit and knew a few things. Yet now and then, not too often, I pretended not to know a major scholarly book or even a great philosopher with which he was thoroughly acquainted. This game was not free of risk: I would act as if I knew only from summaries things he was thoroughly familiar with from the texts themselves. I had to suppress arguments that readily sprang to my tongue during a discussion. Once I could manage to avoid certain quotations during a conversation, I would become bold and commit some gross blunder with true insolence: I would credit Spinoza with a line from Descartes, insisting that I was right and leaving Thomas enough time to roll out his heaviest artillery. I gazed at him with bogus fear while he visibly bristled more and more. And finally, when my cause seemed definitively lost, I pretended to be so miserable and ashamed that Thomas found his magnanimity again and had to comfort me. By then, I knew that my trick had worked; he had achieved and was enjoying a sense of superiority without overly disdaining me, for I hadn't managed so badly in the preceding discussion. I was absolutely delighted when I found the strength to leave him right after such a triumph of his knowledge; and today, it makes me feel no less happy to go back to those moments.

However, Thomas didn't beat me only in the history of philosophy, which was his real object of study, after all. He gave me the feeling that he didn't lack experience in a different and very important area. At first, he spoke about it with some restraint, perhaps to keep from frightening me. Or perhaps he first wanted to find out how far he could go, for he regarded me as prudish. I always thought of him as helpless. When he was given food or drink, which sometimes happened in my presence, I witnessed his inability to bring anything to his body on his own. He made sure I wasn't around when he had to obey a call of nature. If it came upon him suddenly, he would send me away without further ado, calling his mother only after I had gone a few steps away. He would not allow me to return, and I wouldn't see him until the next day. He was prudish about such things, and I liked the fact that he was prudish. Yet how astonished I was when he once told me point-blank that "the girl" had been there yesterday. He said she was pretty and stupid and was good for only one thing; he usually sent her away after an hour. He had been deceived by the way she walked. He felt like exchanging her for another. He sounded as if he owned an entire pondful of girls, from which he only had to help himself. I was speechless. He sensed my embarrassment and told me all about it.

Earlier, he said, he hadn't had any girls; this achievement was something that he likewise owed Professor Gomperz. He had deeply wished to be with a woman. He had often been so unhappy about it that he didn't feel like studying anymore. He then hadn't touched a book for days on end, his tongue had shrunk because it had nothing to do, and he had scorned his sister so cuttingly because of her suitors that she ran out of the house in tears. Professor Gomperz, who could get nowhere with him during his lessons, had asked him what was wrong, and Thomas had confessed that he needed a woman. He had to have a woman, otherwise he couldn't continue his studies. Professor Gomperz, as was his wont in difficult situations, stuck his little finger into his ear and promised to take care of the matter.

Gomperz went into a café on a side street of Kärtnerstrasse, a place where prostitutes hung out, and he sat down alone at a round table. Gomperz had never been to such a place before. He had put on dark glasses to remain incognito; after all, he was a professor at the university and an elderly gentleman. There he sat, in his loden cape, which he never took off, and certainly not in this sort of place; he sat huge and bolt upright. He wasn't alone for long. Three girls sat down at his table. They hadn't pinned great hopes on him; he looked as if he had wandered in by chance. He wasn't proud, however; he spoke to them right away in his slow, emphatic drawl, explaining what he was after: He had a young friend who was paralyzed, and he was looking for a girl for him. He wasn't sickly or repulsive; he didn't have an unsavory illness—on the contrary, he had extremely rich hair and the most beautiful eyes. He was very sensitive and couldn't do anything by himself; he couldn't even reach for food. He had a fine mind and was highly gifted, but everything had to be done for him. He was looking for a young, fresh, healthy girl who could come to his home in Hacking every week, for one afternoon. *He* (the professor) would take care of the fee. When they had agreed on the price, the money would always be lying on the dresser in the bedroom. Before the girl left, she could simply take the money on the dresser, but only if everything had gone well—that was the only condition.

It turned out that each of the girls was willing to come, but only after they were again reassured that the paralyzed man wasn't sickly. They also wanted to know his name, and both his first and last name had a cozy ring for them. A girlfriend of theirs in the tavern was also named Marek. They asked Professor Gomperz to pick one of their willing number, the one he liked best, for "Thomas" (they were already calling him that). Now, all of them were pretty, though in different ways. The professor didn't have such an easy time making his choice, and when he subsequently told Thomas about his adventure, Gomperz dubbed it his "Judgment of Paris."

However, the professor wasn't present the first time the girl came; he said he didn't want to spoil their fun with his gray beard. The girl was warm and zealous, and Thomas got what he had so intensely wished for. He was beside himself with joy and, in his exalted state, he forgot to remind the girl about the payment lying on the dresser. She, in turn, was so absorbed by her new task that she neither looked for the money afterwards nor asked for it, and she promised of her own accord to come back on the following Saturday at three in the afternoon. She came punctually, never missing a Saturday. Thomas had to remind her about the money for her first visit. She did take it; but *after* being with him, she would never take money, and when Thomas asked her to take it, she said, "Don't worry about it! I'll visit you for fun." And a whole week had to go by before she could bring herself to go over to the dresser and pick up her pay, which had, after all, been agreed upon.

This continued for more than six months, and he always had to remind her about the money. In his heart, he wished she would leave it there, and his wish was so strong that he always devised new ways of talking about it. "Someone's poured out his purse on the dresser," he said. "Could you pick it up, please!" Or, "Why do people have to leave their money here! I can't stand it! Am I a beggar?" It had to happen right when she came; for later on, there was no way of getting her to take it. On Saturday, when he wanted to look forward to her arrival, the moment came when that silly matter occurred to him and he had to concoct something new. Also, it offended him that the whole business was connected with the professor, as if Gomperz were still taking care of it after all those months. If Thomas was in a bad mood and wanted to hurt the girl, he said: "Your friend, the professor, sends his best." Or, "Did the professor show up again in your tavern?" The girl was simple; she obeyed him because she didn't want to displease him. He was obstinate, he wouldn't let up, and she didn't dare come near him before doing what he reminded her to do. She would have preferred to bring him something herself, but when she tried to give him small presents, she got nowhere. "There's the present," he said vehemently, twitching his head toward the dresser. "Only the professor gives presents here."

Had she divined his true wish, everything could have gone on nicely; but his pride gave him no peace; he forced her to take what she didn't even want; and what was initially excessive gratitude turned into resentment. During the week, he might sometimes think of her with hatred. He lay in his wagon, basking in the sun, a woman went past with an appealing walk, and he thought with hatred about the impending Saturday visit. He told me how they had broken off, and he didn't seem to regret it. He viewed it as a manly action, worthy of a free spirit, especially since he had no one for quite a while after that. He had said to her, rather gruffly, "You've forgotten something again!" He waited until the despised thing was in her purse and then he said: "You don't have to come anymore." He refused to explain. As she stood in the doorway, turning to him with a querying look, he hissed: "I have no time. I have to study more." She wrote him a letter, awkward and full of mistakes, a love letter such as I have never seen—if only I had memorized it.

He let me read it. He observed me as I read it. He seemed untouched; it had been some time ago. Nevertheless, he had kept the letter, and when he wanted to see it, he said to his mother in the terse way that he felt sufficed for her, "Give me the letter!" He didn't explain which letter, but she knew the one he meant. I read it and understood what had happened. It was obvious how unfair he had been to the girl. He remained adamant, and the last thing he said about it was: "Then she should have sent it back to Gomperz, all of it!"

Meanwhile, he had learned how to impress women, and in conversations he let on that he was experienced in amorous matters. He was visited by women, who were allowed to sit out in the sun by his wagon, telling him about their unhappy marriages and what they suffered from their brutal husbands. He listened to them, and they felt understood. Sometimes he gave them advice, which they followed; they came back and thanked him; the advice had worked. If he didn't like the way a woman walked, he refused to converse with her. He would then signal to his mother, and she would take in the wagon with him, thus breaking off the session, which hadn't really begun.

The miracle he was waiting for occurred after we became friends. A female physician, whose office was located in Ober Sankt Veit, once visited him to treat him for a feverish cold. She came driving up in her little car and was instantly taken to him in his bedroom, so that he didn't even see her walk. The fever made him somewhat numb, and he was dozing. Suddenly, she stood before him and identified herself as a doctor. Even in this condition, he did not fail—as was his wont—to slowly open his eyes wide, and he achieved the usual effect. The doctor fell in love with him on the spot and, when he was healthy again, she invited him on short drives in her car. Whenever she had time and the weather was nice, she came to pick him up.

Initially, she lifted him out of the wagon with his mother's help and placed him in the car like a bundle. Then she asked him what he would like to see; he could select anything he wanted. The drives, brief at first, grew longer and longer, ultimately going as far as Semmering. He intoned his own song when he was lifted into the car for such a drive. I witnessed it several times: I wanted to visit him, and though I already saw the doctor's car in front of his house, I didn't turn back. I approached them, supposedly to say hello, but actually to hear the happy breath of his voice, which was trying to rejoice because the world was opening up to him. The physician, who handled him very cautiously, spending every free moment on these drives, became his mistress; and she remained his mistress all the time I knew him.

Kant Catches Fire

After moving out to my hill at the edge of the city, Vienna, between Veza's home on Ferdinandstrasse and Hacking, that is, Vienna at its broadest, became my province. When I came home from Veza's late at night, I didn't take the urban railroad (the shortest connection) to the last stop, Hütteldorf-Hacking. There were two trolley lines not far from the urban railroad and running parallel to one another through a more densely populated neighborhood. I hopped a trolley. It was a very long ride; somewhere along the way, wherever I felt like it, I jumped out and then walked up and down the dark streets. Throughout this large district, there was no street, perhaps no house, that I didn't get to see during my scouting trips. And quite certainly, I visited every tavern that stayed open late at night.

After my return to Vienna, I was much more eager to go on these trips. I was filled with a deep distaste for *names;* I wanted to hear nothing about names; I would have preferred to bash away at them all. Having lived in the midst of the big name-kitchen—three months the first time and six weeks the second time—I had an afflicting sense of disgust at names. I felt (a vision of horror since my childhood) like a feeder goose, incarcerated and force-fed with names. Your beak was held open and a gruel of names was stuffed into it. It didn't matter which names were mixed in, so long as the gruel contained them all and you thought you were about to choke on it. I opposed this united affliction and harassment by names, I resisted it by means of every person who had no name, everyone who was poor in name.

I wanted to see and hear *everyone,* for a long time, over and over, hear everyone even in the endlessness of his repetition. The freer I became for this and the more time I devoted to it, the greater my astonishment at this variety, and right in the poverty, banality, the misuse of words, not in the braggadocio and bumptiousness of the writers.

If I entered a nocturnal tavern that offered me a favorable opportunity to hear, I would remain for a long time, until the place closed at 4 A.M., I would surrender to the stream of entering, departing, returning figures. I enjoyed shutting my eyes as though half asleep or turning to the wall and only listening. I learned how to distinguish among people purely by hearing. I didn't see a person leaving the place, but I missed his voice; and as soon as I heard his voice again, I knew that he was back. If one didn't shy away from repetition, if one took it in fully and without disrespect, one soon recognized a rhythm of speaking and replying; scenes took shape out of the ebb and flow, the movement of acoustic masks, and these scenes, in contrast to the bare shrieks of self-assertion by those names, were interesting—that is, not calculating. Whether achieving their effect or not, the scenes recurred—or perhaps it would be more accurate to say that the purview of their calculation was so narrow that they were bound to appear unsuccessful to the listener, and hence futile and innocent.

I liked these people, even the most hateful among them, because they were not given the power of speech. They made themselves ridiculous in words, they struggled with words.

They gazed into a distorting mirror when they spoke; they demonstrated themselves in the distortion of words, which distortion had become their alleged likeness. They made themselves vulnerable when they courted understanding; they accused one another so unsuccessfully that insult sounded like praise and praise like insult. After my experience of power in Berlin, which I had perceived up close in the deceptive guise of fame, and in which I had thought I would suffocate, I was understandably receptive to any form of powerlessness. It seized hold of me, I was thankful to it; I was unable to sate myself with it, and it was not the openly declared powerlessness with which others like to operate selfishly: it was the hidden, dyed-in-the-wool powerlessness of individuals who remained apart, who couldn't get together, least of all in speech, which separated them instead of binding them.

There were many things that attracted me to Thomas Marek, most of all his daily strain to overcome his powerlessness. He was worst off of all the people I had ever known; but he spoke, and I understood him. And what he said had meaning. It occupied my mind not only because it cost him such an effort to form words out of his breath. I admired him because with his intellect he had gained a superiority that transformed him from an object of pity into a person to whom people made pilgrimages. He was no saint in the traditional sense, for he was open to life and loved every aspect of it, most intensely those aspects that were denied him. In his childhood, he had begun with *involuntary* asceticism, and now everything that had happened in years of unspeakable toil was devoted to acquiring the faculties and facilities that other people took for granted.

I asked him whether it didn't make a stronger impact on him to be *read to* rather than to read for himself. That had been true earlier, was his answer: when he had been younger, his sister had read to him: poems, stories, plays. That was how their friendship had started, that was how they had become inseparable. But then this had no longer been enough for him, he had wanted to get to more difficult things, which his sister didn't understand. Should she have read to him *mechanically* without knowing what the sentences meant? He considered his sister too good for that, and she considered herself too good for that. Reading something to him, she *communicated* it to him. It had to be equally important for both of them; he didn't want to demean her into a mere reading parrot. Also, he felt the need to reflect calmly at times and, if he couldn't recall the exact wording, he wanted to look it up, as it were, and ascertain it. For both reasons, it became indispensable for him to read on his own. Did I have anything to criticize in his method of doing so?

Certainly not, I said. On the contrary, he had solved the problem so cogently that it seemed like the most natural thing in the world.

Which it was, and yet I never could get used to it. And whenever he read to me (perhaps just one sentence or even a whole page), I always felt as if I were experiencing it for the first time. I felt more than respect: I was ashamed that I had always had such an easy time reading, and I looked forward to what would come out with his method. Each sentence that he formed in this way with his breath sounded different from any other sentence that I had ever heard.

In May 1930, when I began visiting Thomas, I had already spent six months on my sketches. All eight characters of my *Human Comedy of Madmen* existed, and it appeared certain that each one would be the center of an individual novel. They ran about side by side; I preferred none. In rapid alternation, I focused now on one, now on another; none was neglected, nor did any predominate; each had his specific speech and his specific way of thinking. It was as if I had split into eight people without losing control of them or myself. I was apprehensive about giving them names; I designated them (as I have already said) with their dominant characteristics, and I restricted myself to the initials of these characteristics. So long as they had no names of their own, they didn't notice one another. They remained free of residue, were neutral, and did not try to gain the upper hand over what they didn't perceive. There was a huge leap from the "Enemy of Death" to the "Spendthrift" and from the latter to the "Book Man." Yet the road was clear; they themselves didn't block it. I never felt pressured; I lived with an élan and elation such as I have never known since then—the lone arranger and surveyor of eight remote, exotic territories, always traveling from one territory to another, sometimes even changing my place en route, never held anywhere against my will, never overpowered by anyone, a bird of prey, calling eight territories his own instead of one and never landing anywhere in a cage of caution.

My conversations with Thomas were about philosophical or scholarly subjects. He had quite a bit to say and enjoyed saying it, but he also wanted to know what I was occupied with. I talked to him about the civilizations and religions that I was investigating for any traces of crowd phenomena. Even now, during the period of my literary sketches, I devoted several hours a day to this project. He found out nothing about my literary doings; a sure instinct told me that my characters had something that was bound to offend him, whether because their far-reaching motion would strike him as hopelessly unattainable or because their limitations would remind him of his own. I made a point of keeping quiet about my sketches, and it wasn't very difficult, for this way something inexhaustible was left over for our conversations: a work that came into my life at the same time as Thomas and that acquired cardinal importance for me, Jacob Burckhardt's *History of Greek Civilization*. Thomas had familiarized himself with the Greeks long ago, but he had encountered them on the orthodox scholarly route of his period. He could explain to me in what ways the then new scholars deviated from Burckhardt; yet Thomas showed a fine sense for Burckhardt's incomparably deeper interpretations. We agreed that

Burckhardt was the great historian of the nineteenth century, and we felt that he should now come into his own.

This conversation was important to me, but I participated with only part of myself. However, I sensed that my relationship with Thomas, our frequent meetings, also had an effect on my other part, which I concealed from him.

There was more for me here with Thomas than with all other people I knew. This was due not only to the incomparable nature of his existence; he also surprised me with things I couldn't expect. In some ways, he was like one of the characters I had invented: when you knew the condition on which he depended, then everything that happened with him was definite and consistent, nothing could have been any different from what it was. You felt that his conduct was lucid and graspable. He became the heart of my *Human Comedy* and, without appearing in it himself, the crowning evidence of its truth. But because he was so different from my characters, he seemed more alive than any of them. Nor could he be killed: his three suicide attempts, all very serious, had washed over him without a trace; things that would have killed anyone else had had no effect on him. He was now protected against all self-surrender; he knew it and was agreeable to it. Whenever he didn't feel badly off, he was even proud of it; everything he gained from others, even from me, served to strengthen him.

He was more than the characters that I was filled with; for, in his independence, he *procured* his own life. Even in his condition, he was capable of unpredictable metamorphoses; this was what he surprised me with most. You thought you knew him, and yet he turned out to be unpredictable. I believe that, precisely because he was so much stronger and more mysterious, he would have caused the destruction of the eight characters with whom he clashed inside me. He didn't know them; they knew him, and, being nameless, they were at the mercy of his name.

But he himself, who, in the course of just a few months, had become a silent, incessant danger to my project, who had innocently found entrance into every character, hollowing them out from the inside and weakening them—Thomas himself became the cause of a salvation. Seven of the characters perished; one survived. The immensity of my enterprise contained its own punishment; yet the catastrophe in which it ended was incomplete; something—today it is titled *Die Blendung* [*Auto-Da-Fé* in English]—has remained.

Thomas often asked me about experiences that were denied him, and once he even insisted on a precise description of the events of the Fifteenth of July. I told him everything straight out, in details that I had never pulled up and presented together. I felt how vivid this day still was in me after three years. His sense of it was different from mine: it didn't terrify him; the swift movement, the frequent change of location had a stimulating impact on him. "The fire!" he said, over and over. "The fire! The fire!" He seemed almost tipsy. I told him about the man who had stood away from the crowd, clutching his hands over his head and repeatedly and woefully shouting: "The files are burning! All the files!" And Thomas was overcome with mirth, tempestuous laughter; he laughed so hard that his wagon began to roll and took off with him. Laughter had become a driving force; since he couldn't stop, I had to dash after him and catch hold of him, and I felt the powerful thrusts that his laughter gave the wagon.

At this moment, I saw the "Book Man," one of the eight characters, in front of me. He suddenly leaped out in place of the file lamenter. He stood at the burning of the Palace of Justice, and it struck me like lightning that he would have to burn up with all his books.

"*Brand* [conflagration]," I murmured, "*Brand.*" Thomas, when his wagon stopped and his laughter finally died out, repeated: "Conflagration! That must have been a conflagration!" He didn't realize that the word *Brand* had now become a name in my eyes, the name of the book hero. And that was his name from then on; he was the first and only character to receive a name, and it was this name that saved him from self-dissolution, in contrast to the other characters.

The balance among the characters was destroyed. I got more and more interested in Brand. I didn't as yet know what he looked like; he had replaced the file man, but he didn't look like him at all. He didn't just stand at the side. I took him seriously, just as he took the fire seriously, the fire that was his fate, in which he would end voluntarily. I believe it was the expectation of this fire that gradually dried out the other characters. Occasionally, I did sit down and focus on them, trying to continue writing. But the fire, which had now reawakened, was close by; in its presence, these characters got something empty, bookish. What sort of creatures were these, threatened by no death? After all, I had expressly exempted them from death; they were to live, in order to get together in that pavilion, which I had picked for them. There, they were to have the conversation on which I set such great hopes; I had even imagined that this conversation would yield *meaning*, unlike the conversations of "normal" people, who came out with nothing but banalities and yet still failed to understand one another.

Even my picture of this conversation had dimmed since I was having conversations full of surprises, though I tried to give these conversations a precautionary turn. They were supposed to spare another person, whose sensibilities had become more important to me than my own; yet what I heard in these conversations preoccupied me more than anything I could devise. The pavilion in Steinhof, which I still had before me, was soon emptied, like the characters that were supposed to get together in it. I found this pavilion ridiculous; it gave itself airs in front of the other pavilions. I just couldn't understand why I had destined this one to such high honors: any of these pavilions would have done the job. They were all mirror images of one another.

While the characters were left more and more to their own devices without my putting a violent end to them (I didn't reject them, didn't conceal them; I abandoned all of them at some point in midsentence), I was so absorbed by Brand the Book Man that I would look out for him when I was walking. I pictured him as long and scraggy, but I didn't know his face. Before I saw his face, this character too had something of the wraithlike quality that had caused the other seven to go a-begging. I knew he wasn't in Hacking; Brand made his home in the inner city or very close to it, and I now often went into Vienna, assuming that I would run into him.

My expectations didn't deceive me. I found him as the proprietor of a cactus shop, which I had frequently passed without noticing him. At the start of the passage leading from Kohlmarkt to the Café Pucher, there was a small cactus shop to the left. The shop had a single display window, not very broad, in which many cactuses of all sizes were standing, prickles by prickles. Behind them, the proprietor, a long, scraggy man, looked out to the passage; he was a sharp sight behind all the prickles. I halted in front of the display and gazed into his face. He was one head taller than I and gazed over me, but he could just as well have gazed through me without noticing me. He was as absent as he was scraggy; without the cactus prickles, you wouldn't have looked at him; he consisted of prickles.

Thus I had found Brand and he wouldn't let go of me. I had planted a cactus in my body, and it now kept growing, resolute and nonchalant. It was already autumn; I sat down to work; my work progressed daily without breaking off. The year's dissipation was over; rigorous laws prevailed now. I allowed myself no leaps, I gave in to no temptation. What counted was a dense network, something in me that I called "untearability." During my year of dissipation, Gogol, whom I so greatly admired, had been my master. In his school, I had devoted myself to the freedom of invention. I never lost my joy in this freedom, not even later, when I strove for other things. Now, however, in my year of concentration, when I was after clarity and density, a transparency without residue, as in amber, I stuck to a model that I admired no less than I did Gogol: Stendhal's *The Red and the Black*. Every day, before starting to write, I read a few pages of this novel, thus repeating what the author himself had done with a different model, the renowned new book of laws in his day.

I kept the name Brand for several months. The contrasts between the characteristics of this character and the flickering of his name did not bother me at first; but when all the characteristics existed, hard and unshakable, the name began to spread out at the expense of the character. The name kept reminding me of the character's end, which I didn't wish to think about prematurely. I was afraid that the fire might blaze ahead of time and consume something that was only just evolving. I renamed Brand and now called him Kant.

He had me in his power for an entire year. The relentless way this work proceeded was a new experience for me. I felt ruled by laws that were more powerful than I, something recalling the discipline of natural science, which I had, after all, penetrated in a special way, even though I had then turned my back on it so resolutely. The first signs of the impact that this discipline had on me could be felt in the rigor of my book.

In autumn 1931, Kant set fire to his library and burned up with his books. His death affected me as deeply as if I had gone through it myself. This work launched my own insight and experience. For several years, the manuscript, lying untouched in my room, bore the title *Kant Catches Fire*. The pain of this title was hard to endure. When I reluctantly decided to change it, I was unable to separate from fire completely. Kant became Kien [German for resinous pinewood]; the ignitability of the world, a threat that I felt, was maintained in the name of the chief character. However, the pain intensified into the title *Die Blendung* [The Blinding]. This title preserved (recognizable to no one else) the memory of Samson's blinding, a memory that I dare not abjure even to-day.